THE MENTOR'S GUIDE

Facilitating Effective Learning Relationships

SECOND EDITION

Lois J. Zachary

Foreword by Laurent A. Parks Daloz

JOSSEY-BASS
A Wiley Imprint
www.josseybass.com

Published by Jossey-Bass
A Wiley Imprint
989 Market Street, San Francisco, CA 94103-1741—www.josseybass.com

Jossey-Bass books and products are available through most bookstores. To contact Jossey-Bass directly call our Customer Care Department within the U.S. at 800-956-7739, outside the U.S. at 317-572-3986, or fax 317-572-4002.

Wiley also publishes its books in a variety of electronic formats and by print-on-demand. Not all content that is available in standard print versions of this book may appear or be packaged in all book formats. If you have purchased a version of this book that did not include media that is referenced by or accompanies a standard print version, you may request this media by visiting http://booksupport.wiley.com. For more information about Wiley products, visit us www.wiley .com.

Library of Congress Cataloging-in-Publication Data

Zachary, Lois J.

  The mentor's guide : facilitating effective learning relationships / Lois J. Zachary.—2nd ed.
    p. cm.
  Includes bibliographical references and index.
  ISBN 978-0-470-90772-6 (pbk.); ISBN 978-1-118-10330-2 (ebk.);
  ISBN 978-1-118-10331-9 (ebk.); ISBN 978-1-118-10332-6 (ebk.)
    1. Mentoring in education. 2. Learning, Psychology of. 3. Interpersonal relations. I. Title.
  LB1731.4.Z23 2011
  371.102—dc23

                                                                                      2011024034

Printed in the United States of America

SECOND EDITION

PB Printing   10 9 8 7 6 5 4 3 2 1

The Jossey-Bass Higher and Adult Education Series

CONTENTS

Exercises, Examples, Tables, and Figures

EXERCISES

EXAMPLES

TABLES

FIGURE

Years ago, a friend sent me a drawing by artist Brian Andreas with a quote sketched into it: "Most people don't know that there are angels whose only job is to make sure you don't get too comfortable and fall asleep and miss your life." Since the publication of the first edition of *The Mentor's Guide*, these words have resonated in my ears, and a few more angels have been added. I dedicate this edition to my "angels," Ed, Bruce, Lisa, David, Talia, Emily, and Lory, whom I can always count on to make sure I don't get too comfortable, fall asleep, and miss my life.

FOREWORD

ECOLOGISTS TELL US that a tree planted in a clearing of an old forest will grow more successfully than one planted in an open field. The reason, it seems, is that the roots of the forest tree are able to follow the intricate pathways created by former trees and thus embed themselves more deeply. Indeed, over time, the roots of many trees may actually graft themselves to one another, creating an interdependent mat of life hidden beneath the earth's surface. This literally enables the stronger trees to share resources with the weaker so the whole forest becomes healthier.

Similarly, we human beings thrive best when we grow in the presence of those who have gone before. Our roots may not follow every available pathway, but we are able to become more fully ourselves because of the presence of others. "I am who I am because we are," goes the saying, and mentors are a vital part of the often invisible mat of our lives.

There have, of course, always been mentors, but our ability to name them as such is relatively recent. Psychologists discovered them only a generation ago; educators and the business world were not far behind. Since then, mentors have become a hot item, appearing in best-sellers, on television specials, and on film. Generally they are viewed as people who help us find a jewel of wisdom or a promotion at work. At bottom, however, mentors are more than that. As Zalman Schachter-Shalomi says, they "impart lessons in the art of living." Great mentors extend the human activity of care beyond the bounds of the family. They see us in ways that we have not been seen before. And at their best they inspire us to reach beyond ourselves; they show us how to make a positive difference in a wider world.

Lois Zachary knows a lot about that. Coming from a background in human development, she has spent years of direct experience in organizational change, leadership education, and mentoring. In *The Mentor's Guide*, she brings her experience, together with an impressive range of resources, to create a trove of practical knowledge and concrete exercises for all of us who seek to serve as mentors in more adequate and humane ways. True to the essence of mentoring, the activities here are artfully designed not to preach about one right way to be a mentor but rather to help readers see their own mentoring style and preferences more clearly and thus learn from direct experience and observation.

Yet this is no chocolate box of platitudes. Zachary knows that good mentoring is tough, and she peppers her numerous examples with instances of inadequate or failed mentoring. The journey of mentor and protégé runs along narrow and daunting ledges as well as high outlooks and is not for the faint-hearted or indifferent. She bluntly warns of dangers along the way even while offering priceless assistance in the form of savvy observations and solid advice. Chapter Seven alone, on feedback, is worth the price of the book, as is the annotated list of resources in Chapter Nine.

Moving beneath the superficiality and formulas that too often mark the literature on mentoring, Zachary reminds us that it is the particularity of each relationship that really matters, that human development always takes place in a larger context that mentors ignore at their peril. The exercises in the chapters invite us to explore more profoundly our own capacities for establishing genuine trust with others, listening with real respect and compassion, examining clear-eyed our own inflations and convenient delusions. Again and again, Zachary reminds us that the central skill of an effective mentor is no less than the capacity for self-awareness—a willingness to keep a relentless, if forgiving, eye on our own journey, as well as that of our companion.

There is much here for all of us to learn from. One of the speakers in the book plaintively remarks that what she really needs is "a mentor to mentor me about mentoring." With this second edition of *The Mentor's Guide*, Lois Zachary has stepped forward to start us on our way toward becoming more adept in this vital, nourishing, and profoundly human role as we open the way for those coming after us to sink their roots deeper, to grow fuller, to participate more richly in the interdependent mat of life.

Laurent A. Parks Daloz
Clinton, Washington

Preface to the Second Edition

AN OLD AFRICAN PROVERB SAYS, "If you want to travel fast, travel alone; if you want to travel far, travel together." At its core, that is what mentoring is: traveling far, together, in a relationship of mutual learning.

New mentors may be caught off guard, thrust into the role by professional obligations or a chance meeting, but with no maps to show them where the journey might go. A mentor who has traveled this road finds that the need for guidance never ends; every new mentoring relationship comes with its own set of fresh challenges. To both of these mentors, and to you—whatever your mentoring experience—I offer this book as a guide and companion. I hope it will allow you to understand your role as a mentor more deeply and make mentoring the priority it should be.

In that spirit, this book is a practical guide that lays out the processes from beginning to end and provides tools for creating an effective learning relationship. It will ground you in the predictable phases of mentoring and give you strategies and techniques to help you understand how to manage intentional mentoring relationships in a cycle that fully engages both mentoring partners—mentor and mentee.

Mentoring at its very core is a learning relationship, and the phases I discuss and explore in this book are structures and processes that contribute to learning. These phases—preparing, negotiating, enabling growth, and coming to closure—are present in both formal and informal mentoring relationships, and they are in motion even when you are not aware of them. Being able to anticipate and work with them is the key to mentoring partnership success.

WHY ADULT LEARNING AND DEVELOPMENT IS KEY TO MENTORING

The Mentor's Guide draws much inspiration from Laurent Daloz's *Mentor: Guiding the Journey of Adult Learners*.[1] I find his learner-centered focus compelling. By intimately focusing on the learner, the learning connection, and the learning process, Daloz reaches into the very core of mentoring.

Since the first edition of *The Mentor's Guide* appeared in 2000, interest in and knowledge about adult learning and development have grown exponentially. Many major publications on the topic have been revised and updated,[2] some several times over.[3] The breadth of knowledge has expanded, and practitioner research and field practice have added depth and nuance to theories put forth by thought leaders like Daloz, Jack Mezirow, Stephen Brookfield, and Sharan Merriam.

We now recognize that adult learning is more than a cognitive process; it is a multidimensional phenomenon.[4] Social networking and virtual platforms continue to accelerate the pace of learning and the dissemination of knowledge and to create cyberspace learning communities among diverse learners. Along with increasing globalization, these changes have focused more attention on the importance of context and difference. The uniqueness of the adult learner has been accentuated over the past decade as we continue to learn more about the complexities of the brain, multiple types of intelligence, and our emotional selves.

All of this has meant fundamental changes for mentoring. As the learning process has shifted from mentor directed to self-directed, the focus of the mentoring partnership has shifted from knowledge transfer and acquisition to critical reflection and application. The mentee is no longer a passive receiver but an active learner; the mentor is no longer an authority figure but a facilitator of learning.

According to Stephen Brookfield, effective facilitation is characterized by the conditions of voluntary engagement of both partners, mutual respect for the mentee's individuality, collaboration, critical reflection, and empowerment of the learner.[5] Over and over in my work, I have found this approach to be fruitful and compelling for both mentor and mentee: in such a relationship, everyone shares in the learning.

WHAT'S NEW IN THIS EDITION

The practice of mentoring, and knowledge about it, are always evolving—like the mentoring relationship itself. The changes in this new edition of

The Mentor's Guide reflect that understanding. The chapter on learning has been updated, and a full two chapters are devoted to context—the context of difference and the context of how people come together to connect with one another in the relationship.

In response to new understandings, the names of the four phases of the mentoring cycle have gotten more explicit and descriptive. I've renamed the enabling phase based on feedback that I've received. And I've divided the chapter on enabling growth into two full chapters; the first explores the components of support, challenge, and vision, and the second deals with engaging in feedback and working with obstacles. Almost all of the chapters offer new exercises, as well as fresh examples of mentors and mentees drawn from actual mentoring experiences in a variety of situations in business, government, nonprofit, and higher education.

How you use this book is up to you. You can use it as a self-help book, a compendium of resources for helping to facilitate mentee learning, an introduction to mentoring, or a workbook to refer to again and again in specific instances. However you use it, remember that *The Mentor's Guide* offers a framework for informed mentoring practice. It is designed to provide insight into the nature and focus of the mentoring process so that you can facilitate learning in ways that enrich, enable, enliven, and engage the learning of the mentee.

Not all mentoring arises from an institutional base. In fact, many mentoring relationships do not. Because this book concentrates on facilitating learning relationships, you can use it independent of organizational affiliation or by community groups. Its perspective has no institutional walls.

If *The Mentor's Guide* is the extent of your mentoring preparation, it will give you a solid grounding from which to proceed. It is not, however, a comprehensive reference about everything there is to know about mentoring. Rather, it presents an array of practical options, steps, and strategies for action and reflection and is useful in a variety of settings to help facilitate the mentee's learning.

The Mentor's Guide combines discussion and workbook-like elements to support those who are in the process of facilitating learning in mentoring relationships, formal and informal. You can use these exercises and reflections to prepare in advance of your mentoring sessions or use them as they are or modify them. Use the exhibits and exercises as discussion points for mentoring conversations. These resources are meant to be helpful reminders for you to keep the focus on the learning and the learners.

I invite you to begin the journey by starting wherever you are right now.

There are several approaches you might follow:

- *Start with your questions.* Use this book as a reference when you have a question. Frame your question first, and consult the index for where you might find the answer.

- *Start at the beginning.* Proceed step by step, and work your way through the entire book from start to finish. Complete the exercises in logical sequence.

- *Start at the Contents.* Scan the Contents page. Consider the topics that interest you the most, and start with those.

- *Start with your stumbling blocks.* Identify what is getting in the way of your mentoring relationship. What do you need help with first?

- *Start where you are right now.* Locate yourself in relation to the four phases of the mentoring relationship: at the beginning (preparing, negotiating), the middle (enabling growth), or near the end (coming to closure).

We all learn in different ways, so honor your particular learning style as you make your way through the book. Some exercises will mesh with your style and situation; others will not. Choose what is appropriate to your way of learning and your needs. You may find that you need time to reflect before taking action. If you prefer to focus on the concrete and practical, you might be more likely to work through the exercises yourself, as well as with your mentee. If you prefer hands-on experience, try experimenting with a variety of the options presented.

A FEW THOUGHTS BEFORE YOU BEGIN

For me, mentoring is a way of life: it's my job, my passion, and the way I perceive the world. For you, mentoring may be a smaller part of your life, something that you pursue out of interest or curiosity or an urge to give back, or something you agreed to take on as part of your job. However you have come to mentoring, my advice is the same: if you are going to do it, do it right.

My goal is to help you make excellence in your mentoring relationship a personal priority and be more reflective about your own role as a mentor. I hope you will accept my invitation to delve more deeply into understanding your role in a mentoring relationship and how you can more effectively facilitate the learning of your mentee. Before you embark on your journey through the mentoring process, I leave you with these thoughts about the nature of mentoring work:

- Mentoring can be a powerful growth experience for both mentor and mentee. Mentors will learn new things about their mentee, themselves, and their organizations.

- Mentoring is a process of engagement. No one can mentor without connection. In fact, mentoring is most successful when it is done collaboratively. Commitment by and engagement of mentoring partners is a key element in establishing, maintaining, and experiencing successful mentoring relationships.

- Facilitating successful mentoring is a reflective practice that takes preparation and dedication. It begins with self-learning. Taking the time to prepare for the relationship adds value to it.

- Mentoring with staying power focuses on the learners, the learning process, and the learning. *The Mentor's Guide* models that approach by providing exercises to stimulate more informed mentoring practice.

- When mentoring is consciously and conscientiously grounded in principles of learning, the likelihood that the mentoring relationship will become a satisfactory learning relationship for both partners dramatically improves.

Mentoring can be a joy, and it is always a privilege. I hope that this book will inspire you to make it a priority, learn as much as you can, commit time and attention to each of your mentoring relationships, and continue to learn and grow as a mentor.

Acknowledgments

I ACKNOWLEDGE my very talented, creative, and spirited developmental editor, Naomi Lucks. Thank you for your time, commitment, and contagious sense of humor.

I acknowledge the gifts of a great storyteller, loyal friend, and business partner, Lory Fischler. I couldn't ask for a better fellow traveler.

I acknowledge the rich and powerful ideas of teachers Stephen Brookfield and Jack Mezirow. Little did I know thirty years ago how much your work would continue to inform my thinking and enrich my practice.

I acknowledge the wisdom of a true mentor and believer in the power of learning to transform the human experience. Larry Daloz, I appreciate your insights, probing questions, and friendship more than you know.

I acknowledge my publisher, Jossey-Bass. I am very grateful to be part of its extended family. To David Brightman, senior editor, Adult and Higher Education, and Sheryl Fullerton, executive editor, my sincerest appreciation for your continuing support and encouragement.

About the Author

LOIS J. ZACHARY is an internationally recognized expert on mentoring excellence and has been cited as "one of the top 100 minds in leadership" today. Since *The Mentor's Guide* was first published in 2000, it has become the primary resource for organizations interested in promoting mentoring for leadership and learning and for mentors seeking to deepen their mentoring practices. With her best-selling books *Creating a Mentoring Culture* (2005) and *The Mentee's Guide* (2009), Zachary has created a comprehensive set of resources for promoting organizational mentoring sustainability.

Zachary is president of Leadership Development Services, LLC, a Phoenix-based consulting firm that specializes in leadership and mentoring, and director of its Center for Mentoring Excellence. Her innovative mentoring approaches and expertise in coaching leaders and their organizations in designing, implementing, and evaluating learner-centered mentoring programs have been used by her wide array of clients, including Fortune 500 companies, government organizations, and educational, profit, and nonprofit institutions. Zachary received her doctorate in adult and continuing education from Columbia University. She holds a master of arts degree from Columbia University and a master of science degree in education from Southern Illinois University.

THE MENTOR'S GUIDE

SECOND EDITION

CHAPTER 1

LEARNING
GROUNDING THE WORK OF MENTORING

LEARNING ON THE PART of both mentor and mentee grounds the work of mentoring. It is the reason we do it, the process we engage in during a mentoring relationship, and the outcome that both mentor and mentee seek. Genuine learning evolves through a process of exploration and discovery. It requires collaboration between the mentoring partners and a safe environment that honors the mentee's integrity and learning style. In this paradigm, mentor and mentee travel a parallel journey.

LEARNING

Mentoring relationships that are not grounded in learning, especially those based on the traditional model of wisdom transmitted from "master" to "apprentice," are not very successful. Let's begin by looking at how these two very different styles of mentoring operate:

Randy and Pat

Randy, a manager in a multinational corporation, had been assigned to mentor Pat, a new employee. Pat was bright, energetic, highly motivated, and eager to make his mark. Their mentoring relationship started out on a positive note, and they developed rapport easily. Anxious to please this high-level executive, Pat worked on Randy's projects and researched whatever topics he assigned; he even carried Randy's briefcase to meetings.

Before long, however, the level of interaction dramatically shifted. Over the weeks and months, Randy's responsibilities increased, and he had less and less time for Pat. Soon they drifted away from two-way information sharing and discussion to transaction and information giving. There was no time available for raising or answering questions, and their e-mails were brusque and matter of fact.

Pat soon became frustrated. He had learned a great deal by shadowing Randy, but he needed more. What was missing was the opportunity for Pat and Randy to discuss and process the learning that was taking place.

This mentoring model is not unique to the corporate world. There are similar examples in academia, where the mentee is so eager to get ahead that the exposure that comes with "carrying a professor's briefcase" makes the experience worthwhile. In Pat's case, however, that benefit was short term.

Jocelyn, too, had high ambitions and realized that she needed some specific skills to get ahead. She approached Carmon, a high performer and much-admired manager in her organization, to be her mentor. Jocelyn and Carmon's mentoring relationship, collaborative from the beginning, was much more successful.

Carmon and Jocelyn

At their first meeting, Carmon worked with Jocelyn to crystallize her amorphous learning goals. They set ground rules for the relationship and agreed that it would be Jocelyn's responsibility to initiate the contact between them.

Each time they met, Carmon and Jocelyn reviewed the progress they were making toward Jocelyn's learning goals. They also set aside regular time to talk about their levels of satisfaction with their interaction and how each felt things were going.

They had to work through one potential rough spot: Jocelyn was eager to do as much as possible, and she wanted more of Carmon's time than Carmon felt she could spare. Because they had intentionally built time to reflect into their regular meetings, they were able to talk openly and honestly about Jocelyn's concerns. They also identified other areas Jocelyn could explore for learning on her own, including several projects, client meetings, and strategic internal meetings. This gave Jocelyn more ways to approach her goals, and freed Carmon to do her own work.

What made the difference in these two very different examples? Randy and Pat's more traditional mentoring relationship is one-way, with knowledge transmitted from mentor to mentee. Jocelyn's more successful relationship with Carmon was a collaborative learning partnership in which learning was allowed to flow freely in both directions.

At a deeper level, these two examples illustrate the difference between the old and new paradigms of mentoring. In the more traditional authoritarian teacher–dependent student–supplicant paradigm, a passive mentee is expected to receive and absorb knowledge.

Today mentoring has become collaborative; it is now a mutual discovery process in which both the mentor and mentee have something to bring to the relationship ("the give") and something to gain that broadens each of their perspectives ("the get"). Wisdom is not passed down but discovered and nurtured. This shift frees both partners to learn together.

Creating a Learning Partnership

The collaborative mentoring paradigm you will learn about in this book is rooted in principles and practices of adult learning. Mentor and mentee work together to achieve specific, mutually defined goals that focus on developing the mentee's skills, abilities, knowledge, and thinking; it is in every way a learning partnership.

The learner—in this case, the mentee—plays an active role in the learning, sharing responsibility for the priorities, learning, and resources, and becoming increasingly self-directed in the process. The mentor nurtures and develops the mentee's capacity for self-direction (from dependence to independence to interdependence) over the course of the relationship. Throughout the learning relationship, both mentoring partners share accountability and responsibility for achieving the mentee's learning goals.

Today's mentoring relationships are usually short term: when the learning goals have been accomplished, the relationship comes to closure. If goals have not been achieved by a prearranged deadline or the partners agree on more goals, the mentoring partners are free to review, assess, and renegotiate their relationship.

Elements of the Learning-Centered Mentoring Paradigm

The learning-centered mentoring paradigm has seven critical elements: reciprocity, learning, relationship, partnership, collaboration, mutually defined goals, and development:

1. *Reciprocity.* The presence of reciprocity and mutuality in a mentoring relationship frequently surprises first-time mentors. Each partner has specific responsibilities, contributes to the relationship, and learns from

the other. Both partners say that as a result, their perspectives have expanded and they have gained new knowledge; mentoring is a value-added relationship for them.

2. *Learning*. Without the presence of learning, mentoring doesn't exist. It is the purpose, the process, and the product of a mentoring relationship. That's why it is essential that you understand your mentees as learners and yourself as a learning facilitator. As a mentor, you will need to know how to engage and guide your mentee appropriately and create a climate that supports learning. And you must also be open to learning yourself.

3. *Relationship*. Strong relationships motivate, inspire, and support learning and development. But good mentoring relationships take time to develop and grow. From the beginning, both mentor and mentee must be open and trusting and honor each other's uniqueness. Both partners need to work at establishing, maintaining, and strengthening the relationship through their mentoring time.

4. *Partnership*. A good relationship forms the basis for a strong mentoring partnership. You and your mentee respect one another and are attuned to each other's needs. This will help you establish agreements that are anchored in trust. With a strong partnership, you will both feel secure enough to work at building and strengthening the relationship and to hold yourself and each other accountable for results.

5. *Collaboration*. Partnership is, by definition, collaborative. Together you and your mentee build the relationship, share knowledge, and come to consensus about the focus of the mentee's desired learning; then you actively work together to achieve it.

6. *Mutually defined goals*. Mentoring must flow in the direction of defined goals—otherwise, like a river without a clear channel, your relationship will meander until it dries up. It is vital to clarify and articulate learning goals at the beginning and to review them throughout the mentoring relationship. This means asking questions, listening to answers, and engaging in ongoing conversation to ensure that you select meaningful goals that will guide the work of the relationship.

7. *Development*. Mentoring needs to promote the mentee's development and growth. When development is future directed, it creates its own momentum. As a skilled mentor, you can consciously facilitate movement forward by providing appropriate support, challenge, and "help in anchoring the vision of the potential self."[1] This means helping mentees

to develop the skills, knowledge, abilities, and thinking necessary to achieve their success.

MENTORING BASED ON PRINCIPLES OF ADULT LEARNING

The shift in mentoring practice aligns with basic principles of adult learning first laid out by Malcolm Knowles:[2]

- Adults learn best when they are involved in diagnosing, planning, implementing, and evaluating their own learning.
- The role of the facilitator is to create and maintain a supportive climate that promotes conditions necessary for learning to take place.
- Adult learners have a need to be self-directing.
- Readiness for learning increases when there is a specific need to know.
- Life's reservoir of experience is a primary learning resource; the life experiences of others enrich the learning process.
- Adult learners have an inherent need for immediacy of application.
- Adults respond best to learning when they are internally motivated to learn.

Table 1.1 defines the elements of the learner-centered mentoring paradigm.

Over the past three decades, knowledge about adult learning has expanded far beyond these basic principles. Research has opened new areas of understanding, and we have become more attuned to the complexities of facilitating adult learning.[3] Many related theories inform adult learning practice today. We will focus on three of them: emotional intelligence, self-directed learning, and transformational learning.

Emotional Intelligence

Emotional intelligence is the ability to recognize and understand our own emotions (self-awareness) and the emotions of others (social awareness) and then to use this ability to guide our behavior (self-management) and manage our relationships (relationship management).[4] For example, an emotionally intelligent mentor is easy to relate to and always makes her mentees feel comfortable, even when her own workload is demanding. Her door is always open, both literally and figuratively. She listens carefully and asks good questions, so her mentees believe that she "gets them."

TABLE 1.1

Elements in the Learner-Centered Mentoring Paradigm

Mentoring Element	Changing Paradigm	Adult Learning Principle
Mentee role	From: Passive receiver To: Active partner	Adults learn best when they are involved in diagnosing, planning, implementing, and evaluating their own learning.
Mentor role	From: Authority To: Facilitator	The role of the facilitator is to create and maintain a supportive climate that promotes the conditions necessary for learning to take place.
Learning process	From: Mentor directed and responsible for the mentee's learning To: Self-directed with the mentee responsible for own learning	Adult learners have a need to be self-directing.
Length of relationship	From: Calendar focus To: Goal determined	Readiness for learning increases when there is a specific need to know.
Mentoring relationship	From: One life = one mentor; one mentor = one mentee To: Multiple mentors over a lifetime and multiple modalities for mentoring: individual, group, and peer models	Life's reservoir of experience is a primary learning resource: the life experiences of others enrich the learning process.
Setting	From: Face-to-face To: Multiple and varied venues and opportunities	Adult learners have an inherent need for immediacy of application.
Focus	From: Product oriented: knowledge transfer and acquisition To: Process oriented: Critical reflection and application	Adults respond best to learning when they are internally motivated to learn.

And she checks in regularly to make sure that they are getting what they need from her when they need it.

To move learning forward, you must become a student and steward of emotional intelligence. This means:

- Being self-aware and managing your own emotions
- Being other aware and able to read your mentees
- Being able to manage your mentoring relationships

Everyone has, to a lesser or greater degree, an innate level of emotional intelligence. As with most other things, emotional intelligence gets better with practice.

The following story of Janine and Roger illustrates a mentor's emotional intelligence at work:

Janine and Roger

Roger, Janine's current mentee, is quiet and shy to the extreme. In their first few conversations, he made no eye contact and literally talked to the wall. She is well aware that he needs time to frame his thoughts and talk about them and has patiently given him leeway to do so. But during their most recent session, he seemed so distant that she doubted if he would even notice if she left the room. She wondered what kind of an impact his one-way conversational style was having on his relationships with work colleagues.

During their next mentoring meeting, Janine stopped Roger when he started "talking to the wall."

"Roger," she began, keeping a neutral tone, "I sense that you have something on your mind that you need to work out. While part of our purpose in working together is to help you deepen your thinking, I'm not sure that the way we're going about it now is the best way to use our time. My observation is that you come here not to get additional perspective, but to actually form your thoughts during our meeting. I can see that when you are working out your ideas, you are staring at the wall—totally in your head. You don't seem to know that I'm here, and it makes me wonder if I really need to be present." She paused a moment, but Roger was quiet, so she continued.

"We're supposed to be in partnership, but you aren't asking for help. You aren't asking for input. Sometimes I do want to offer a comment, but you can't see that in my body language or facial expression because you aren't looking at me. What's your take on that?"

Roger looked down at his hands, his lips pressed together. Janine could see that he did not know how to respond, so she continued with concerned questions, seeking to understand. "First of all, Roger, I'm wondering if perhaps you've been doing this for so long you're not even aware of it. Maybe you're not conscious of the impact it has on other people, especially those you work with. I think that's something that we should be talking about."

Janine could see that Roger lacked the emotional intelligence to understand the impact of his behavior on others. She also was aware that Roger wasn't taking optimum advantage of her time as a mentor to sort out his thinking in advance.

Janine is an experienced and excellent mentor. She always tries to turn situations into learning opportunities, and she creates a climate for openness. She makes her mentees feel confident even when they are clearly wrong, and she does this by giving them feedback in a way that can lead to new understanding rather than embarrassment or anger. She shares her own stories and experiences, and reveals her vulnerabilities as a way of demonstrating her support. She doesn't solve problems for her mentees but empowers them to do it for themselves.

Although Roger was resistant at first, Janine's understanding and nonthreatening approach finally got through to him. He needed structure in order to marshal his thoughts, and she provided it. As a result of her feedback, Roger began to come to the sessions more prepared with his thinking, so that he could present ideas to Janine and be ready to listen as well as talk. Janine challenged him to bring that same intention to his other meetings and to become more aware of his tendency to engage in one-way communication. By raising his awareness and challenging him to monitor his behavior, Roger was able to more fully engage in the relationship. Over time, he became an active mentoring partner and more engaged with colleagues.

Lack of self-awareness is the biggest impediment to developing emotional intelligence. Parker Palmer reminds us that "encounters with mentors . . . can awaken a sense of self and yield clues to who we are."[5] Janine "gave Roger a clue" and, as a result, stimulated the growth of his emotional intelligence.

Effective mentors are emotionally intelligent and foster emotional intelligence in their mentees. Table 1.2 offers some questions for you to consider in thinking about your own emotional intelligence.

Self-Directed Learning

Malcolm Knowles popularized the term *self-directed learning* (SDL) to describe how adults take initiative and use resources to further their own learning efforts.[6] Today SDL has become a hot topic and buzzword. But what does SDL really mean?

On the surface it seems self-explanatory: adults should, by nature of their adulthood, be self-directed. Knowles was explicit as to what was involved: diagnosing learning needs, formulating learning goals, identifying learning

TABLE 1.2

Questions to Consider About Emotional Intelligence

Four Components of Emotional Intelligence	Questions to Consider
Self-awareness	Do you recognize and understand your moods, your emotions, and what drives you? Do you understand the impact of your moods and emotions on other people?
Self-management	Do you control or redirect your impulses, behaviors, and moods? Are you able to suspend judgment? How flexible are you when circumstances change or you have to overcome obstacles? Do you consistently strive for your personal best?
Social awareness	Are you aware of other people's emotions, needs, and perspectives and take them into consideration? Do you pursue your goals with persistence and energy? Do you maintain optimism even in the face of failure? Do you have a passion and strong drive to achieve something for others?
Relationship management	Do you respond to the emotional reactions of others appropriately? Do you exhibit cultural sensitivity when dealing with other people?

Source: Adapted from Goleman, Boyatzis, and McKee (2002).

resources, selecting and implementing learning strategies, and evaluating learning outcomes in his framework. And yet adulthood does not necessarily grant the knowledge or capacity to do this work.

Is SDL more of a destination than a journey? To what extent does cultural context bear on the amount of initiative a learner will take? Researchers continue to wrestle with these questions and define SDL as a phenomenon.[7]

Although the term *self-directed learning* suggests learning through one's own efforts, SDL assumes that it takes place in connection with others as resources, not in isolation. The principles and practices of SDL honor the uniqueness and adulthood of the mentee by shifting control from the facilitator to the learner. Ultimately mentees must accept responsibility for their own learning.

The capacity for SDL exists in varying degrees in each person. The mentor's role is to facilitate the process, keeping the mentee's development front and center. As Cheryl Lowry has said, facilitating self-directed learning means inspiring "learners to view knowledge and truth as contextual, to see value frameworks as cultural constructs, to appreciate that they can act on their world individually or collectively to transform it."[8]

Mentoring is the quintessential expression of SDL. In a mentoring relationship, both parties mutually define and share responsibility. Together they develop strategies, find resources, and evaluate learning together. At its core, the mentoring agreement (discussed in Chapter Five) is a learning contract that defines the objectives, strategies, resources, time line, and evaluation methodology of the relationship. To that end, as a mentor it is important to:

1. Create a learning partnership.
2. Help mentees identify goals for learning.
3. Negotiate a learning contract.
4. Help learners discover what objectives they should set.
5. Use multiple modalities and resources to achieve the objectives.
6. Manage the learning experience.
7. Help mentees stay focused on the goals, objectives, and learning strategies.
8. Periodically revisit goals to stay on track.

Transformational Learning

We often hear someone describe mentoring as a transformational learning experience and assume that something has changed as a result. But transformation is really about becoming open to possibilities and perspectives by critically reflecting on one's lived experience.[9] This generates new insights and signals a change in how we see and make sense of the world, and it brings about more aligned, sustainable, and synergistic behavioral patterns and action.

Mentoring can be transformational for both mentors and mentees. For example, although she had informally supported various colleagues for years, Lauren had never been a mentor. But because she had had several great mentors, she welcomed the opportunity to "pay back" by mentoring Jonas, who was quite ambitious and talented but was having trouble getting ahead. The experience, however, did not go quite as she had planned:

Lauren and Jonas

Lauren enthusiastically shared her experiences with Jonas. She told him stories about how she got started, her career journey, the people who supported her, and how she learned to network her way to the top. After several months, she began to notice that Jonas seemed interested in her stories but was not really engaged.

"What's wrong?" she asked. Jonas shrugged, but said nothing. With a start, Lauren realized that although he now knew everything about her path, she still didn't know much about Jonas.

"Jonas," she said, "here I've been going on and on about my experiences—let's talk about you for a change!" Jonas perked up. But as he told her his stories, she realized that Jonas really didn't know very much about himself. He was so busy climbing to the top that he hadn't taken time to reflect on what he was doing.

Lauren began to listen more attentively and ask questions to get Jonas to reflect on his experiences. As he became more comfortable talking, she invited him to explore his underlying behavioral assumptions and examine why he did what he did in specific situations.

This was new territory for Jonas, but he got the hang of it fairly quickly. Soon Jonas's insights led to extended conversations about values and beliefs, and the realization that his values did not align with his leadership behaviors and future aspirations. Jonas began to see that leadership was not about moving ahead from one stepping-stone to the next. He needed to make some deeper changes to be successful. He would have to let go of behaviors that were holding him back and consider alternatives.

Working with Jonas also had a profound effect on Lauren: she began to reflect on her own leadership journey and saw some areas in which she too might become more self-aware. When she looked at her own assumptions about her leadership team, she decided to make significant changes in how she was leading her team. The positive feedback was immediate. Several direct reports commented that she seemed to be listening more. The questions she raised reengaged her team, created more ownership, and enabled them to reach new goals.

Lauren was amazed at how dramatically subtle shifts in her behavior affected the productivity of the team and led to changed behavior in other parts of her life as well. She was more conscious of her behaviors and assumptions and how they drove her responses and behavior. She continued to be more self-aware and was able to catch herself more quickly when she occasionally slipped back into old habits.

Mentors can help mentees become more aware of how their beliefs, assumptions, and behaviors affect their daily lives by letting go of self-limiting and unrealistic assumptions that hold them back. Because the relationship is collaborative and both partners are learning, mentors can have similar transformational insights about their own behavior and make changes they never before considered.

The Four Levels of Learning

Inevitably both mentors and mentees bring different levels of experience and competence to the relationship. The competence model contributes to understanding the learning cycle by breaking it into four stages: (1) unconsciously incompetent, (2) consciously incompetent, (3) consciously competent, and (4) unconsciously competent.[10] If you remember the process of learning to ride a bicycle, you already understand the nature of these four levels.

Table 1.3 summarizes the four stages. You can use the chart to gain some insight into your own competency level and gauge your mentee's competency level in relation to the four levels.

- *Level 1: Unconscious incompetence.* Learning begins when we become conscious of what we do not know. In the first level, we "don't know what we don't know." As a result, we may appear overconfident. You may have a mentee who is new to his professional role and thinks he knows what he needs to learn—but in reality, he doesn't have a clue because he is essentially blind to what he doesn't know. Similarly, if you have never mentored anyone, reading this book may shine a light on knowledge gaps you didn't know you had.

- *Level 2: Conscious incompetence.* At this second level, we become aware of our lack of knowledge or understanding. As these gaps surface, we become less confident. For example, you may realize that you need to learn more in order to become an effective mentor. You may opt for training, surf the Internet in search of pointers, or talk to other mentors.

TABLE 1.3

Levels of Competence and the Mentor's Role in Learning

Level	Learners	Mentor's Role
Level 1: Unconsciously incompetent	Learners are unaware of what they do not know, or they may assume they know something when they really don't. Confidence exceeds ability.	Support discovery of how much the mentee needs to learn (blind-spot awareness).
Level 2: Consciously incompetent	Learners become aware of what they do not know (the gaps) and can articulate, "I don't know how to do that." Confidence drops.	Encourage by helping the mentee understand mistakes. Ask questions to deepen his or her thinking. Facilitate application of new knowledge.
Level 3: Consciously competent	Learners want to take learning deeper. They know the information, process, and skill but still need to carefully think through the process. Confidence rises.	Provide opportunities to practice. Offer feedback.
Level 4: Unconsciously competent	Learners know the information, process, and skills and demonstrate competency at using them, but they no longer have to think through the steps. Confidence is demonstrated.	Engage in reflection on practice to facilitate continuous improvement. Watch for signs of complacency.

- *Level 3: Conscious competence.* By the third stage, we are aware of what we don't know and develop competency through concentration and practice. The more we practice, the more confident we feel. Let's say you have read this book and are starting to implement what you've read. You will find that you are very attentive to what you are doing as you integrate theory and practice.

- *Level 4: Unconscious competence.* In the fourth stage, unconscious competence, using the skill or knowledge has become habitual and second nature. We move confidently, without having to think through the steps.

When you've read this book and practiced its concepts long enough, that knowledge will become part of your approach. But rather than getting lulled into complacency and saying, "Aha! Now I've got it!" stay humble: always be reflective about your practice, and realize that there is more to learn.

LEARNING STYLES AND COGNITIVE FRAMEWORKS

Everyone has his or her own learning style. When both you and your mentee are familiar with your mentee's learning style, you can use that knowledge to help facilitate learning.[11] For example, if your mentee is a logical person who is data driven and fact oriented and you operate more intuitively, you will need to remember that your mentee approaches learning in a more structured, specific way than you are normally comfortable with. Adjusting the learning in a way that meets your mentee's needs rather than your own is a good rule of thumb in creating an environment that facilitates learning.

Our cognitive framework—how we make meaning—also influences how we learn and act. William Perry describes a developmental continuum of progressively more complex meaning structures (ways of thinking) that affect how we act (ways of being).[12] Perry offers four frameworks: dualism, multiplicity, relativism, and commitment. Essentially these are lenses through which individuals may view the world. Knowing which lenses your mentee is wearing is fundamental to your success in facilitating an effective learning relationship:

- *Dualism.* This individual sees dichotomy and concreteness everywhere: right or wrong, we or they, should or should not. As a mentee, this individual sees the mentor as an authority figure dispensing knowledge and truth. This mentee will expect you to direct the mentoring process, so you will need to emphasize the collaborative nature of the mentor-mentee relationship.

- *Multiplicity.* This individual sees each person as having his or her own truth because "everyone is entitled to their opinion." Relying on feelings rather than logic, the mentee sees all knowledge as equal. As a mentor, you will need to help this mentee assess the value of different options and see how knowledge fits together.

- *Relativism.* This individual sees diversity of opinion everywhere and analyzes these opinions relative to each other. Reality takes on a qualitative dimension, depending on its context. Your mentee sees you as mentor as one of many resources with whom he or she is interacting. As a mentor, you can facilitate learning by helping your mentee contextually analyze his or her thinking.

- *Commitment.* Perry's fourth framework is qualitatively different because it describes ways of being rather than ways of thinking. A committed mentee is internally motivated to act out of an awareness of relativism.

As mentor, you can facilitate learning by helping your mentee connect thinking with acting.

APPLYING ADULT LEARNING CONCEPTS TO MENTORING

Over a century ago, Louis Agassiz was a natural history professor at Harvard University.[13] One day, he assigned his student the task of observing a fish and then left him alone. The student quickly grew bored with the assignment and concluded that he had "seen all there is to see." To fill his time while waiting for Professor Agassiz to return, he took a pencil and paper and drew the fish. And as he drew, he discovered features he had not previously observed.

When the professor returned, the student eagerly reported what he had found from observing and drawing the fish. At first, Agassiz praised his student and remarked, "A pencil is one of the best of eyes." Then he challenged him, saying, "You have not looked very carefully! Why, you haven't even seen one of the most conspicuous features of the animal, which is as plainly before your eyes as the fish itself. Look again, look again."

This scene between Agassiz and his student repeated itself over and over. And with each new observation by the student, Agassiz offered a compliment, followed by a challenge to "look, look again." In this way, Agassiz offers valuable lessons in adult learning and mentoring. For example, rather than telling the student the answer, Agassiz provided an opportunity for self-discovery and reflection. In addition, he paced the learning to be sensitive to the student's need. And he kept encouraging the student to examine the fish from many different perspectives: to look more deeply. That is exactly what I hope you will do.

Polly Berends writes, "Everything that happens to you is your teacher. The secret is to learn to sit at the feet of your own life and be taught by it."[14] Research supports this: one of the best ways adults learn and also retain the knowledge they learn is through critical reflection on experience. According to Stephen Brookfield, who has made a study of the process of critical reflection and adult learning, critical reflection is an attempt to uncover and explore the assumptions that underlie what we do and how we do it so that our actions become more informed, integrative, and aligned.

The exercises throughout this book offer you the opportunity—and challenge—to "look, look again" and learn from experience. When you can use that learning to full advantage in your mentoring relationships, you will be in a better position to enhance the learning of your mentees. You will also be better prepared to encourage your mentees to learn from their experiences.

THE MENTOR'S JOURNEY

Let's begin by making sure you have a clear understanding of your own personal journey. Each of us is an amalgamation of our own life experiences. By becoming a student of your own journey, you will be better able to understand its flow and pattern. Observing the journey is also a telling way to test out assumptions—a healthy sense of perspective is useful in guiding your mentee's learning.

This is a vitally important step. When we fail to differentiate between self and other in a mentoring relationship, we run the risk of projecting our own lived experience onto our mentee. The result is that the mentee's learning becomes formulaic rather than individualized, and the mentee ends up front and center on your stage rather than creating his or her own.

Reflecting on Your Personal Journey

The metaphor of the mentor's journey captures the meandering quality of the movement that follows us as we face new challenges and go off in new directions. We experience unexpected delights, lurking dangers, doors opening and closing, change, and ennui. It's easy to be distracted in the moment, and this exercise gives us the time we need to properly observe and reflect. "In the mentoring process," say Huang and Lynch, "reflection enables us to slow down, rest, and observe our journey and the process of self-knowledge that is so important along the way."[15]

There are three steps in the observation process:

1. *Gain self-awareness*: This step is triggered by self-reflection. It is fundamental to understanding your role in facilitating effective learning relationships.

2. *Understand the mentee's journey*: Mentees bring their own history of experience to the mentoring relationship. When you engage the mentee in a discussion of that experience, you can avoid the "mentor cloning" trap—inadvertently training your mentee to become another version of yourself.

3. *Gain perspective*: Look again at your own journey and that of your mentees. What you learn from observing these separate and distinct paths has direct implications for the learning outcomes.

There are many ways to depict a journey. The way you choose will be uniquely your own. You may choose to construct a time line (as in Exercise 1.1) by making notes, or you may prefer a more graphic approach. The means for completion are not as important as taking the time to reflect on your

EXERCISE 1.1

Your Personal Journey Time Line

The line in the box below represents your journey as an adult from the past to today. Using words, symbols, or drawings, sketch your journey on the time line.

1. Draw a time line horizontally on a sheet of paper, like this, allowing as much room as you need above and below the line:

2. In the space above the time line, note significant life events that have influenced you the most. Do not feel constrained to stick to work-related events or even those that have to do with mentoring. Focus on the events, milestones, and transitions (positive and negative) that have had an impact on your development.

3. Now turn your attention next to the space below the time line:

   - Identify opportunities that made a difference in your life and helped you grow and develop.

   - Identify obstacles that got in the way of your journey.

   - Note "unexpected delights"—events and experiences that were not planned but just happened.

4. Review your time line of events, and add the names of individuals who contributed to your development.

5. What lessons did you learn, and how did they change your thinking?

6. What new understandings emerge for you as you review your time line of experience?

personal journey and consider the movement that has brought you to the place you are in your life. Here's one example.

Miriam's Time Line

Miriam volunteered to be a mentor to women who wanted to make a transition in their careers. In preparing for her role, she constructed a time line of her own career journey, which had taken a unique course.

A utility company had hired Miriam immediately after she completed her associate degree at the local community college. After ten years in a variety of jobs, she was promoted to a managerial position. A number of years later, her daughter was fatally injured in a hit-and-run accident. Not long after, she decided to pursue a nursing degree, which she completed three years later. She left the company to take a job as a floor nurse at a local hospital, where she now holds a supervisory position.

In constructing her time line from line worker to nursing director, Miriam identified seven significant life events as having shaped her development: two marriages, a divorce, the death of her daughter, going back to school, specific job promotions, and a fortieth birthday celebration.

She also identified three specific opportunities that helped her grow and develop: a mentoring relationship with a woman who was "a fabulous role model for the possible," the educational opportunity provided by the company, and a spouse who was her "cheerleader, guide, and support." But many experiences also blocked her development along the way: living with a spouse who could not understand her dreams and ambitions, tedious work, and coworkers who tried to undermine her educational advancement.

She would be the first to say that serendipitous events and experiences contributed to her growth and development. One of these was meeting Charlotte, her mentor, at a neighborhood holiday party. Another was spending hours visiting her critically ill daughter in the hospital.

In reviewing her time line, Miriam realized that there were more hidden helpers—individuals who contributed to her growth and development—than she had realized. Among these were her mother, her eldest son, a ninth-grade teacher, her first supervisor, the head nurse at the hospital where her daughter lay dying, a favorite aunt, and a motivational speaker at a conference she had attended.

She realized how much her thinking had changed over time. Instead of letting change happen to her and push her around, she learned how to deal with it and ultimately became a change agent for others. She became a can-do person, taking responsibility for her own life through accepting risks and daring to dream.

Completing the time line exercise helped Miriam become aware of how many people had helped her on her journey. "I never realized how privileged I've been; I knew on some level, but not to this extent. I was overwhelmed with gratitude, and felt a need to reconnect with some of these people. I also was more clear about why I wanted to be a mentor: I needed to give back some of the gifts from others that I'd been privileged to receive."

Reflecting on Your Mentoring Journey

In *Composing a Life* (1989), Mary Catherine Bateson describes her developmental journey through life as a composition of connections with women friends who flow in and out of her life at different stages, times, and places. Each has contributed to making her who she is. She reminds us that "the past empowers the present, and the groping footsteps leading to the present mark the pathways to the future."[16]

In Exercise 1.2 you will construct a mentoring time line. In it you will reflect on what you have learned from the mentors (or other people) who have been part of your life's composition and explore how that learning might affect you as a mentor. You can use a piece of blank paper, or write your thoughts in your journal.

The Mentee's Journey

It is human nature to make assumptions about others and project our own experiences and reality onto them. Sometimes, with relatively little real information, we blithely fill in the blanks and become convinced—mistakenly, as it usually turns out—that we understand the other person. Mentors especially need to guard against this temptation and be aware of what sets their journey apart from their mentees'. One way to do this is to understand not only your own journey but the mentee's journey. Here's a cautionary tale:

EXERCISE 1.2

Reflecting on Your Experiences as a Mentee

Think about your mentoring experiences and the people who were there to guide, support, and strengthen you:

My mentors were:

When did they come into my life?

What wisdom have I gained from each of them?

What were the most satisfying aspects of those relationships, and why?

What were the least satisfying aspects of those relationships, and why?

What did I learn about being a mentor from these experiences?

What did I learn about being a mentee?

Madeline and Gordon

Madeleine moved to the Southwest after working as a real estate broker on the East Coast for more than thirty years. In a matter of months, she became active in her condominium association and was elected one of its officers. After eight years chairing the association board, she was eager to move on. However, there were no apparent successors with previous experience or knowledge of property management issues. In order to develop a new generation of leadership quickly, she and her board agreed to set up strategically paired mentoring relationships with future association leaders.

When Gordon heard about the vacancy on the board, he immediately volunteered to serve. He said that he "was looking for something to keep him busy" and thought that this opportunity might be "just what he was looking for." Madeleine was not convinced that he could provide the necessary leadership, but she was outvoted by her fellow officers. She thought that Gordon was "a nice enough person" but just looking to fill up his time. She was concerned about gaps in his knowledge of issues and problems and offered to mentor Gordon.

Madeleine spent a week putting together an agenda and materials to orient Gordon to what she felt he needed to know. But when she presented her list to him, he was affronted—and rightly so.

It turned out that Madeleine's assumptions about what Gordon knew were erroneous. Gordon was the former owner of two construction companies and held an M.B.A. His son managed his properties. Gordon's learning needs were not the same as Madeleine's because his experience was different from hers. Had she known more about her mentee's journey before she prepared an agenda and materials, their relationship could have started on a more positive note.

Exercise 1.3 asks you to think about your current or prospective mentee's journey. It is intended to help you gain a better sense about the person you are mentoring, but you will not be constructing a complete time line with details as you did in the previous exercise. If you already know something about this person, the exercise offers an approach for testing out your own assumptions and gaining a clear understanding of factors that may affect the learning relationship.

EXERCISE 1.3

Your Mentee's Time Line

The line in the box below represents your mentee's journey as an adult from the past to today. Using words, symbols, or drawings, sketch this journey on the time line.

1. Draw a time line horizontally on a sheet of paper, like this, allowing as much room as you need above and below the line:

2. What do you imagine your mentee's journey has been? Start with the present and work backward. Think broadly, filling in known milestones, experiences, and events.

3. What more do you need to know about your mentee in order to have a better sense of his or her journey?

4. If you need to gather more information, what questions will you ask your mentee? What information can you gather from other sources?

5. What insights does your mentee's journey raise for you about his or her readiness to learn?

Use a pencil (rather than a pen) to complete Exercise 1.3 because the data you have now, particularly if this is a prospective mentee, will probably be incomplete. If you lack information to fill in the time line, this may be a clue that you need more baseline data from your mentee. Ask questions, and gain the information you need to complete the mentee journey time line. One way to avoid the tendency to use a one-size-fits-all approach when mentoring several individuals simultaneously is to think about the answers to the questions in Exercise 1.3 and become aware of your knowledge gaps about a particular mentee's developmental journey. Completing this exercise will help you identify potential needs and conversation starting points.

Awareness of Self and Other

The mentoring relationship is innately complex because it involves two unique individuals. It is important to preserve the differentiation between self and other and not attempt to homogenize journeys. As Bateson notes, "Work relationships of any kind are enlivened by difference combined with mutual commitment."[17]

In Exercises 1.1, 1.2, and 1.3, you've considered your journey and your mentee's journey separately. In Exercise 1.4, you will consider your mutual journey: Where are you on your journey time line relative to where your mentee is or will be? What implications does this gap present in how you will facilitate learning? The brief story that follows illustrates how you might use what you learn in the exercise.

Niles and Juliana

Niles began his career as a schoolteacher and subsequently switched to city government, where he worked for ten years. As a community service volunteer, he was a mentor in a school-to-work program. He attempted to fill out the mentee time line in Exercise 1.3 with the information he had been given before his first meeting with Juliana, a prospective mentee. After his first several conversations with her, he was able to fill in several missing pieces and gain a better understanding of her needs. But when he completed the self and other exercise in Exercise 1.4, merging their two separate journeys, he discovered a fresh perspective that would completely change the mentoring relationship.

Niles had recently decided to return to school to get a law degree, and he needed the next few months to prepare for the LSATs. He realized that as much as he wanted to be of assistance, the time he had available might not be adequate in view of the

EXERCISE 1.4

Journey Worksheet: Implications for Facilitating Learning

Look at your own time line in Exercise 1.1 and your mentee's time line in Exercise 1.3. Consider where you are right now on your time line and where your mentee is on his or her time line. Then answer the following questions:

1. What concerns and issues does this comparison raise for you as a mentor? Are there significant differences in your life experiences? Where are the biggest gaps in your experiences?

2. What concerns and issues does the comparison raise for you about your (prospective) mentee's learning needs and learning goals?

3. What specific actions or approaches could potentially have a positive impact on the learning relationship?

4. What specific actions or approaches could potentially adversely affect the learning relationship?

5. What strategies might you use to overcome them?

immediacy of Juliana's need. He struggled to find a way to do both and decided to be candid with both his mentoring coordinator and Juliana. They were both grateful that he was open about his personal needs, and they were able to identify workable strategies that would satisfy both his time constraints and hers.

Experience and Reflection

Our own lived experience is the text for self-discovery and learning.[18] It is the most powerful learning resource we have at our disposal. When we are able to reflect critically on our own varied life experiences and learn from them, we can model this critical reflection in our mentoring interaction. For example, Barry learned that his golf game improved when he was able to slow down, concentrate, and maintain his focus. He realized that if he made these same changes at work, he would be more efficient, productive, and focused there as well.

Exercise 1.5 demonstrates how to bring your personal experience to your mentoring work. Jot down quick responses in bullet form. Then revisit them more extensively later, or use the data you generate in conversations with your mentee. If the space provided here is insufficient, you might choose to begin a journal with these questions as the topics, noting the first words and phrases that come to mind as you read the questions. You may also choose to engage in conversation as a way of addressing the questions. Answer the reflection questions only after you have completed the first four items to your satisfaction. Assess the level of difficulty you experienced in addressing these questions.

Use this exercise as a reference point as you raise these same kinds of questions with your mentee. For example, if you experience difficulty in answering these questions, you can say authentically to a mentee, "Look, I know these questions are difficult to respond to. I ask myself the same kinds of questions, and frankly, it takes me a while to come up with answers that satisfy me. Still, I've found that really thinking about what I've learned from my personal experiences helps me improve my performance."

Here's how Angela incorporates reflection on experience into her work:

Angela's Story

Angela is a mentor in a distance learning program. She has several student mentees and has found an effective way to help them reflect on their experiences. Whenever she works with her mentees on a practicum project, she advises them to write in their journals about their learning as it occurs. She encourages them to review

EXERCISE 1.5

Reflecting on Your Experience

This exercise offers the opportunity for a fresh perspective on how it feels to reflect on experience consciously and to learn from it. It will put you in touch with some experiences you have had that can assist you in facilitating your mentee's learning.

Your Experience

1. Working quickly, jot down bulleted responses or words that come to mind for these questions:

   • What lessons have you learned from your successes?

   • What lessons have you learned from your mistakes?

   • What dilemmas do you face daily?

   • What lessons have you learned from grappling with those dilemmas?

2. Let your answers sit for a while. Later, review your answers to see if they trigger additional responses. Then complete these questions:

   • What was it like to address these questions?

   • How would you rate the level of difficulty?

   Easy _____ Difficult

3. What did you learn about yourself in going through this exercise?

   Alternatively (or in addition), you may want to ask mentees to complete this exercise and discuss what the experience of reflecting on experience was like with them. In this way, you can position the learning, saying, "Part of learning is reflecting on experience; this will give you a preview of what that is like."

their entries before starting the next project. At the end of each project, she encourages them to make another entry. And again, before beginning the next practicum project, she asks them to review all prior entries.

Getting to know a mentee does not mean knowing everything about that person. Rather, gaining a good sense about who this person is and what he or she brings to the learning relationship helps the mentor connect and facilitate a more meaningful learning experience. Listening well and asking thoughtful questions are often just enough to elicit the relevant information. Making notes at the end of each mentoring session about events, special people, or concerns your mentee has talked about is helpful. At the same time, identify specific points of connection for the next mentoring session. When you deeply understand the power of experience and reflection, you are better prepared to facilitate learning relationships.

Facilitating Adult Learning

As a mentor, you need to be skilled at facilitating adult learning—engaging mentees as active participants in their own learning by encouraging self-reflection and self-authorship. In essence, you are creating conditions that enable mentees to learn.

Facilitation is rooted in Malcolm Knowles's principles of adult learning. According to Knowles, these practices promote effective facilitation:[19]

- Establish a climate conducive to learning.
- Involve learners in planning how and what they will learn.
- Encourage learners to formulate their own learning objectives.
- Encourage learners to identify and use a variety of resources to accomplish their objectives.
- Help learners implement and evaluate their learning.

"Facilitators of learning," as Brookfield puts it, "see themselves as resources for learning, rather than as didactic instructors who have all the answers."[20] You can facilitate learning in many ways, all the while listening, empowering, coaching, challenging, teaching, collaborating, aiding, assisting, supporting, expediting, easing, simplifying, advancing, and encouraging. The flow of your facilitation will always depend on the needs of the mentee. Some learners may need more support and direction to feel comfortable with the process, while others feel prepared and are ready to go to work immediately.

EXERCISE 1.6

Reflecting on Facilitation

Think about your experience in facilitating someone else's learning. Or recall an experience of someone you observed facilitating another person's learning. Now answer the following questions:

1. Describe an experience in which the goal was to facilitate someone else's learning.

2. What did you do? What did the learner do?

3. What factors affected the success or derailment of your efforts?

4. What metaphor best describes how that experience felt for you?

5. What, if anything, would you do differently in facilitating your mentee's learning?

TABLE 1.4

The Facilitator's Reference Guide

1. Engage mentees and tap into their unique experiences.

2. Encourage mentees to reflect on their past experiences and use them as learning opportunities.

3. Inspire and build mentee confidence and competence.

4. Create a positive, safe learning environment.

5. Relate to mentees' situations, issues, and concerns.

6. Consider the timing.

7. Pace the learning.

8. Allow adequate time for mentees to integrate and reflect on the learning.

9. Use a variety of approaches that draw on different learning styles.

10. Be flexible and open to new ideas.

11. Respect mentees' unique needs and cultural differences.

12. Be clear about the purpose, direction, and boundaries of the learning.

13. Ask for feedback on your facilitation techniques.

14. Be open to suggestions for improving the process.

Exercise 1.6 will help you appreciate some of the complexities of learning facilitation and ways in which you will approach it with your mentees.

Mentoring is a process of becoming for both partners. Although we want to encourage mentees "to look, look again," we also need to be our own diligent observers of the process. I encourage you to refer to the facilitator's reference guide in Table 1.4 to help you stay on track.

WHAT MENTORS DO

Mentors facilitate learning by keeping the learner front and center. To mentor effectively, you will use the learning approach most appropriate for your mentee. Asking questions, reformulating statements, summarizing, listening for the silence, and listening reflectively will help you do this. These strategies should always be part of your toolkit.

Ask Questions

Questions encourage learning by allowing us to reflect. Asking questions that require thoughtful answers (like those in the exercises in this chapter) is a good way to help mentees articulate their own thinking. Use questions to engage the mentee in the conversation. Remember: ethical, role-appropriate questioning is a must. When you stray outside these boundaries, it is easy to exceed limits of appropriateness and fairness.

- Ask questions that support and challenge—for example: "That's a nice way of describing the culture. How would you apply some of that thinking to the staff?"

- Ask questions to stimulate reflection—for example: "Could you tell me a little more about what you mean by . . . ?" "Is there another way to look at this?"

- Ask specific questions that draw on your mentee's unique thinking and learning style—for example: "That seems logical, but let's take a moment to brainstorm some other possibilities." "It sounds like you have a lot of good options! Is there one that you really resonate with?" "That's a great idea. How do you think we might put it into action?"

- Allow time for thoughtful reflection—for example: "It sounds as if we've only begun to scratch the surface. Let's think about this some more and discuss it further in our next conversation."

Reformulate Statements

When we rephrase what we've heard mentees say, we can clarify our own understanding and encourage the mentee to hear and reflect on what they have articulated. This offers an opportunity for further clarification:

- Paraphrase what you heard—for example: "I think what I heard you saying is . . ."

- Continue the process of rephrasing and paraphrasing until you clearly understand and the mentee is no longer adding new information—for example: "My understanding is . . ."

Summarize

Summarizing what you've learned during a session reinforces the learning. It also serves as a reminder of what has transpired and acts as a way to check assumptions:

- Share the content of what you have heard, learned, or accomplished— for example: "We've spent our time today doing . . . During that time we . . . As a result, we achieved the following outcomes . . ."

- Leave judgments and opinions out when you summarize—for example: "Did you say that . . . ?" "I understood you to say . . . Is that correct?"

- Deal with the facts of the situation, not the emotions—for example: "So, I am hearing three things. Number 1 is . . ., number 2 is . . ., and number 3 is . . ., Have I got that right?"

Listen for the Silence

Silence provides an opportunity for learning. Some individuals need time to think quietly. Silence can also indicate confusion, boredom, or even physical discomfort:

- Don't be afraid of silence.

- Encourage silence.

- Use the silence as an opportunity for reflection—for example: "I notice that whenever we started to talk about . . . you get kind of quiet. I'm wondering what that is about."

Listen Reflectively

Often we hear but do not really listen. When you listen reflectively, you hear the silence, observe nonverbal responses, and hold up a mirror for the mentee:

- Be authentic—for example: "What I'd like to see is . . ."

- Clarify—for example: "What do you mean by . . . ?"

- Provide feedback—for example: "You did a great job with that. I like the way you . . . I also thought that . . . Next time you might try . . ."

When your work is solidly grounded in principles of adult learning, you and your mentee can be colearners who both benefit and grow from the relationship. The two chapters in Part One will broaden your understanding of the learning process by exploring the role of context and its influence in the mentoring process.

PART ONE

CONSIDERING CONTEXT

SHAWN WAS A SELF-DESCRIBED military brat who lived in five different countries when he was growing up and going to school. As a child, he was disciplined and self-directed and never questioned authority. This worked to his competitive advantage while he was in engineering school. Once he started working, however, he found himself out of context. His company did not worry about whether employees came to work on time or worked a set number of hours. It put a higher value on building relationships and measured success by the quality of the team's effort rather than individual contributions. After a few months, Shawn was beginning to wonder just how he fit in and even whether he had chosen the right career. The context of his experience just didn't mesh with the new context of his work environment.

Shawn's mentor, Todd, was thirty years older than Shawn. He had spent his early career in more structured work settings and had to find his own flexibility to navigate changing times and processes. He was sympathetic and quick to grasp how Shawn's discomfort and disconnects grew out of these conflicting contexts—the one he had been raised in and the one in which he needed to work. Todd facilitated a mentoring experience that engaged Shawn in learning how to look at various approaches to solving a problem and being willing to entertain other opinions in the process.

ALL MENTORING RELATIONSHIPS ARE EMBEDDED IN CONTEXT

Context influences how we perceive reality, what we see as possible and achievable. From it, we draw our identity and formulate our thinking and attitudes.[1] When I entered the work world, I was immediately struck by the disconnects between what I had been raised to expect and the professional options that were available to me. I had the good fortune to have mentors who helped me see beyond the myopia of my institution, gender, and job contexts. Rather than label me, they facilitated my learning by helping me understand that I was not a context but a contextual being and that I could be working with these multiple contexts rather than against them.

All mentoring relationships are grounded in context: the circumstances, conditions, and contributing forces that affect how we connect, interact with, and learn from one another. Context plays a critical role,[2] yet it is an elusive and difficult concept to grasp because our contexts are multilayered: we never operate in just one context.

Think for a moment about the contexts of your daily life: your home, your workplace, your profession, your social situation, your upbringing, your country or family of origin. As mentoring partners, we each bring our own multiple contexts and create a new context of partnership, which itself influences our relationship. Individually and collectively, we respond to contextually derived behaviors and values, and the context or environment also responds to us.[3]

As Jack Mezirow writes, "The justification for much of what we know and believe, our values, and our feelings depends on the context . . . in which they are embedded."[4] Context is always at play, in subtle and overt ways. It helps us understand the values that drive our behavior, affects our emotions, and colors how we read a person or a situation. Ignoring context, overlooking it, or taking it for granted dramatically affects the learning that takes place in a mentoring relationship.[5]

Mentoring relationships exist both across and between contexts. For example, many educational institutions have well-entrenched mentoring programs for fledgling teachers, and many graduate schools offer graduate education using mentoring as a vehicle to support, promote, and accelerate learning across contexts. Mentoring has become a professional responsibility in specific contexts like teacher education, law, health care, and leadership. Community mentoring partnerships foster economic development between contexts: between business and education. Senior centers offer opportunities for cross-generational mentoring—again, between contexts. The array of mentoring opportunities is as varied as the contexts themselves.

The context of a mentoring relationship adds its own unique layers of contextual complexity. Is the relationship formal, informal, sponsored, situational, incidental? Does the relationship operate in a group? Is it a one-to-one partnership? Is it virtual or face-to-face? Because all of these contextual layers affect an individual simultaneously, learning partners in a mentoring relationship need to communicate expectations and establish ground rules and processes that work for them in the specific context of mentoring. Otherwise they may soon find themselves working at cross-purposes.

CONSIDERATION OF CONTEXT FACILITATES LEARNING

Context is a formidable consideration in facilitating the learning that takes place in mentoring relationships. A mentoring learning goal that is set without taking into account the mentee's context—the bigger picture, the strategic objectives, and the mentee's fundamental priorities—is doomed from the start. The feedback a mentor provides also needs to be situated in context if it is to be relevant and useful to the mentee.[6] The relationship itself is context specific, and variations in context determine how mentoring is experienced and the outcomes derived from the relationship.[7]

"The learning that adults do arises from the context of their lives," says Sharan Merriam.[8] As mentors, we must develop our contextual intelligence and consciously use it as a tool to ensure the integrity of the learning process. We need to become context sensitive to abundant difference.[9] Ultimately, as Nye writes, "Contextual intelligence also requires emotional intelligence. Without sensitivity to the needs of others, pure cognitive analysis and long experience may prove insufficient."[10]

The two chapters in Part One focus on the context of difference (specifically, cultural difference, generational difference, sexual preference, gender, race, and power) and the context of connection (various configurations of mentoring and virtual and distance connections). The scope of possibilities for discussing context in relation to mentoring is both broad and deep; in this book, we only begin the process of digging.

CHAPTER 2

THE CONTEXT OF DIFFERENCE

BRINGING WHO WE ARE TO WHAT WE DO

THE SAYING, "WE SEE THE WORLD not as it is, but as we are," has been attributed to many sources—Anaïs Nin, Charles Lamb, and the Talmud, among others. As a mentor, it's vital to be aware that no two people—including you and your mentee—see the world through precisely the same lens. Too often we make meaning through "difference filters" that blind us to our own biases and lead us to misunderstand people who are communicating with us through their own difference filters.

It's easy to make the mistake of thinking our mentees are just like us. Yet it is far more likely that you will notice the differences between you and your mentee first—especially if he or she is from a different culture or religion, is older or younger than you, has a different sexual orientation, or is of a different race, and it's not unusual that there will be a power differential. Ultimately the context of mentoring is difference: who we are shapes our thinking, our conversation, our relationships, and our behaviors. Too often we become unwitting prisoners of our own stereotypical assumptions. Becoming aware of these filters, and understanding that we can put them aside, opens up possibilities for learning you may never have dreamed of.

THE CONTEXT OF CULTURE

How we define and understand the word *mentor* varies from culture to culture, and this understanding can alter the very essence of the mentoring relationship. In one cultural context, it may be closely related to teacher, supervisor, or expert; in another, it might not translate directly. In other cultures, the word may even have a negative association with the perception that it is "weak" to seek or need a mentor. None of these understandings are the same as that of the mentor in the mentoring relationship we are talking about in this book.

Cross-cultural understandings frame how we see the world and how we act within it. If the role of teacher is traditionally revered, as it is in China, the mentee's perception of mentor as teacher might affect the openness and directness of communication or how conflict is resolved. If your mentee comes from a culture in which the expectation is that the teacher must initiate contact, communication is seen as tied to credibility and control. If the words *teacher* and *mentor* are interchangeable terms in that culture, you will need to help your mentee understand that your relationship will not be one of knowledge given, knowledge received.

Your effectiveness in a cross-cultural mentoring relationship rests on your cross-cultural competency and your communication skills.

Cross-Cultural Competency

Cross-cultural competency means being able to understand cultural differences and use that understanding to communicate and interact effectively with people from other cultures. Global and cross-cultural experts identify an array of competencies for establishing successful global relationships in business, many of which pertain to mentoring relationships.[1] These include becoming culturally self-aware, having an authentic desire to learn, becoming attuned to other cultures, and developing a flexible cultural lens.

Become Culturally Self-Aware

Technology allows mentoring relationships to flourish despite great distances—both temporal and cultural. In this example, the mentor, Peter, is located in the United States, and his mentee, Wen, is in Beijing. Differences in their cultural understanding get in the way of the relationship almost immediately.

Peter and Wen

Peter Jensen, an executive in a fast-expanding publishing business, and his mentee, Liu Pei Wen, agreed to conduct their mentoring sessions by videoconference. Peter set up a meeting and confirmed the time for the videoconference with Wen. But that morning, Wen's manager in Beijing asked her to attend a meeting with him, which was scheduled at the same time as the videoconference with Peter.

When Peter called in for the videoconference and found that Wen was not there, he was annoyed, but he decided that something must have happened and waited to hear from her. After two days had passed and Wen still had not checked in, Peter called Wen to ask if something was wrong. She apologized profusely for the misunderstanding. When Peter offered to set up a meeting for the following morning, Wen responded that she needed to "recommend it to her manager" first.

Now Peter was angry. He felt that his time was valuable and that Wen was not taking this relationship seriously. When he complained to one of his colleagues who had spent time at the Beijing office, she explained that for Wen, punctuality was not as important as honoring hierarchy—and her boss took precedence over Peter. Hearing this, Peter was taken aback. He had never considered how different ways of thinking might play out in his mentoring relationship.

Until he was confronted with a problem, Peter was unaware of his how own cultural biases limited his receptivity to Wen's cultural assumptions. Even if the gap is not as wide as Peter's and Wen's, a good strategy is to identify culturally derived values and assumptions that could affect your relationship with your mentee. It may be that you were brought up in a culture where sharing feelings is inappropriate or that a one-on-one learning relationship is seen as a weakness. Self-knowledge is the most important cross-cultural competency for a mentor to possess because it keeps the mentor on course and focused. It will certainly help you in your understanding of others, and as Mezirow points out, those who become conscious of their own values and assumptions and critically examine them will be rewarded with a deeper understanding of their own behavior.[2]

Exercise 2.1 is an opportunity to think about cultural assumptions that may guide your actions yet are virtually invisible to you.

Have an Authentic Desire to Learn

The expanding global workforce has made the need for awareness of other cultures very important; for mentors, it is imperative. But awareness may not be enough. An authentic desire to learn about another culture will give you a new perspective on your own cultural perspectives.

Even if you don't feel genuinely interested at first, make an effort to try acting as if you do. Be open and willing to listen to your mentee without making value judgments, and ask questions if you are puzzled about why your mentee does things in a way different from what you expect.

EXERCISE 2.1

Reflecting on Your Own Cultural Assumptions

Look at the examples of assumptions and behaviors provided in the first three lines of this table, and then complete the exercise by reflecting on your own values and assumptions. Consider what values and assumptions you hold that someone from a culture other than your own might not readily understand. How do these values and assumptions get played out on a daily basis in what you do and how you do it?

Value or Assumption	How They Are Reflected in Your Behavior
Elders are to be revered.	I am deferential to people who are older than I am even if I don't agree with their opinion.
It is impolite to raise your voice in a business meeting.	If someone is impolite, I can't relate to them.
Relationships are important.	I need to connect with people before I do business with them.

And remember too that cross-cultural mentoring encompasses individual and cultural diversity. Don't assume that every cultural tendency you have read about will apply to your mentee. Check out your assumptions with your mentee before you act on them.

Finally, give yourself and your mentoring partner permission to make mistakes—and then create ways to learn from mistakes together. If you are not making mistakes, you are not learning.

Develop a Working Knowledge of and Appreciation for Other Cultures

Even when both mentoring partners speak the same language and are born in the same country, their cultural expectations can get in the way of a productive relationship. Let's look at what happened to Hugo and Ed:

Hugo and Ed

Hugo Schröeder and his mentee, Ed Yazzie, both engineers in a multinational architectural firm, were paired as mentoring partners in the organization's formal mentoring program. The program focused on fast-tracking high-potential employees by matching them up with senior associates from different cultural backgrounds who had broad corporate experience, business savvy, and specialized expertise. Both mentee and mentor were expected to work on the same client project during the year of mentorship.

Hugo and Ed held their initial mentoring meeting in an office on the project location. Hugo greeted Ed with a handshake, invited him to sit down across the table, and tried to get down to business right away. He drove the agenda and tried to steer the conversation in such a way that a mentoring agreement would result from the meeting. But Ed seemed to offer resistance at every turn. Ed wanted to get to know his mentor—not just what he did but who he was. He wanted to understand Hugo's family background and ancestry, and he wanted to share his own experience and talk about his family. Hugo saw this as a waste of time, but he didn't want to insult Ed by cutting him off. He figured if he got this over with now, they could get down to business next time.

But the second meeting was the same. Hugo wanted to define learning goals for the relationship, but the harder he pushed, the quieter Ed became. Progress toward goal setting proceeded at a snail's pace. Hugo became increasingly impatient and frustrated with Ed, who seemed only to want to get to know more about him and to hear and tell more family stories. Hugo, for his part, was only getting more and more uptight.

Hugo's parents were first-generation German immigrants; he was raised in an austere, orderly home, and that's what he was comfortable with. He had little patience for relationships in the workplace and didn't understand why Ed felt that establishing a personal relationship was so important. Ed was a Native American raised in a large extended family. His vision of a mentor was someone who could be a kind of surrogate uncle—someone who would get to know him as a person, feel proud of him, support him, and befriend him.

Hugo was puzzled and frustrated but said nothing. In fact, he didn't know what to say. Ed avoided the issue altogether and swallowed his disappointment. His cultural tradition and upbringing had taught him to defer to elders and, for him, the term *elder* included mentors. After the fourth meeting, Hugo couldn't hold back his frustration. He told Ed that he was sabotaging the mentoring relationship. Ed was left with a sense of shame and hurt.

It became evident very quickly that this mentoring partnership was not the one either had envisioned. Hugo might have been able to head off this compounding misunderstanding if he had taken Ed's cue during that first session and gotten to know his mentee. He might also have gotten some valuable clues if he had asked Ed why these stories were so important and then explained his own perspective. It's easy to get boxed in by our own ways of thinking. We begin to believe and act as if ours are the best or even the only ways of thinking and behaving, and we close off other ways of doing things. Getting locked into someone else's stereotypes in mentoring is just as possible and troublesome as it is in any other context. Mentors who are in the best position to facilitate learning are willing to learn about the basic functional elements of their mentee's culture.

A good strategy in this case is to seek information about your mentee's country—its people, politics and government, key historical and cultural achievements, dominant religious beliefs and practices, family and social structure, educational system, economics and industry, geography, sports, entertainment, and symbols. This will help you begin to see the world through your mentee's lens—and it may look very different from your own.

Become Attuned to Other Cultures

Culture influences the way people express themselves, including everything from tone of voice, being "polite" or "argumentative," using lots of gestures, and even saying yes when the real answer is no. Understanding the norms of the culture a person comes from can help communication enormously, as Nancy discovered.

Nancy and Mario

Mario Lombardo, the distribution manager for an Italian winery, was eager to move from Italy to his company's corporate offices in the United States. To prepare himself, he found a U.S. manager in the Wisconsin branch—an experienced and knowledgeable insider—who agreed to be his mentor. Nancy was looking to expand her leadership skills and saw mentoring Mario as an opportunity to broaden her own cultural awareness.

The relationship did not go the way Nancy had hoped. Right from the beginning, each encounter with Mario was fraught with tension. Mario would ask good questions but constantly interrupted her as she attempted to provide answers. His frequent emotional outbursts became a constant irritant. Nancy found herself beginning to doubt his intentions, but when she told her friend Barbara about her frustrations, she laughed and said, "I guess you haven't met many Italians." Nancy was taken aback. She decided to do some research about his culture.

Nancy soon learned that Mario's emotional responses were expressive of a culture where subjective feelings are valued. Mario's need for discussion was not about her, but what he needed to do to gain clarity. She realized that her own need for results did not match Mario's need for process.

"Becoming culturally attuned" means being able to read the culture of a mentee and understanding what is happening and what is expected through the context and nonverbal behaviors. Through conversation, mentor and mentee become aware of different perceptions and values that can facilitate or hinder their communication.

These values inform the expectations and agreements that will flow out of the relationship and can be about almost anything. One partner's cultural expectations may be results oriented. This may not be true for the other partner. Decision making in some cultures takes several meetings to achieve. Waiting for consensus may be difficult for one partner personally and yet may be very much a part of the way another culture conducts its business. Joking between men and women in some cultures is considered inappropriate. Be aware that people from many cultures do not always express their feelings verbally. Avoid asking questions that are personal, embarrassing, or probing. Remember that even such seemingly basic concepts as time, cultural distance, and what constitutes politeness vary widely.

A global mind-set will give you the ability to expand your own knowledge and deal more effectively with the complexity of the world. Because our world is indeed shrinking, a number of books have been written on the subject of cultural behavior. I urge you to seek them out and begin to tune up your cultural IQ.[3]

Develop a Flexible Cultural Lens

Mentoring in a cross-cultural context requires preparation and flexibility. Cross-cultural expert Gloria Sandvik identifies four action strategies for maintaining a flexible cultural lens: prepare, remember, observe, and show. For each, she offers specific recommendations.[4] Exercise 2.2 offers a concrete to-do list based on her work.

No matter how prepared you are, you will inevitably find a great deal of individual variation within a particular cultural context. Each individual you mentor will be operating not only in the context of culture; he or she will also be a composite of learning styles, family values, economic circumstances, and so forth. As Oyler points out, "The key to cross cultural mentoring is knowing that you must also add all of the complexity of any human interaction after somehow becoming culturally attuned."[5]

Communication Skills

Dominick grew up in an Irish American family in an Irish American neighborhood, and most of his friends were people he had grown up with or friends from work who were much like himself. He had never given much thought to people outside this narrow range—not because he actively avoided them but because he never had the opportunity to meet them. That changed when he met his new mentee, Luann, a new employee from Southeast Asia.

Dominick and Luann

After three meetings with Luann, Dominick was becoming increasingly frustrated. He tried different approaches, but he couldn't get Luann to open up and talk about her work situation or the challenges and issues she was facing. How was he supposed to mentor her if she wouldn't say anything?

EXERCISE 2.2

Intercultural Communication Checklist

1. Prepare

   ❑ Research your mentee's culture before you meet.

   ❑ Identify your intention. What do you want from this relationship?

   ❑ Clarify the goals of the mentoring relationship.

2. Remember

   ❑ Use active listening skills to clarify and confirm.

   ❑ Show interest, attention, and empathy.

   ❑ Respect differences in learning pace, and respect silence.

   ❑ Experiment with different approaches, questions, and expressions.

   ❑ Suspend your judgment.

   ❑ Before concluding on any point, clarify meaning and support connection using descriptor questions (who, what, when, how, how much, how many).

   ❑ If you need to think about something that comes up in a session, say so. Engage in appropriate reflection and research, and then get back to the other person.

   ❑ Be patient.

   ❑ Accept differences.

3. Observe

   ❑ Your own assumptions, biases, and stereotypes.

   ❑ Consistency and relevance in responses and feedback to make sure that adequate communication is taking place.

   ❑ Your own values and the underlying contrasting values that might be operating in the relationship.

   ❑ Any discomfort, disconnects, or feelings that might be at play.

4. Show

   ❑ Respect.

   ❑ Reliability.

   ❑ Expertise and knowledge.

   ❑ A learner-centered focus.

Source: Sandvik (1996). Adapted with permission.

Dominick vented his frustration to a coworker, Jeb. "So what do you know about her?" Jeb asked.

"Nothing," said Dominick. "She's just too closed off. She looks down all the time. I know she speaks English, but we can't even have a normal conversation. I think it's a waste of my time."

Jeb pressed him further. "When did she come to this country? How did she get here? Does she have a family here? Where did she go to school? What inspired her to become a financial analyst? What is she interested in learning?"

Dominick shrugged. "I really don't know. We never went there. I know that she's from Singapore, and she's an account manager in our new division. That's about it. You know, I'm really not into the personal thing—this is about business."

Jeb was honest with Dominick. "You know, Dom, your alpha male, business-is-business style might be pretty intimidating to someone like Luann. From what I know, in her culture, people in authority get the final say and you learn not to push back. You're her mentor, so she probably sees you as being in charge. And maybe talking about her problems and challenges isn't part of her culture either."

The more Dominick thought about Jeb's feedback, the more he had to admit that Jeb had raised some valid points. He was suddenly seeing himself from Luann's point of view, and it shook him. Maybe it wasn't that she was closed off, but that he didn't get it. He decided to focus on learning more about Luann and developing the relationship rather than immediately driving for results.

It was difficult at first; he felt awkward and out of his element. But he was trying, and that got through to Luann. They spent one session just getting to know each other, and she told Dominick how hard it was adjusting to the new culture and how out of sync she felt. Soon they were able to move on to work issues. As she began telling Dominick about some of the challenges she was facing, they were finally able to focus on identifying learning goals. Dominick began to see that if he slowed down, invested his time in getting to know people, and established relationships at the start, he might become better at this mentoring thing—and he might also be a more effective leader.

Communication is the essential building block for facilitating all learning relationships, and it is integral to a successful cross-cultural mentoring experience. The inventory in Exercise 2.3 is designed to help you assess

EXERCISE 2.3

Cross-Cultural Mentoring Skills Inventory

For each skill listed, indicate in the second column how comfortable you are in using that skill by writing in one of these three abbreviations: V = very comfortable, M = moderately comfortable, or U = uncomfortable. Next, identify an example that illustrates a concrete situation when you were either comfortable or uncomfortable using the skill. Insert a check mark in the last column for each skill that you feel you need to improve to develop a comfort level. Once you have completed the skill inventory, rank your overall comfort level of cross-cultural mentoring on a scale of 1 to 5, with 5 being the most comfortable and 1 being the most uncomfortable.

Skill	V, M, or U	Example	Needs Work
Reflective listening: Using the skills of attending, clarifying, and confirming			
Checking for understanding			
Maintaining cultural self-awareness			
Providing and receiving feedback			
Maintaining global perspective			
Reading between the lines (keying into feelings)			
Suspending judgment			
Maintaining emotional versatility			
Exercising cultural flexibility			
Creating culturally appropriate networking opportunities			
Modifying communication style to accommodate cultural differences			
Sensitivity to varying cultural perceptions of time, space, authority, and protocol			

Overall comfort level of cross-cultural mentoring:

1   2   3   4   5

your comfort in relation to many of the communication skills you will need in mentoring individuals from other cultures.

Make the best use of the exercise by following these steps:

1. Assess your comfort on each skill.

2. Review any items you assess at a level of moderately comfortable (M) or uncomfortable (U).

3. Determine which skills you need to work on.

4. Prioritize the skills you have identified according to what you need to work on the most.

5. Separate your priorities into short-term and long-term categories.

6. Develop a plan.

7. Seek feedback on the plan.

8. Revise the plan accordingly.

9. Set target dates for completing the plan.

10. Get started.

Listening is a critical aspect of any mentoring relationship. This is doubly true in a cross-cultural mentoring relationship, where the initial enthusiasm and excitement about learning are often followed by a period of confusion and frustration that can be exacerbated by poor communication skills. Being a good communicator in these circumstances requires a high level of interpersonal skill and respect for cultural practices.

Asking open-ended questions is a good strategy—What do you enjoy about your work? Why did you come to this country? If you could set the agenda for our mentoring session today, what would it be? Be comfortable in the silences; they are telling you something about this person. Work on your emotional intelligence, and use the communication skills we discussed in Chapter One. Then talk about areas where there might be cultural misunderstanding. Check for understanding by asking what specific words, phrases, or expressions mean. Avoid examples that are regionally or culturally specific. Whenever possible, use universal examples—ones that can be understood across cultures, such as the weather, education, career, hobbies, travel, and family—and be as descriptive as possible. Keep in mind that phrases that are commonplace in one country may be difficult for others to understand (for example, "put up with," "butt of a joke").

It is easy to get lulled into complacency, especially when things appear to be going well in a relationship. Keep yourself cross-culturally fit by reflecting on the following questions:

- What am I doing to modify my communication style to accommodate cultural differences?

- In what ways am I improving at reading nonverbal messages such as pauses and silences?

- What do I do when I find myself in a culturally inappropriate situation?

- Am I getting better at suspending judgment in my mentoring relationship? If not, what gets in the way? How can I improve?

THE CONTEXT OF INTERGENERATIONAL UNDERSTANDING

People who travel through time together share a common historical journey that informs the assumptions they make, their values, the language they use, their points of reference, their preferred mode of communication, and how they learn. When we mentor someone much older or younger than ourselves, we need to remember that we are each seeing things through the context of our particular generation's worldview.

Being aware of generational context gives you a rich frame of reference for understanding your mentees. There you will find clues as to how best to relate to them, how to engage in the relationship, and how to best facilitate mentee learning. Let's take a look at two examples that illustrate how generational differences might show up in a mentoring relationship.

Jeanne and Emily

Emily, an account manager at Marketing and Advertising Company, was recently promoted to her current job after two years with the company. She had been expecting the promotion for over a year, even though the industry standard was a three-year stint as assistant account manager before advancing. In order to fast-track her development, the company included Emily in its talent management program and paired her with a mentor, Jeanne, a senior partner in the firm.

Since her promotion, Emily and Jeanne have met three times. Although the relationship started out strong, it is not going well now. Jeanne, a ten-year veteran in the field and a high school teacher before that, is annoyed with Emily's constant griping about how long it took her to get her new position. Jeanne thinks that Emily is, like most other people in her twenties, arrogant and entitled—attitudes that Jeanne remembers from her teaching days and finds frustrating and infuriating.

Sylvia and Jon

At age thirty-five, Jon is being considered for a promotion along with three other financial analysts. His work product is excellent and he has demonstrated talent, but his department manager, Sylvia, wonders about his dedication and work ethic. No matter how backed up the workload, Jon leaves the office by six every evening. Everyone else, including Sylvia, stays until much later.

Even though he shows maturity and promising leadership potential, Sylvia wonders if Jon will be willing to adjust his lifestyle for the responsibility that comes with going to the next level.

Both of these examples speak to the challenges of intergenerational mentoring. We will revisit them as we discuss three of the four generations in the workplace today: boomers (born between 1946 and 1964), Gen X (born between 1965 and 1979), and Gen Y (born between 1980 and 1995).[6] One caveat: these are general categories and represent clusters of common traits and characteristics. It's important to remember that although people are born into a specific generation, they might not have the mind-set of that generation for a variety of reasons, or they may have some overlap with an earlier or later generation if they were born at the extreme end of a range. Finally, generational typology may be more about the assumptions we make than about reality.[7]

Boomers

Boomers, born between 1946 and 1964, were raised by the fourth generation, traditionals: parents who lived through hard economic times and had traditional values. Boomers tend to be the opposite of their parents in status, wealth, and idealism. As a generation, they are optimistic, confident, competitive, and goal driven. They measure self-worth by the quantity and quality of accomplishment. In fact, their identity is often intertwined with their job.[8]

Work focused and willing to put in long hours to achieve career advancement, they seek prestige, recognition, and reward for their effort. They are self-reliant and independent thinkers who feel comfortable challenging the status quo. Boomers are idealistic and want to make a difference in the world. They want others to hold the same values and work ethic they do, and that means working just as hard and being just as committed. Younger generations, however, see boomers as workaholics and technological laggards who are set in their ways.

Boomers are often the first to be tapped as mentors because of their accumulated experience, wisdom, and expertise. They are particularly open to being mentors at this stage of their careers because it is a way of making a difference and "giving back" to their organizations. Like Gen Ys, they find working collaboratively tremendously fulfilling and meaningful.

Emily's mentor, Jeanne, is a boomer. After teaching for twenty years, she was ready to make a change. So at age forty-five, she redirected her creativity and made a career shift. She worried about this midlife transition and wanted to be accepted and credible, so she set out to prove herself. She sought out mentors, put in long hours, and advanced her career. She looked for guidance from people who were like her, seeking out the more mature managers who were the most committed and successful.

Mentoring Boomers

Like Jeanne, boomers may also be mentees. Lifelong learning continues to be a priority for them. Having a mentor makes sense as boomers find themselves seeking new ways to work, taking on different responsibilities, and moving to other roles. They want mentors who will be warm and caring. They want to be challenged, and they want the learning to be interesting and fresh.

Here are some pointers for mentoring boomers:

1. Challenge them. Boomers are not looking for "more" as much as they are for fresh ideas and new opportunities. Many feel bored, stale, and stalled out.

2. Acknowledge their accomplishments, hard work, and effort. Praise and recognition are important to everyone, particularly to boomers.

3. Make them feel your interest. Connect with them on personal and professional levels.

4. Show respect, as you would to any other mentee. Use a tone of respect, and engage them as a collaborative partner in the relationship.

5. Use appropriate language, but don't talk down to them. Avoid using slang and highly technical terms that are not commonly understood.

Gen Xers

Born between 1965 and 1979, Gen X is also known as the "me" generation. As a group they are entrepreneurial, productive, cynical, and often skeptical. They want to get their own needs met, take on individual responsibility, be inclusive, and feel that others trust them.

Sylvia's mentee, Jon, has two young children and shares child care and household responsibilities with his wife, who is also on a fast track at her company. Controlling both his work life and his family life is a priority, as is spending quality time with friends and family.

Like Jon, many other Gen Xers are challenged by the desire to make work meaningful and rewarding, even though it is not their primary focus. They work hard and pride themselves on being highly reliable and loyal workers.[9] They find work most enjoyable when they are creating something of lasting value, feel they are on a predictable, upward path to success, and feel their expertise allows them to be valuable contributors on a winning team.

Mentoring Gen Xers

Gen Xers seek mentors who are competent and direct and yet informal. They look to their mentors to gain a big-picture perspective, to help them define career expectations and develop a career path.

Being mentored by boomers like Sylvia is a challenge for them because they sense that boomers just don't "get them" (their parents are probably boomers). The result, according to Erickson, is that many get caught up in doing something because they think it is "going to lead to something else even though they don't enjoy it or think about it."[10]

Because Gen X is not impressed by authority, it is best for mentors to take a hands-off approach. Encourage creativity and initiative. Help Gen X mentees discover new approaches, set expectations, raise the bar, and then turn them loose to figure out how to achieve their goals. Talk about how to measure progress, put a process in place to measure it, and then give them regular feedback on their progress.

Here are some pointers for mentoring Gen Xers:

1. Set clear expectations, and identify measures of success. This frames the arena of action and encourages Gen X mentees to take control of their own learning.

2. Communicate regularly and give feedback. Touching base increases Gen Xers' self-confidence by letting them know whether they are on track. It also creates an opportunity for connection.

3. Build a trusting relationship, as you should with mentees of any age. Get to know your mentees in a collegial way. Stay in contact. Let them know that you trust them.

4. Make yourself available to answer questions and give just-in-time support. This keeps Gen X mentees moving forward.

5. Don't micromanage. Step back to let the mentee take charge of the assignment. Remember that learning to deal with setbacks is an opportunity for learning. You can speed the process by asking Gen X mentees questions that get them to reflect on their experience.

Gen Yers

More has been written about Gen Y—also known as millennials, echo boomers, net generation, first digitals, the iPod generation, and the "we" generation—than about any previous generation. With nearly 62 million members born between 1980 and 1995, they are the largest generation since the boomers.

Jeanne's mentee Emily is the poster child for Gen Y. Unlike Jon, she didn't need to balance her work and her life because she sees no separation between them; to her, they are seamless. Gen Yers like Emily are extreme multitaskers, obsessed with their career development. They want to get ahead and get it right. They have high expectations and crave feedback, but it needs to be authentic, continuous, and direct. They know what they believe and value. They want to be in the middle of the action and trusted to make it happen.[11] They bring high energy and full engagement to their work.

Mentoring Gen Yers

Gen Yers look for mentors who can offer them hands-on experiences that will empower them to take the next step. They prefer positive, collaborative, achievement-oriented mentors who will take them seriously. They naturally seek mentoring because they see their growth and development as a priority.

According to Sujansky and Ferri-Reed, "Nowhere is the difference between two generations more apparent than in how each of those generations uses language. The Millennials . . . communicate with each other using a rich mixture of slang language, colloquialisms, technical jargon and chat speak."[12] These "sound bites" offer a view of their world, their context, and their 24/7 dependence on technology.

Here are some pointers for mentoring Gen Y:

1. Tell them the truth, as you should with all other mentees. It sets the tone for the relationship.

2. Gen Yers want to be treated as equals. This means treating them with respect and acknowledging what they bring to the table.

3. Ask for and listen to their thinking. They want their opinions to be heard and taken seriously.

4. Make the relationship personal, fun, and engaging.

5. Offer challenging stretch assignments and a variety of learning opportunities.

6. Break goals into small pieces with realistic deadlines. Make sure they have the resources and the information that they need to achieve their goals.

7. Use technology. If you don't know how, ask them; they are masters of it.

8. Provide regular feedback, especially praise and affirmation.

Know Your Own Generation

We live in the context of our own generation, and we bring it into relationships. Just as we see our mentees as part of their generation, with whatever assumptions we may have about it, they see us through their own generational lens. Being effective in the role of mentor depends on being aware of how this might impact our relationship. Use Exercise 2.4 to reflect on the first time you became aware of generational differences between yourself and someone else and how that affected your relationship.

Table 2.1 offers a list of generational do's and don'ts that you can use as a guideline to review generational differences. Remember, though, that these are generalities: your mentees are all individuals.

Don't "Generationalize" Your Mentees

To a large extent, our current relational paradigm of mentoring reflects generational shifts as well as what we now understand about how adults learn. Not so long ago, we thought of learning in two big boxes: the learning-of-children box and the learning-of-adults box. Today learning has become more differentiated. Boomers and the previous generation, traditionalists, are probably more comfortable with mentor-directed relationships; they need to make more of a shift in their approach to mentoring, especially when dealing with Gen Y and the technological advances.

An effective mentoring relationship requires that each partner understand something about the other person's generational context and yet not make

EXERCISE 2.4

Reflecting on Generational Differences

Think about the first time you were aware of a generational difference between yourself and someone else:

- What did you observe?

- How did those differences positively or negatively affect your relationship?

- How might those differences affect your current and future mentoring relationships?

TABLE 2.1

Generational Do's and Don'ts

	Do	Don't
Boomers, 1946–1964	Give them challenging work with the opportunity for prestige. Focus on professional accomplishments. Expect hard work. Make them feel special. Talk optimistically about opportunities for change.	Micromanage. Create dependent relationships. Assume traditional or conservative values. Be cynical. Get bogged down in bureaucracy. Be afraid to try new things.
Gen Xers, 1965–1979	Demonstrate your own competence. Share information. Ask for their opinion. Set expectations. Talk about end results. Be collegial. Provide recognition for individual achievement. Provide support and suggestions, and get out of their way. Identify measures of success. Be technologically up to date.	Micromanage. Focus on the "boss" role. Exclude them from the communication loop. Ignore their opinion. Make it about "being a family". Make their goals too easy to reach. Protect them from making their own mistakes. Just give them "atta-boys" ("Great job!" comments that give them no real information).
Gen Yers, 1980–1995	Tell them the truth. Treat them as equals. Acknowledge what they bring to the table. Make the relationship fun. Let them have a voice and a veto in the relationship. Challenge and stretch their minds with a variety of assignments. Provide opportunities for teamwork.	Micromanage. Just give them orders and assignments without the rationale. Provide just negative, critical feedback. Assume they can't learn as quickly. Be unavailable. Be disrespectful even if they are your junior. Be afraid to learn new ways to use technology.

"generationalizations." Guidelines like those in Table 2.1 are helpful, but stereotypes are misleading. Aim to fully understand the uniqueness of each of your mentees regardless of generation. Without this understanding, it is easy to make assumptions that can disrupt the relationship and take it off course.

Remember Sylvia and Jon? Sylvia didn't understand Jon's priorities of trying to balance work life and home life, so she applied a familiar generational stereotype: she began to write him off as a slacker who was not a viable candidate for future leadership. In Jeanne and Emily's case, Jeanne was turned off by and impatient with Emily—not for what she did at work but for her attitudes. She told herself that Emily was "entitled," the product of "helicopter parents," and would never change. Both mentors needed to work to move past the generational misunderstandings that were getting in their way.

The primary value of generational analysis is to provide another frame of reference, a language and a lens for understanding forces that contribute to the human dynamics that take place in a mentoring relationship.[13]

THE CONTEXT OF OTHER DIFFERENCES: SEXUAL IDENTITY, GENDER, AND RACE

So far we've looked at two kinds of mentoring in which difference plays a role, but there are many other contexts in which difference is played out—many more than we can include in this book. In this section we focus on three stories as windows to understanding how the contexts of sexual identity, gender, and race can play out in the mentoring relationship.

The Context of Sexual Identity

With the end of "don't ask, don't tell" in the military, openness about sexual identity at work is more widely accepted. However, talking about it may still make some people feel uncomfortable, especially when they've never known anyone who is a member of the bisexual, gay, lesbian, transgender community. We begin with Darra, a college professor, and her reflections on a lesbian in one of her classes:

Darra and Eve

One of my colleagues told me that there were several gay and lesbian students in my class, but he didn't tell me who they were. I tried to figure it out myself but never found out who they were for sure. When one of my students, Eve—one of the women I had on my "list of possibilities"—approached me and asked me to mentor her, I liked everything about her. She was energetic, intelligent, and insightful. And I immediately thought to myself, *I hope she isn't a lesbian.*

As soon as I realized what I was thinking, I slapped myself. I knew I needed to challenge my own residual prejudice toward people of a same-sex orientation and said to myself, *So, Lord, please help me, if she is. I need to be accepting and open to her as a valued human being.*

During our first meeting, Eve mentioned something about her partner using the pronoun "she," and I froze in my tracks. What do I say? Do I ask her about it? Do I ignore it? Is part of our mentoring conversation supposed to be directed toward issues of her acceptance? I really felt paralyzed. Eve, who had noticed my reaction to this information, helped me through it! She actually said to me, "Darra, do you know many lesbians?"

I was honest with her: "No, I don't know any personally, although I think my neighbors are gay. Is that going to be a problem for you?" You know, I think I was asking that question for both of us.

Eve was relaxed and calm and said, "Not at all! I am many things, and being a lesbian is just one of them."

Thus began a year of a wonderful relationship. We met regularly, and I helped Eve sort through her thesis and career goals. I hope I taught her a few things, both in and outside class. But, oh, she taught me so much more. It has been really hard for me to overcome a lifetime of bias and prejudice, but since we began meeting, I've gotten to know several gay individuals—my two neighbors, a student, and my realtor—as people, and I appreciate them as I would any other individuals. So while Eve was working through her career path, I was working out some of my own issues.

Darra had some long-held beliefs about people whose sexual orientation was different from hers. These biases and stereotypes made her uncomfortable and created blind spots in her ways of thinking. When Eve became her mentee, the situation brought up negative feelings that Darra needed to work through. Example 2.1 shows Darra's reflection on the situation and how it helped her work it through.

The Context of Gender

Much has been written about the dynamics of mentoring relationships between men and women. The literature suggests that the old stereotypes hold fast: women are generally more internally focused and put a priority on building relationships, valuing care, concern, and connection. Men tend to focus externally first, on the tasks of procreating, providing, and protecting.[14] It's easy to see how these characteristics get played out in a mentoring relationship. The traditional model of mentoring reflects a more paternalistic approach to mentoring. Today's definition reflects a shifting paradigm that blends the best of both approaches.

Harry considered himself a man's man. He knew how to build relationships, develop customers, and bring in business. He was a natural-born schmoozer—the company's unofficial caretaker of high-maintenance customers. Harry was great at taking them to ball games, playing golf, going out for drinks and cigars, and shooting the breeze. As a senior executive just a few years away from retirement, he was also the go-to-guy for mentoring. But

---

EXAMPLE 2.1

Darra's Reflection

My underlying biases and stereotypes:

- *All gay people are different from me.*

- *Gay women have a hard edge to them.*

- *Only interested in women's issues.*

- *Don't like men and are angry about it.*

My discomforts, disconnects, or feelings that might get in the way:

Discomforts	Disconnects	Feelings
Never before met a gay person	*Have nothing in common*	*Negative*
I don't know how to talk to a gay person.	*I am very feminine.*	*Morally uncomfortable*
Afraid gay woman will come on to me	*Traditional marriage*	*Fearful*
	Church looks down on it	

---

when he was asked to mentor a recent Ivy League M.B.A. graduate named Aimee—his first experience doing this sort of work with a woman—he came up against a wall of assumptions and prejudices he didn't know he had.

Harry and Aimee

Harry was stymied. This was his first time mentoring a woman, and he was plenty uncomfortable. First of all, he found Aimee's good looks, and the way she dressed, distracting. The businesswomen he knew wore suits, not tank tops and skirts.

Second, he was used to getting to know people (that is, men) over drinks in a bar or on the golf course or at a football game. There was plenty to talk about to get started: the teams going to the playoffs, the toughest hole of the course, or the quality of the scotch. His tough-talking style and snarky sense of humor had always helped him be successful with clients. With Aimee, however, none of these settings were going to work and none of his usual topics applied. He was lost at sea.

During their first meeting, Harry played it safe. He told Aimee stories about his career. He was conscientious about cleaning up his language and held back on cracking jokes. He thought things went okay, although in retrospect she'd been pretty quiet.

But Aimee left the meeting feeling both intimidated and disheartened. She had to listen to his pointless stories, and he hadn't let her get a word in edgewise. Wasn't mentoring supposed to be about meeting her needs? Harry held a key position in the company—he was a guy's guy, like so many other C-level power players, even the women—but she knew that she was lucky to have him as her mentor, and she was anxious to learn from the master. Still …

Over drinks with a friend that evening, she vented her frustrations. "I need help figuring out how to navigate this company, and I've got a boatload of questions about options and approaches. But Harry just kept reeling off his war stories, one after the other. He didn't ask one thing about me, including what I wanted to learn from him!" Aimee was also was put off by Harry's tone, which struck her as demeaning and paternalistic.

She was ready to quit the relationship, but her friend suggested giving Harry another chance: he was the master, after all, and he must have some wisdom to impart. "Look, just send him an e-mail saying what you're looking for from his mentoring, and what you hoped to accomplish. Be neutral. If he doesn't get it, move on."

Halfheartedly, Aimee agreed to give it one more try.

Harry was surprised to receive Aimee's e-mail, which struck him as surprisingly businesslike and intelligent, and he was grateful for it. At least now he had some direction. He felt more comfortable with a list of questions to address, and the next meeting seemed to go better. They were even able to engage in an awkward kind of conversation. Having questions on a piece of paper to work from also gave Aimee an edge into the discussion and gave both of them a way to stay focused on her issues. Harry really was an expert.

After a few weeks, both Harry and Aimee felt that the mentoring meetings were generally fine. But Harry was having trouble figuring out how to give Aimee feedback on a few issues he felt that she needed to deal with. First of all, Aimee wasn't tough enough. She seemed to take everything personally and was defensive about feedback others were giving her. If Aimee were a guy, Harry would have just looked him in the eye and told him to "man up." If he tried that with Aimee, he was afraid she would burst into tears, and he had no tools to deal with that reaction.

Another challenge he faced with Aimee was talking to her about the way she dressed. The style she was wearing was probably hip and cool for her generation, but it seemed more "girls' night out" to him—certainly inappropriate for their company's culture. A couple of times he had alluded to her short skirt with a little snarky barb, hoping she would take the hint, but nothing changed. In fact, she seemed to be getting annoyed. Harry found himself doing some hard thinking. Clearly his usual tactics did not work with Aimee.

Harry hadn't gotten to where he was in the company by being stubborn. He saw that maybe his old material and delivery were stale. The last thing he wanted to be was out of touch with this generation: they were making news in business, and he was in business to stay in business. In the process of learning to mentor Aimee, Harry began to reflect on what to say and how to say it, and anticipating how his message might be received. (Harry's reflection is shown in Example 2.2.) In the end, he decided to be straight with Aimee. This was definitely new territory for him, and it felt exciting.

EXAMPLE 2.2

Harry's Reflection

My underlying biases and stereotypes

- *One way to build relationships.*

- *Snarky humor builds relationship.*

- *Sometimes I just don't understand women.*

- *Young people don't dress professionally anymore.*

- *Women need to learn how to build customer relationships the good old-fashioned way.*

- *Women just can't make it in a man's world.*

My discomforts, disconnects, or feelings that might get in the way:

Discomforts	Disconnects	Feelings
Aimee is really hot	*What to say and how to say it*	*Don't want to hurt Aimee's feelings*
Small talk	*How to relate to her*	*Aimee is attractive*
Talking about personal issues		*Not going to let the relationship fail even if I am uncomfortable*
Not confident about how to mentor a woman		*I need to protect her*
How Aimee dresses		

As he mentored Aimee, Harry discovered that he was becoming not only more gender sensitive but also more compassionate. He began to think hard about other relationships in his life and at work that he had taken for granted, and he realized that he could be more sensitive to what others brought to those relationships. For her part, Aimee found that having a no-nonsense male mentor was just what she needed to get ahead. It toughened her up and gave her language she could use to relate to other men at work. Babcock and Laschever explain, "In the workplace, people who mentor women can encourage women not to accept the status quo. They can teach them that the world is more 'negotiable' than it often seems, and they can demonstrate that seeking out opportunities to improve their circumstances can be an effective and often necessary strategy for getting ahead."[15]

The Context of Race

As an African American woman, Betty had been struggling for four years to find acceptance and trust from the people in her organization. There were very few women or people of color in the company—and in her own division, she was the only one. Although she had moved up quickly, she never really learned that much about the organization or how to navigate the system. Finally, she asked to be mentored. Not surprisingly, her mentor was a white male, George. Here are her reflections on that relationship:

George and Betty

I think George saw that I had a lot of frustration, and that is why he agreed to help me. It took a while for me to feel that I could trust a white man enough to share how alone I was really feeling. I was battling a system that didn't support someone like me. When I told my mentor that I felt like an underdog, he reminded me of all my accomplishments. He helped me realize that a lot of my thinking was based on my own very limited perception. These self-discovery moments were enlightening for me. I always assumed that people weren't interested in my story. My mentor made me feel that I could take a risk and open myself up. He helped me recognize that I should be proud of who I was and what I had accomplished on my own. He made me feel that I could tell my story and it would be all right.

Over the course of the year, I learned to see myself differently. I have found my voice and achieved greater self-understanding. George helped me build stronger bonds and learn how to network with people throughout the company. Our mentoring relationship has helped me in other ways too.

There have been some personal relationships that have been a source of stress for me. My mentoring experience has shown me that it's okay to trust people. I now am so much happier personally and professionally. By the way, George really surprised me last week. He was telling me how much he was learning by mentoring me. Apparently he had never mentored an African American before and even got some advice from colleagues at the beginning of our relationship to make sure that he understood where I was coming from. He really gets me, and I feel and appreciate his support.

George found it useful to reflect on Betty's underlying biases to try to get a handle on the best way to facilitate her learning. Example 2.3 shows his reflections.

Everyone has biases and stereotypes. As a mentor, work on increasing awareness about yours and bring them into consciousness by reflecting

---

EXAMPLE 2.3

George's Reflection

My underlying biases and stereotypes

- *She sticks with her own kind.*

- *She is not very trusting.*

- *She has a chip on her shoulder.*

- *She is afraid of me.*

My discomforts, disconnects, or feelings that might get in the way:

Discomforts	Disconnects	Feelings
Never mentored an African American	*Can't seem to connect with one another*	*Maybe I should go talk with one of my African American colleagues and get some advice*
Afraid that I will say the wrong thing	*We are talking but not communicating*	*I have to try harder to understand where she is coming from*
	Can I meet her expectations?	

EXERCISE 2.5

Your Self-Awareness Reflection

My underlying biases and stereotypes:

My discomforts, disconnects, or feelings that might get in the way of mentoring relationships:

Discomforts	Disconnects	Feelings

on your experience and taking yourself to task. This is challenging to do because we aren't accustomed to thinking about it. Many people automatically respond to their discomforts, disconnects, and feelings by choosing to avoid certain people or dealing with them inauthentically. Others are frequently surprised at what surfaces when they allow themselves time to think about their stereotypes and biases, and they are often caught off guard when they realize how their biases and stereotypes affect their relationships.

Use Exercise 2.5 to reflect on your underlying biases and how they affect your interactions.

THE CONTEXT OF POWER

The learner-centered mentoring paradigm is based on a relationship of reciprocity, collaboration, and partnership. Power in the relationship is shared, yet positional power is still a formidable presence. If you are your mentee's superior at work, that understanding is always part of the unspoken context of your relationship.

To facilitate learning effectively, mentors must become aware of power dynamics that relate to difference. According to Hansman, "The biggest paradox surrounding mentoring relationships is that although mentors seek to 'empower' their protégés, the relationships themselves are entrenched with power issues."[16] *Entrenched* is a great word to describe power issues.

Think for a moment about a time when you felt powerful. Now contrast it with a time when you felt powerless. Chances are that each image conjures up different reactions and feelings. *Power* might evoke words like *pride* and *achievement*; you may even stand up straighter. *Powerless* might suggest words like *fear* and *humiliation*, and you may find yourself feeling angry or sad. Both power and powerlessness can have a negative impact on the mentoring relationship and result in conflict, withdrawal, and inauthenticity, among other things.

For example, Betty brought a feeling of powerlessness to her relationship with George. Her mentor recognized this and empowered her to find her voice in the relationship and at work. Harry had positional and personal power that could compromise his mentoring relationship, but Aimee had come to him because of his positional power, and he had to make the relationship work. Earlier, we saw how Dominick's alpha-male style was intimidating Luann and leaving her powerless.

Mentors like Harry often have positional power. Positional power, however, doesn't belong in the mentoring relationship because it puts distance between people.[17] What belongs is the mentor's sensitivity to difference. It is hard to be sensitive to the "other" unless you know something about the person you are mentoring. To really know that person is to be authentically curious, check out assumptions, and explore rather than ignore difference. To be indifferent renders others powerless. Facilitating learning means being sensitive to the abundant shades of difference among and between the individuals in the mentoring relationship.

In a mentoring relationship, difference is always at play in both subtle and overt ways. Even when we mentor people who are "like us"—same culture, generation, gender, race, orientation, or anything else—they are still their own person, the sum total of much difference. We need to be curious about difference and understand it better to be effective mentors. Even if it seems difficult and barriers seem insurmountable, stay in conversation. Acknowledge that conversations are hard and that it is going to take work on your and your mentee's part.

"Mentoring across barriers," say Ensher and Murphy, "offers a fresh perspective and is the ultimate in building empathy for a person whose perspective or interests may diverge radically from your own."[18] To have meaningful mentoring relationships, mentoring partners must be willing to engage in truth telling that extends across difference.

My friend and colleague Stacey Blake Beard says, "Mentoring is always fraught with the concern of how to cross boundaries, how to bridge cultural differences to show yourself, and to accompany another on their journey."[19] It is the sum total of our differences and idiosyncrasies that makes us uniquely who we are. Some of these differences can be attributed to cultural differences, some to generational differences, some to gender, race, or power differences: the list goes on. Understanding difference is of paramount importance in facilitating effective mentoring relationships.

We think we are objective when we see difference, but none of us truly is. Objectivity is a journey. "We all carry cultural baggage," says Daloz, "perhaps most of all those who claim to have none." What matters, he says, is the willingness to acknowledge our own biases and stereotypes and to "continue working at more adequate, permeable and inclusive ways of knowing."[20]

In this chapter, we've looked at the context of difference and some specific examples and how they play out in mentoring relationships. In the next chapter, we explore the context of connection in terms of how people come together in the mentoring relationship.

CHAPTER 3

THE CONTEXT OF CONNECTION
LINKING UP AND LINKING IN

THE SPACES AND PLACES in which mentoring partners convene, connect, communicate, and learn with one another add another context for learning. In this chapter, we' look at some of the approaches and configurations in which mentoring partners connect and then turn to distance and virtual mentoring connections. Finally, we look at the deeper connections of mentoring, which keep the relationship alive and evolving.

FORMAL AND INFORMAL MENTORING

As a mentor, you may be involved in a formal mentoring program, or you may be asked to mentor someone informally. Some mentors, like Nevin, are engaged in formal and informal mentoring relationships simultaneously:

Nevin

Everyone in the company knew Nevin—he was a superstar, recruited away from a competitor. Nevin knew the business, how it operated, and how to drive a high-performance team. He also knew the value of mentoring and quickly became its champion. When the company initiated a mentoring program, he was the first to sign up. By the end of the year, he had a couple of mentees of his own. In addition, several other individuals had approached him and asked him to mentor them informally.

Each of his informal mentoring relationships was different. One mentee, who had been at the company for ten years, was very clear about her goals; he worked with her to lay out a time line and work plan to achieve them. The other mentee, fresh out of college, wanted career advice and asked to meet with him on an ad hoc basis.

Formal mentoring is commonly associated with words like *organized, proscribed, structured, facilitated,* and *supported*. But the term itself actually refers to mentoring that is conducted under the umbrella of an organizational entity, such as a business or a school. Program parameters are defined for the mentoring partnership and include both structural and accountability mechanisms. Programmatic and relationship expectations, requirements for eligibility, and program goals and outcomes give this mentoring formality.

Informal mentoring relationships are usually described as unstructured, casual, need based, and natural. For example, you may see great promise in an individual, someone who could benefit from your experience; or someone looking for a mentor may see you as a good candidate and ask if you are interested. Informal mentoring relationships can run the gamut from casual conversations or situational and information sharing to structured and "formalized" relationships. Each relationship proceeds at its own pace and on its own timetable.

Even in formal mentoring, each relationship structure varies depending on the learning needs and style of the mentoring partners. Once you are inside and working the relationship, it becomes a dance of two or more people coming together in partnership to move learning and development forward. As Huang and Lynch so beautifully capture it, "It is the dance between willing and consenting partners, a dance of giving and receiving each other's gifts."[1] The chapters in Part Two of this book discuss strategies for making the most of both approaches.

MENTORING CONFIGURATIONS

The traditional form of mentoring involves two individuals: an older, more experienced person and a younger, less knowledgeable one. The classic model of one-on-one mentoring is that of Odysseus's son, Telemachus, and Mentor, from Homer's *Odyssey*. When Odysseus goes off to fight in the Trojan War, Mentor (in the form of the goddess Athena) guides Telemachus in his quest to find his father. In the process, Mentor teaches the young man enduring lifelong lessons.

But that was then, and this is now. As we discussed in Chapter One, mentoring today is a partnership between individuals of varying ages, stages, and experiences. The mentor is not always the older partner in the relationship, and the relationship can be informal or formal, face-to-face, distance, or virtual. It can also involve younger people bringing older colleagues up to speed on new ideas, peers mentoring each other, and supervisors mentoring direct reports. Mentoring may even be done in groups.

Reverse Mentoring

In 1999 Jack Welch, former CEO of General Electric, initiated the concept of reverse mentoring by asking a group of senior executives to tap into the technical expertise from within the rank and file of his company. Although the concept of reverse mentoring (also known as R-mentoring or RM) has been around for more than a decade, it was not until the large number of Gen Ys entered the workplace that it gained traction.[2]

In reverse mentoring, a senior leader or manager seeks to quickly gain technical or knowledge expertise (or a different point of view) from a younger person or someone from the rank and file of the organization who has the knowledge he or she needs. The other person also benefits by interacting with and developing a relationship with someone he or she may never otherwise have gotten to know—a senior leader or manager—and gains valuable insights about the organization. Here's an example:

Daniel and Elinor

Elinor, executive vice president of human resources, was worried. As the economy tanked, she had to let almost a third of the company's workforce go. When things eased up, she brought new and younger talent into the organization. The culture of the company started to shift, and those who had been there for years were feeling uneasy.

To the older workers, their new Gen Y colleagues were speaking a different language. They were eager to get to work, in a hurry to participate in decision making and to advance their careers. They were asking for opportunities that didn't exist, and they wanted as much information as they could get about how things really worked in the company. The older employees felt threatened; the new ones felt thwarted. When one of Elinor's colleagues suggested reverse mentoring, she thought it was worth a try. In fact, she tried it herself.

Elinor's reverse-mentoring relationship with Daniel turned out to be a gift. At first, she thought he was speaking in tongues—he used so many expressions and acronyms that she couldn't always follow or even understand his thinking. But she persevered, asking lots of questions, and she soon found his perspectives perceptive and thought provoking.

Daniel was enthusiastic and genuinely excited to be part of the culture shift that was taking place in the organization. They talked about the changes in depth and how they were affecting the rank and file. Elinor solicited Daniel's opinions about what would create value for him as an employee. She asked him if he thought his coworkers would agree. Daniel gave her a thumbs-up, and suggested that she set up a blog and create an employee wiki to find out.

This was foreign territory to Elinor, so she asked Daniel to show her examples of effective employee wikis. Once he demonstrated how a wiki worked, Elinor was amazed that it was so easy. She began to wonder about what other tools and technologies were available for employees to connect with each other. She felt as if she were entering a new world of possibility. And Daniel found that reverse mentoring was helping him feel more connected to the company. He appreciated the opportunity to share his expertise, have personal time with Elinor, and see how open higher-ups were to employee input.

The real value of reverse mentoring is not only its ability to pass technical expertise to those who didn't grow up with it. On a deeper level, it serves to create connections between people who have traditionally been separated by the visible and invisible barriers of hierarchy.

Peer Mentoring

In peer mentoring one peer may mentor another peer, or both peers might mentor each other. They share some level of commonality—job title, academic success, experience, cohort, or something else. It works because even people in the same job inevitably have different skill sets.

Peer mentoring can take place in a one-to-one or group setting, either formally or informally. The Chicago Bar Association Alliance for Women developed a peer mentoring program (mentoring circles) in which each member is both a mentor and a mentee. Not only do junior members learn from those with more experience, but midlevel and senior attorneys gain an opportunity to hone management skills, build relationships, and develop referral networks. Each circle (group) comprises eight to ten women of varying levels of experience and from a wide range of practice areas. They meet at least four times a year; some meet as often as once a month. One of the members acts as a coordinator of the meetings, although the meeting logistics are determined by each circle. Another member acts as a facilitator for the discussion.[3]

Group peer mentoring, like one-to-one peer mentoring, is self-managed by individuals with similar job functions, experiences, interests, or needs.

The group takes responsibility for crafting its own learning agenda and managing the learning process to meet members' learning needs.

Peer mentoring has found a niche in education, from elementary through postsecondary. A student peer mentor, for example, may help another student learn the ropes, stay on course, and achieve academic success. Nonprofit boards use peer mentoring to orient new board members. Peer mentoring has been useful in getting new employees up to speed and in facilitating cross-functional learning.

Supervisory Mentoring

Owen is one of Ramondo's direct reports, and he is also Owen's mentee in the company's formal mentoring program. Not surprisingly, both men are struggling to keep their mentoring relationship separate from their work roles:

Ramondo and Owen

"Owen works hard, puts in long hours, and really wants to succeed," Ramondo told his mentoring coordinator. "I want him to succeed too …, although sometimes I think he is too conscientious and overconfident. I try to spend a few minutes mentoring him every day."

"Every day?" his coordinator asked.

"It's not that I am micromanaging him," Ramondo said quickly. "'It's just that I want to make sure that he's doing the right thing in the right way. I don't know … he seems defensive or something."

"Can you give me an example?"

"Like yesterday," Ramondo replied, "we sat down and talked about the company's direction, our department goals, and his role as a contributor. I asked him to tell me his strengths and challenges as a contributor, and he reeled off a list of strengths a mile long. When I brought up two challenges I thought he was going to have, he immediately dismissed them by saying, 'I'm on top of it. No biggie.'"

Admittedly, engaging in a formal mentoring relationship with someone who reports directly to you is not ideal. But the reality is that if you are a supervisor, you probably informally mentor your direct reports every day. This type of job performance–related mentoring is situational; it becomes a series of additive and spontaneous mentoring moments and mentoring conversations.

In a formal mentoring program, supervisory mentoring can potentially be problematic. Most mentees will find it difficult to be candid and open with a mentor who is also responsible for evaluating their performance. They will have difficulty taking risks and being vulnerable.

If you find yourself in this position, you must be mindful that you have two separate roles—mentor and supervisor—and keep your boundaries clear. Here are some strategies:

- If conflict exists in your relationship, don't take on the mentoring role.

- Acknowledge the potential role conflict at the beginning of the mentoring process, and make respecting those boundaries part of your ground rules. (I discuss ground rules in Chapter Five.)

- Make sure your mentee is clear about when you are moving from one role to another. For example, you might say, "I am stepping out of my role as your mentor now. In my role as your supervisor, I need to let you know that . . ."

- Set aside a regular block of time specifically dedicated to mentoring. Don't combine supervision and mentoring time into one session to save time.

Group Mentoring

More and more organizations are embracing the innovative concept of group mentoring as a way to manage human, knowledge, and time resources. Inevitably this was Nevin's choice:

Nevin

As other managers learned about Nevin's expertise in managing high-performance teams, they called him and asked for his mentorship. He was flattered to be asked to mentor so many people, but it was also draining on his time. When Nevin talked with his own manager about these issues, she suggested that he consider group mentoring. He liked the idea and decided to give it a try.

He began by making a list of people who had called him to learn more about high-performance teams. Nevin asked each of them to elaborate on the questions they had and what specifically they wanted to learn. He collated the list and sent it to all of them for feedback. Based on the responses, he created a six-session agenda from the final list and posted an invitation. Most of them said yes, but several declined.

When the group convened, they discussed ground rules and put an accountability process in place. As they worked together, it became apparent that people were connecting with each other in new ways, and the opportunity to bounce ideas off one another generated a level of excitement none of them had experienced before.

Nevin was delighted with the results. He had found a way to make an impact while learning more about the organization and creating new networks for himself and others. The success of the mentoring group produced great interest throughout the company, and soon other mentoring groups began to form.

In group mentoring, individuals either mentor each other or rely on one or more individuals to facilitate the learning of a group of mentees. Facilitated group mentoring can involve diverse individuals from different parts of the organization, individuals with similar interests and experiences, or even an intact work team. The mentor-facilitator asks questions to keep the dialogue thought provoking and meaningful, shares personal experiences, provides feedback, and serves as a sounding board.

A new concept, mentoring quads, is a variation on this theme. As the name suggests, four people are involved: three mentees learn from a mentor and from each other. Mentoring quads often begin a one-to-one mentoring relationship; at some point, with the permission of the mentor, the mentee invites other mentees into the relationship.[4]

Personal Board of Directors

There is one more mentoring configuration to mention here: the personal board of directors. Let's look at Margo's story:

Margo

Margo appeared to have it all: early success, the admiration and respect of her peers, job offer after job offer, and multiple leadership opportunities. Her success took on a life of its own. Before she knew it, she found herself totally swept up in a constant bustle of activity, until the day she met the love of her life. That chance meeting and the relationship that ensued gave her pause to reflect on her career choices and what was really important to her.

Margo used the same skills that had already taken her far. Instead of wasting time going around in circles by herself, she looked around for others who could help her think through her issue—people who had experience that she thought would be relevant to her situation. She found five people who agreed to serve as mentors. To expedite the process, she brought them all together at the same time and place and convened a personal board of directors meeting to begin the process of helping her "figure out the rest of her life."

Increasingly, individuals seek personal mentors (apart from or as an adjunct to organizational mentors) to guide them at various transition points along their life's journey. In Margo's case, a group of hand-picked mentors functions as a personal board of directors to help facilitate an individual's achievement of a clear and specific learning goal.

The board of directors model has the advantage of providing multiple perspectives and diverse feedback from a variety of mentors at the same time. The mentors meet together with the mentee at regular intervals. The mentee manages the learning process, calls and hosts the meetings, and (together with her mentors) shares accountability for the learning process and achievement of desired results.

Engaging in this process as a mentor is very exciting. The synergy of bringing multiple mentors together (most of whom probably don't know each other) is uplifting and generates new learning for everyone. I speak from experience when I tell you that the joy of being a mentor on a board of directors multiplies when you are engaged in group mentoring.

DISTANCE AND VIRTUAL MENTORING CONNECTIONS

The first edition of this book included a lengthy discussion about long-distance mentoring. Technology has changed so rapidly since then that the term now feels outdated, irrelevant, and redundant. Even the traditional and rather cumbersome definition of *distance mentoring* ("a geographically diverse mentoring relationship that takes place when it is not feasible, desirable, or convenient for mentoring partners to meet on a regular face-to-face basis") has changed. Rather than a second choice or a substitute for face-to-face mentoring, distance mentoring today is a real choice: a broad and generic descriptor for mentoring relationships in which the partners are geographically separated.

The global workplace, generational preference, changing demographics, and technology have influenced how mentoring connections are made, maintained, and sustained. In the past, most mentoring took place in one-on-one meetings, with an occasional telephone conversation or written communication to supplement them. Today, a new lexicon of distance and virtual mentoring options exists for doing that, and those options have extended contact on a real-time basis.

Marla and Tammy managed their virtual mentoring with aplomb:

Marla and Tammy

Marla and Tammy worked for the same large medical products company. Marla had been in field sales for many years and was based at company headquarters. Tammy telecommuted from her home office in another state, where she had her field sales territory. Although the two women had never met face-to-face, they felt as if they had. Their mentoring relationship had begun with several e-mail exchanges and morphed into monthly Skype connections. They used e-mail to send agendas and stay connected between meetings, and they'd attended webinars together in real time.

Frequently when Marla was online, she noticed that Tammy had logged onto Skype and poked with an instant message just to say "hi." They continued to connect for the next nine months until they discovered that they would both be attending the same conference. Meeting in person was a perfect way to celebrate their mentoring relationship.

Virtual technology is not the only way that mentoring partners connect when they live or work in different geographical locations. Like Robert and Marsha, their connection may be limited to a series of telephone conversations. And as in their case, partners may easily get off to a rocky start:

Robert and Marsha

Marsha had never had a mentor—until now, she had never needed one. But after two weeks in her new position at the university, she felt uneasy. She was excited about her new responsibilities— she was quite capable, and she knew it. But she was anxious nonetheless. She just didn't understand the ins and outs of the system and its politics, and she felt that she was always one step away from making an unwitting mistake.

Robert, a full professor and dean of the health science school located on the main campus seventy miles away, agreed to be her mentor. Their initial conversation, which was brief and matter-of-fact, was followed by a series of frustrating telephone "conversations." Marsha was always late, apologized for her tardiness, talked about the weather, and then bombarded Robert with questions about university news and people.

> Robert tried to answer her barrage of questions but couldn't wait to get off the phone. Her nonstop questioning was wearing him out. After another week of frustration, he told Marsha she might want to find another mentor.

What happened here? First, as her mentor, Robert failed to establish ground rules for their communication. He also needed to be more candid with Marsha about her lack of regard for his schedule. Both partners had just jumped in with no real understanding of the other's needs. Clearly the goals and ground rules of this mentoring partnership had not been clearly articulated. Had they been, Robert would have been able to refocus the conversation on Marsha's goals. Instead, Marsha's anxieties and her unfocused need for information dominated the conversation. Robert and Marsha had no real points of connection to sustain the relationship past the many stumbling blocks.

POINTS OF CONNECTION

When mentoring takes place face-to-face, we have any number of cues to let us know if we are connecting or getting off track. But when the medium of communication is phone, e-mail, or social networking like Linked-In groups or Ning, we have far fewer cues and nonverbal ways into the conversation.

As we will see in Part Two, all mentoring depends on establishing and maintaining meaningful points of connection—the building blocks for effective interaction. By connecting first, we are better able to develop fruitful and productive learning relationships. When we're talking about effective distance or virtual mentoring, where misunderstanding is easily caused by a typo or a misinterpreted offhand remark in the absence of nonverbal cues, these points of connection deserve special attention.

Table 3.1 identifies seven points of connection and what you can do to facilitate each of them.

Let's look at Robert and Marsha's relationship in terms of Table 3.1. First, it's clear that Robert never set the climate for learning (point 1). He took on the responsibility of mentoring Marsha in good faith. He thought Marsha had great potential and wanted to help her.

By talking about her learning needs and his own time demands (point 2), Robert probably could have avoided some of his frustration. He didn't really know Marsha. Certainly he knew her "on paper" and

TABLE 3.1

Seven Points of Connection

What You Can Do	Making the Connection
1. Invest time and effort in setting the climate for learning.	Determine your mentee's learning style and learning needs and how that might play out in your relationship, given that it is not face-to-face.
2. Be sensitive to the day-to-day needs of your mentee.	Spend time connecting with your mentee. Ask enough questions to give you sufficient insight into his or her work context.
3. Identify and use multiple venues for communication.	Explore all available options: e-mail, videoconference, e-learning technologies, telephone, mail, and emerging technology—and use more than one of these. Look for opportunities to connect face-to-face, even at a long distance.
4. Set a regular contact schedule, but be flexible.	Agree on a mutually convenient contact schedule, and make sure it works for you and your mentee. If you need to renegotiate a scheduled appointment, use that situation as an opportunity for connection and interaction.
5. Check on the effectiveness of your communication.	Ask questions: Are we connecting? Is what we are doing working for us? What can we do to improve the quality of our interaction?
6. Make sure that connection results in meaningful learning.	Is learning going on? Is the mentee making progress?
7. Share information and resources—but never as a substitute for personal interaction.	Set the stage to share information. Then share the information and follow up.

had met her at a recent retreat, but he really did not know who she was as a person.

Marsha and Robert had many communication options available in addition to the telephone (point 3). Perhaps they could have taken care of some of the basic "information" questions by e-mail.

Scheduled times for contact—and an agreement about impromptu contact or delays—are crucial (point 4). Had expectations been set more clearly, Marsha would have realized that she needed to call Robert to let him know she was running late. Robert then would have the option to renegotiate the time frame.

Some of Robert's frustration could have been avoided had he checked on the effectiveness of the communication from the very beginning (point 5).

Marsha may be learning from her mentoring relationship with Robert, but he has no sense of what that is; in fact, he feels that it is the "wrong kind" of learning. They have not had the learning conversation (point 6). And information—too much information, Robert would say—is being shared at the expense of interaction (point 7). It is helpful to keep these points of connection in mind in any mentoring relationship. It is crucial if you are engaged in distance or virtual mentoring.

MAKING TECHNOLOGY WORK FOR YOU

Technology can be a powerful tool for building and maintaining mentoring connections. Murphy and Tanner used it well from the beginning:

Murphy and Tanner

In preparation for their first mentoring meeting, Murphy dropped his new mentor, Tanner, a brief e-mail to introduce himself. He knew very little about Tanner's background and asked him about it. Within minutes, Tanner shot back a bio and a link to his blog, along with an e-mail response.

Following their first face-to-face mentoring session, Tanner sent Murphy his notes and reflections on their session. Murphy added some comments and his own reflections and promptly returned them to Tanner for comment. Several times during the month, he checked out Tanner's Facebook page.

Virtual mentoring can fast-track the learning, but it requires preparation on your part.

Get Comfortable with the Technology

If you are not comfortable with technology, you will need to learn to overcome your discomfort or resistance to it.

Staying ahead of the technology curve is hard. What is popular today may be a passing trend tomorrow. As I write, many mentoring partners use virtual meeting and Web conferencing sites, such as Go-to-Meeting, Adobe Connect, Web 2.0, and Skype. Social networking sites like Facebook, Twitter, Ning, and Linked-In offer opportunities to create mentoring communities, and many have created online group mentoring sites. These platforms are not mutually exclusive. You will probably use many of them during the course of your relationship depending on your mentee's comfort level and preference.

Manage Your Social Presence

Your social presence is the person you appear to be when you communicate online. You need to know how to be present when you are in that space. Read your e-mails before you press Send to make sure they reflect the message you are sending. If they are too casual, too formal, full of misspellings, and so on, you may be sending an unintentional message about yourself.

Take a look at your social networking presence, and make sure that what you post on these sites reflects the image you want the world to see. Remember that once information goes into cyberspace, it may be there for a very long time.

Manage Your Time Commitment

There is no doubt that time is a major factor in establishing, building, and sustaining mentoring relationships. Many mentors underestimate the time commitment required for distance mentoring relationships. Know that you will need to invest time and effort in creating the climate for learning.

Set up a regular schedule for communicating that allows flexibility. Decide when to connect, how to connect, and who will initiate the contact. Be sensitive to the day-to-day time availability of your mentee. Check in to make sure you are using your connecting time well. Distance mentoring often takes place in a rapid-fire volley of back-and-forth conversation. Take care to make sure that your connections do not become transactions.

Use Multiple Virtual Modalities

You have many options for connecting with your mentee. Take advantage of as many as you can. It is not unusual for a mentor and mentee to exchange regular e-mail, use instant messaging, or connect on Skype or Google or iPhone's FaceTime so that they can "see" each other, and use a share-point site to exchange materials. Some modalities work better than others when it comes to different purposes. For example, if you need to give feedback to your mentee and you know that it is going to be hard for her to hear it, connect in person (face-to-face or virtually) or by telephone.

CONNECTING ON A DEEPER LEVEL

Technology can accommodate most types of mentoring relationships. However, being virtually connected with your mentee doesn't necessarily mean that you've connected on a deeper level. Palloff and Pratt suggest six essential elements that can help you connect to your mentee and successfully facilitate learning: honesty, responsiveness, relevance, respect, openness, and empowerment.[5] I would add one more: time. Let's examine these one by one.

- *Honesty*. It is impossible to have honest dialogue with your mentee unless you first create a climate of safety and trust. Few people can just meet, shake hands (in person or virtually), and jump into honest give-and-take without ruffling feathers. Taking the time to develop rapport will help you connect with your mentee on a meaningful level. If telephone conversations are not providing that human connection, consider other means. Sometimes it is easier for people to be more frank in an e-mail than they are in person or on the telephone. Be willing to experiment, and find a way to connect that is comfortable for both you and your mentee.

- *Responsiveness*. Regular and timely communication maintains the feeling of connection. Let your mentee know when you are too busy to talk or to provide a thoughtful response. When you travel across time zones, take the time difference into consideration in communicating with your mentee. If a particular kind of online interaction is your preferred mode, discuss it with your mentoring partner. You don't want to be sending instant messages if your mentee doesn't give them priority.

- *Relevance*. Mentoring is a learner-centered relationship, so you must understand what is relevant and meaningful to your mentees. Find ways to connect to their life experiences. Become familiar with what else is going on in their lives, what they are thinking, what they value, and what they are doing. And make sure that the learning goals you agree on are relevant to their needs.

- *Respect*. You can demonstrate respect by listening in ways that affirm and value what your mentee has to say. Be considerate, and recognize that he or she may have ways of doing things that are different from your own but are equally valuable. You must be a learner yourself and genuinely curious about your mentee. Check out assumptions. Ask questions. Stay in conversation. Value difference and learn from it.

- *Openness*. Demonstrate openness by being open yourself. Share your story, and invite your mentees to tell their stories. Set a climate for openness by establishing ground rules that clarify mutual expectations. Discuss confidentiality, and agree on what should be discussed in virtual space and what should not.

- *Empowerment*. Palloff and Pratt say, "In a learner centered environment, the learner is truly the expert when it comes to his or her own learning."[6] Engage in open, honest, and respectful conversation so that you can be attuned to your mentees' learning needs and ensure that learning is appropriate to their context. Encourage ownership by supporting your mentees so they can successfully apply new learning. Be available to answer questions, and encourage them to reflect on what they have learned.

• *Time*. One of the most important elements of deep connection between mentoring partners is time—in particular, committing yourself to give the relationship the time it needs to flourish, even if that means rearranging your other tasks to make that space possible.

When mentoring becomes an add-on to the rest of your day, the connection you need to get work done may never get a chance to grow. Here is what one teacher mentor had to say about how time, or lack of it, affected her relationship: "It wasn't her fault. It was mine. I thought I was committed. It was only when I tried to schedule time and couldn't find any of it that I realized mentoring wasn't enough of a priority for me at this time in my life."

Time for mentoring requires more than willingness and dedication, or even meeting time. It needs to be an ongoing commitment throughout the mentoring relationship. It needs to be considered during the preparation process (particularly self-preparation), discussed as you negotiate goals and ground rules, honored and monitored during the enabling phase, and adhered to as you and your mentoring partner come to closure. Before you commit to a mentoring relationship, be sure you are prepared to block off a realistic amount of time—and then protect that time.

CONNECTING THROUGH REFLECTION

I was browsing in a store this past summer and picked up a notepad that had the following quote on it: "Words matter . . . Write to learn what you know." Whether you are a mentor or a mentee, keeping a journal stimulates ongoing reflection and facilitates learning throughout the mentoring cycle, starting with the preparation phase and continuing until closure is reached.

Using a Journal

Using a journal facilitates connection because it helps focus your attention on the work of mentoring. The world goes on in between mentoring conversations, and it is easy to get distracted. When you make regular time to reflect in your journal, it creates a continuous placeholder for where you are in the relationship and points to the sweet spots of connection.

Some mentors find that including factual material (such as notes capturing the content of the conversation), reactions, feelings, and process notes helps them reflect on their mentoring experience. Others record their mentee's progress in achieving articulated learning goals. Through this process, they find that reflection informs their mentoring conversations by revealing questions and issues to pursue with their mentees.

Sentence Stem Reflection Triggers

There is no perfect way to reflect; choose the approach that works best for you. You may find writing a regular diary entry or using the ship's log method, which charts specific details of the relationship, to be helpful. Sentence-completion stems can stimulate the flow of thoughts and ideas. Progoff, for example, uses a three-step process (see Exercise 3.1):[7]

1. Begin reflection with the phrase "at first." Write a paragraph or two.

2. Switch to "and then," writing whatever comes to mind.

3. Follow with completion of the sentence stem: "and now."

In the following example, a mentor reflects on using this approach following his initial mentoring session:

Reflecting on Dani

At first, when I met Dani, I was put off. She seemed flighty, and even the way she dressed seemed to say, "Don't take me seriously." *And then* we started talking, and I was amazed at the depth of her insights and breadth of her experience. She knew far more than I had given her credit for. *And now* I am looking forward to working with her and learning from the diversity of experience she brings to the relationship.

Regular reflection requires discipline. It is easy to procrastinate when it comes to recording reflections unless you make it a habit. The best advice is just to get started—and stay with it. You can use Exercise 3.1 to get started and write as much as you like.

The reflection triggers in Exercise 3.2 are particularly useful immediately following a mentoring session.

Use whatever methods you like, and don't be discouraged. Stay with it: with practice, reflection flows easily.

Finally, here are some tips for successful journaling:

- Schedule it. Engaging in reflection regularly is more important than the time spent on this activity.

- Personalize the format; for example, use bulleted items.

- Don't get bogged down in detail. Capture a brief description or note some specifics. Make sure you have written enough so that when

EXERCISE 3.1

Progoff's Reflection Triggers

At first,

And then,

And now,

EXERCISE 3.2

Sentence Stem Reflection Triggers

1. About my mentee:

What I am thinking:

What I am wondering:

My most difficult mentoring challenge so far:

What is working well:

What could be working better:

A new learning that has affected me:

you review your entry later, you will be able to recall the mentoring experience clearly.

- Note your feelings at the time. Remember that whatever it is that you experience or that stimulates your thinking will help you better understand your own behavior.

- Note frustrations, learnings, curiosities (ruminating questions), and magic moments (peak experiences or synchronicities).

- Describe particularly meaningful mentoring that you have observed or experienced.

- If you find yourself grasping at straws, sit down and write anything, even if it is that you have no thoughts. Reflect on why that is so. You may find that all you needed was a starting point. Once you have begun, it is easier to continue the process.

Mentoring partners can connect in various configurations of mentoring relationships, formal and informal. They connect by valuing difference. They connect through virtual space and distance. They also connect on a deeper, more fundamental level as human beings, borne out of understanding who they are and what each brings to the relationship.

The learning that takes place within a mentoring relationship is connected as well. The learner—the mentee—remains front and center at all times, but the mentor is learning as well. In Part Two, we look at the phases of the mentoring relationship and the components and processes that keep the mentoring relationship in connection and on course.

The Predictable Phases of Mentoring

THE CHAPTERS IN PART ONE explored mentoring in the context of who we are. In Part Two, we shift our focus to what we do: the work of mentoring and the predictable phases that guide this work.

THE FOUR PHASES OF MENTORING

For new mentors and those who have mentored without formal guidance, the knowledge that mentoring relationships have a predictable structure can be liberating:

Phase 1: Preparing (getting ready)

Phase 2: Negotiating (establishing agreements)

Phase 3: Enabling Growth (facilitating learning)

Phase 4: Coming to Closure (looking back, moving forward)

Although these phases are predictable and naturally build on one another, they are not linear. In fact, we generally portray them as a cycle, as shown in the figure below. The phases are less bound by time definition and psychological milestones; rather, you will know where you are, where you are going, and where you need to be because of the behaviors required to move through each of the stages. With one mentee, for example, you may cycle through the phases smoothly; with another, you may find that although you are actively engaged in one phase, you need to revisit the previous phase.

Simply being aware of these phases—and knowing that they are indeed predictable—provides significant signposts for both mentor and mentee.

The Mentoring Cycle

Movement through the four phases follows a fluid yet foreseeable cycle and usually with some overlap between them. For example, during the enabling growth phase, when mentoring partners are most likely to face potential obstacles, they may need to renegotiate aspects of their mentoring partnership agreement in order to move forward and maintain the relationship. Sometimes mentoring partners move into the coming to closure stage prematurely and find that they have unfinished goals to complete before they bring the relationship to a close.

Phase One: Preparing

The preparing phase is a discovery process. Because every mentoring relationship is unique, you and your mentoring partner must take this time to set the tone for the relationship by engaging in conversation, getting to know each another, and understanding each other's contexts.

Clarity about both expectation and role is essential for establishing a productive mentoring relationship. You can also explore your personal motivation and readiness to mentor this individual. Assess your mentoring skills to identify areas for your own learning and development.

Phase Two: Negotiating

Negotiating is the business phase of the relationship—the time when mentoring partners come to agreement on learning goals and define the content and process of the relationship. Although you will establish goals and create a work plan during this phase, negotiating the relationship is not as simple as drawing up an agreement.

The heart of the negotiating phase has to do with creating a shared understanding about assumptions, expectations, goals, and needs. It involves talking about some of the soft issues in a relationship—important topics like ground rules, confidentiality, boundaries, and hot buttons, which often are left out of mentoring conversations because the partners find these issues difficult to talk about. Establishing boundaries in this way lays a solid foundation for building trust.

Another way to describe the negotiating phase is "the detail phase." This is when the details of when and how to meet, responsibilities, criteria for success, accountability, and bringing the relationship to closure are mutually articulated.

Phase Three: Enabling Growth

The enabling growth phase is the work phase of the learning relationship, when most of the contact between mentoring partners takes place. Although it offers the greatest opportunity for nurturing learning and development, the mentoring partners are also most vulnerable to the obstacles that can contribute to derailment of the relationship—even when obstacles and goals have been clearly articulated. Inevitably each relationship must find its own path and maintain a sufficient level of trust to develop a quality mentoring relationship and promote learning.

The mentor's role during this phase is to facilitate learning by establishing and maintaining an open and affirming learning climate and providing thoughtful, timely, candid, and constructive feedback. Both you and your mentee will monitor the learning process and learning progress to ensure that the mentee's learning goals are being met.

Phase Four: Coming to Closure

Coming to closure is much more than simply marking the end of the mentoring relationship; it is an opportunity for both partners to recognize and celebrate what they have learned. This evolutionary process has a beginning (establishing closure protocols when setting up a mentoring agreement), a middle (anticipating and addressing obstacles along the way), and an end (ensuring that there has been positive learning, no matter what the circumstances). All three components are necessary for satisfactory closure.

Successful closure encompasses evaluating, acknowledging, and celebrating achievement of learning outcomes. Both mentors and mentees can benefit from closure. It is an opportunity to harvest the learning and apply what you have learned to other relationships and situations.

THE ROS MODEL: READINESS, OPPORTUNITY, SUPPORT

The four-phase model is a map you can use to keep your mentoring relationship on a steady course and to see where you are and where you need to be as you follow the unique twists and turns of each mentoring experience. As you will soon discover, every phase of the mentoring relationship presents specific learning challenges. The combination of three primary elements—readiness, opportunity, and support (the ROS model)—facilitates successful movement through each phase.

Readiness relates to receptivity and openness to the learning experience. It addresses the issue of preparedness for every phase. Opportunity refers not only to the venues, settings, and situations available for fostering learning, but also to the quality of that opportunity. Support pertains to relevant and adequate assistance to promote effective learning.

When a third party determines the mentoring pairing, as often happens in a formal mentoring program, readiness may be the last element of the ROS model to fall into place for the mentoring partners. There may be ample opportunity to foster learning, and the mentor may be able to provide adequate support, but the mentor or the mentee (or sometimes both) may not be open to this particular relationship at this time.

Many reasons can account for lack of readiness—for example, lack of perceived need, a belief that the need for mentoring is a "weakness," or that the teachable moment has not yet arrived or has already passed. Charging headlong into a mentoring partnership when readiness has not yet been achieved spells disaster. Situations like this can be overcome by paying attention to the conversational possibilities of the preparing phase, allowing adequate time for both parties to come to a shared understanding of the purposes of the relationship before moving into the negotiating phase.

The framework of the ROS tool can help mentors and their mentees analyze which elements are in place and which are missing before moving to the next phase of the mentoring relationship. Gauging the presence or absence of these primary elements helps keep the mentoring relationship on track by identifying possible stumbling blocks. For example, before moving into the enabling phase, you and your mentee must make sure that you have completed the necessary groundwork, have some ground rules in place, are clear about the purpose of the relationship, have determined the opportunities for enabling the relationship, and understand the kind of support that is required.

You can use the ROS tool on the next page before moving to the next mentoring stage, or when the relationship seems out of kilter. This grid will help you identify strengths and weaknesses in the relationship and target areas for improvement.

The example below shows how one mentor used the ROS tool to determine that he and his mentoring partner were not yet ready to move into the negotiating phase of the relationship. Although he knew this was the situation, completing the grid helped him pinpoint some areas for discussion with his mentoring partner during their next conversation.

The knowledge that preparation, negotiating, enabling growth, and coming to closure are all necessary pieces of the mentoring puzzle will help you understand where you and your mentoring partner are and where you are heading. It will also alert you that you may have rushed through a phase, or skipped it, or need to return to do a little more work. It is this very opportunity to improvise in the moment that lifts mentoring into the realm of adult learning.

EXAMPLE

Using the ROS Tool to Reflect on the Preparation Phase

	Mentor	Mentee	Mentoring Partners
Readiness: Receptivity to learning	*Have had prior experience mentoring and am looking forward to the experience once again.*	*Not sure. Don't know mentee very well. Not yet clear about expectations.*	*Not enough time spent together to determine if we are ready to move into the negotiation phase. Don't have a good handle on this yet.*
Opportunity: Settings and venues to foster cognitive, affective, and relational learning	*Limited personally, but I have lots of good contacts and networks I can tap into.*	*Worried about opportunities to apply learning on the job.*	*I have a few ideas about this. May be able to bring mentee along to board meetings as an observer. Want to introduce her to a variety of people.*
Support: Appropriate, relevant, and adequate assistance to facilitate effective learning.	*I feel pretty good about this.*	*I need to check out how much support my mentee feels he is going to need.*	*We are going to need to talk about boundaries around this.*

EXERCISE
The ROS Tool

	Mentor	Mentee	Mentoring Partners
PREPARING			
Readiness: Receptivity to learning			
Opportunity: Settings and venues to foster cognitive, affective, and relational learning			
Support: Appropriate, relevant, and adequate assistance to facilitate effective learning			
NEGOTIATING			
Readiness: Receptivity to learning			
Opportunity: Settings and venues to foster cognitive, affective, and relational learning			
Support: Appropriate, relevant, and adequate assistance to facilitate effective learning			
ENABLING GROWTH			
Readiness: Receptivity to learning			
Opportunity: Settings and venues to foster cognitive, affective, and relational learning			
Support: Appropriate, relevant, and adequate assistance to facilitate effective learning			
COMING TO CLOSURE			
Readiness: Receptivity to learning			
Opportunity: Settings and venues to foster cognitive, affective, and relational learning			
Support: Appropriate, relevant, and adequate assistance to facilitate effective learning			

The chapters in Part Two guide you through each of the four phases. (The enabling growth phase, the most complex one, spans two chapters.) Chapters Four through Eight discuss the components of the particular phase and offer exercises and approaches you can use to make the most of your mentoring relationship. In Chapter Nine, we explore ways you can contribute to your own growth and development as a mentor and dig deeper into many of the topics presented in this book. It contains an annotated list of resources to further your learning.

CHAPTER 4

PREPARING
GETTING READY FOR A MENTORING RELATIONSHIP

FEW RELATIONSHIPS IN LIFE give us a real opportunity to engage with the other person, to begin to know them, to understand their contexts and motivations, and to let them see who we are—before we jump in. For the mentoring relationship, the preparation phase is just that opportunity. Although it may be tempting to skip this phase—especially if you feel pressed for time or you and your mentoring partner seem to have instant rapport—resist that impulse with all your might. Consciously setting aside the time needed to prepare yourself and your relationship promises a satisfying and productive mentoring experience for you and your mentee.

Just as a good gardener always prepares the ground before planting a tender seedling, preparing readies the mentor for the important work that lies ahead. Self-awareness—understanding our own motivations, our strengths and challenges—is the key to getting ready to mentor. And getting to know your mentee engenders respect, trust, and understanding, all necessary ingredients for a productive relationship. Taking time to prepare for a new mentoring relationship nurtures the meaningful connections that build a productive mentoring relationship and sustain it over time.

PREPARING YOURSELF AS A MENTOR

Considering your own motivation for engaging in a mentoring relationship is a good place to begin your preparation. Your motivation will have a direct impact on your behavior and attitude and on the quality of the mentoring interaction. Mentors who have a deep understanding of why they are engaging in a mentoring relationship end up being more committed to it and are more effective in the long run.

Understanding motivation requires introspection and candor. We all have internal and external motivations for doing things, but we are often unaware of what these are. Even when we can articulate our reasons for mentoring, we may be surprised by new insights.

Perhaps you are motivated by the satisfaction of passing on knowledge, helping to build a business, expanding someone else's knowledge base, achieving recognition, receiving reward for the effort, or increasing your own productivity. Or perhaps you believe mentoring will help you expand your personal network, become better known at work, gain different perspectives, repay the debt of what others have given to you, leave a legacy, or be in a position to exert positive influence: the possibilities are unlimited.

Let's look at the motivations of one mentor:

Sylvia and Lester

Lester was a rising star in the training and development department of a public utility company. He had just asked Sylvia, a twenty-three-year department veteran, to mentor him. He admired how easily she developed training curricula and how agile and confident she was, and he hoped to possess those same abilities himself someday.

Sylvia was flattered, but she was ambivalent about accepting the invitation to mentor Lester. She felt a sense of duty, but she knew that alone was not sufficient reason to say yes. A colleague suggested she explore her motivation using the checklist shown in Exercise 4.1. What she found after filling out the checklist surprised her.

She saw that most of her reasons for mentoring were externally driven by what others expected of her—her coworkers often sought her advice, and she liked that feeling. She did find helping others personally rewarding—she could point to a number of coworkers whom she had positively influenced at some point in their careers. But now she was feeling the limits of her own knowledge. In looking for opportunities to further others' learning, she had been neglecting her own, and she was not confident that she could adequately fill Lester's learning needs.

Sylvia was honest with Lester. She told him that before she could consider saying yes to his invitation, she needed to learn more about his learning goals. Then she could determine if his goals would fit with her experience and knowledge.

EXERCISE 4.1

Mentoring Motivation Checklist

For each item below, check yes if the reason listed reflects your motivation for mentoring and no if it does not. For each item, list a concrete example to illustrate your answer.

Motivation	Yes	No	Example
I have specific knowledge that I want to pass on to others.			
I find that helping others learn is personally rewarding to me.			
I enjoy collaborative learning.			
I find that working with others who are different from me is energizing.			
I am always looking for new opportunities to further my own growth and development.			
I want to see this person succeed.			
I am seeking an opportunity to enhance my visibility, reputation, and contribution to my organization or community.			
I am committed to leadership succession.			
I need to meet a performance requirement at work or in my profession.			
I want to do the right thing.			
I want to pay it forward.			
I am interested in mentoring a particular person.			

Source: Adapted from Zachary and Fischler (2009, p. 115).

What Is Motivating You to Be a Mentor?

What is driving your decision to participate in a particular mentoring relationship? It may feel like an organizational imperative or a voluntary engagement, or both. But if you dig a little deeper, you may find other reasons you didn't suspect. Discovering your core motivation is a little like peeling back the layers of an onion and finding even more layers underneath. Exercises 4.1 and 4.2 are designed to help you do just that. What you find in each case will depend on how truly candid and self-reflective you can be.

Now let's explore your motivation further. We'll begin with the outer layer of the onion, and gradually get to your core motivation. You may be tempted to stop after you have identified the first reason, but I encourage you to continue to work your way down through all three reasons. If you run out of steam, push yourself to keep going or put the exercise aside for now and come back to it later.

In Example 4.1 you can see how Lou, an account manager in a consulting firm, used Exercise 4.2 to help him arrive at the root cause of his motivation.

When you have completed Exercises 4.1 and 4.2, you may find that your actual motivation was different or more complex than you originally thought. Or you may discover that you are even more committed to your original reason. For example, Leonard, a retired small business owner, completed Exercise 4.2 and discovered that his real motivation for mentoring Sally was quite different from what he had believed:

Leonard and Sally

Sally was looking for assistance in developing her fledgling packaging business, and Leonard had volunteered to mentor her as part of the Small Business Association's business mentoring program. He felt an obligation to give back some of the wisdom he had received from the businesspeople who had helped him get started years ago, and he identified this as his primary motivation.

But as he began to look more deeply, he discovered that his underlying motivations were a feeling of loneliness and a lack of stimulation. He missed the give-and-take with other business owners that he used to have on a regular basis. Leonard found that his new understanding of his motivations actually made him feel more enthusiastic about his new mentoring relationship with Sally.

EXERCISE 4.2

Identifying Mentor Motivation

My motivation for mentoring is …

Reason 1: Jot down what you think might be the underlying reason for the sentence above:

Reason 2: Reflect on what you wrote as reason 1 and ask yourself what might have contributed to that response. Jot it down here:

Reason 3: Reflect on reason 2. What might underlie that response? Jot it down here:

Now analyze your responses and jot down your motivation here. It may be the same one you began with or very different.

My primary motivation for mentoring is …

EXAMPLE 4.1

Lou's Motivation for Mentoring

My motivation for mentoring is: *I've worked here for fifteen years and feel that I have gained important insights that may help accelerate someone else's career development.*

Reason 1: *Other people have made it possible for me to be where I am today. As a senior leader, this is something I need to do.*

Reason 2: *It is my responsibility to help our employees become better contributors.*

Reason 3: *I have a particular area of expertise that is in great demand at this time.*

My primary motivation for mentoring is: *To share what it is I really know and am valued for within the company. I realize that I have a responsibility here. If I don't share my expertise, the company won't have that expertise in its next generation of managers.*

Evaluating a Potential Mentoring Relationship

Your motivation has a great bearing on your commitment to a particular mentoring relationship. If your only motivation is external, you will not be likely to work at sustaining it. Nor will you be at your personal best in facilitating the learning relationship effectively and ultimately growing from it personally. That's why it's important to prepare for each new mentoring relationship by evaluating what you can meaningfully contribute to a particular mentoring relationship and determine if you are ready for it. Exercise 4.3 will help you do just that.

Once you've analyzed your motivations, you may find that you are indeed ready and even eager to enter into this mentoring relationship. But you may also discover that although you would like to participate in the relationship, you cannot add value to it. Or you may find that although you are highly motivated to be a mentor, this relationship is not for you. In either case, you may then choose to forgo this opportunity.

Getting Comfortable with Mentoring Skills

The more comfortable we are with a skill, the more likely we will use it. Often, even if we are knowledgeable about specific skills, we may not feel comfortable using them. A person who has received training in managing conflict, for instance, is not necessarily proficient at or comfortable with using those skills.

Some skills, discussed in the sections that follow, are more powerful than others in facilitating mentoring relationships. How well you use these skills will relate in whole or in part to your emotional intelligence. If you are self-aware and socially aware and can effectively manage yourself and your

EXERCISE 4.3

Am I Ready for This Mentoring Relationship?

1. I want to be a mentor because …

2. I want to participate in this particular mentoring relationship because …

3. My experience and expertise will contribute to this relationship by …

4. Specific things I *can* do to help this individual:

5. Specific things I am *willing to do* to help this individual:

relationships, you will be more likely to feel confident and comfortable with these skills. If you are not comfortable, consider this an opportunity to contribute to your own growth and development by finding assistance in this area.

Brokering Relationships

Brokering relationships involves using your own networks to connect your mentees to the people and the resources that will be of assistance in achieving their learning objectives. Mentors need to be experienced networkers and have a stable of diverse contacts from whom to draw expertise, resources, and information in order to be successful.

Building and Maintaining Relationships

Too frequently we put great energy into starting a relationship and assume that this momentum will continue to drive the relationship. In fact, relationships that continue over time require ongoing tending, patience, and persistence. Some people are better at building than maintaining. Mentors need to be adept at both.

Coaching

Coaching and mentoring are kindred spirits. Although the terms are sometimes used interchangeably, they are not the same thing. Coaching focuses on enhancing performance by helping an individual close his or her knowledge and skill gaps. Mentoring focuses on facilitating the future growth and development of the mentee. Mentors often need to use coaching skills to help a mentee in determining knowledge or skills gaps that are holding him or her back and assist in closing these gaps so that this person can reach identified learning goals.

Communicating

Effective communication—being authentic, listening effectively, checking for understanding, and articulating clearly and unambiguously—is a critical part of any relationship. Facilitating a learning relationship requires ongoing communication. Effective communication also involves silences: understanding nonverbal cues and being able to pick up on what is behind the words another person is saying.

Encouraging

Mentors who are good at encouraging come in many guises: cheerleaders, confidence builders, gentle persuaders, critical friends, inspirers, and motivators. Encouragement keeps the mentee focused on the future by first holding out an optimistic vision of what is possible and then keeping up the momentum up while working toward achieving learning goals. Positive reinforcement and validation is important; the right word said at the right time can make all the difference.

Facilitating

Artful facilitation is the key to promoting shared learning, reflective practice, and deeper insight for a mentee. This is the means by which mentors support and challenge mentees to learn, grow, and develop. Mentors must be aware of learning styles and use that knowledge as a basis for enlarging the mentee's thinking and perspective. Respect for different perspectives is critical to creating a shared learning experience and demands that mentors be flexible and open to learning. When you engage your mentees as active participants in their own learning, you encourage self-reflection and ownership.

Goal Setting

Well-defined goals drive the learning process of a mentoring relationship, but setting those goals requires time and good conversation between mentor and mentee. As a mentor, your role is help your mentee clarify, crystallize, and set realistic goals. This means engaging your mentoring partner in a collaborative, robust goal-setting process that culminates in a game plan for how to achieve those goals.

Guiding

Mentors act as guides on the learning journey, leading mentees as they create and grow into their desired future. The mentor guides by being a role model and leads by example. This means that mentors must be familiar with the path so that they can adequately prepare mentees for what lies ahead and help them stay focused on their destination. A good guide can interpret the language, help mentees make meaning of the experience, and arrive safely.

Listening

Being a good listener is the attribute that mentees value most in a mentor. Effective listeners balance talking and listening, and they grasp the content and context of what is being said. Good listeners listen for the noise and for the silence, and they use what they hear as teachable moments to encourage reflective thinking. Effective listening makes mentees feel heard and sends the message that you genuinely care.

Managing Conflict

Conflict can occur in any relationship. Managing it effectively requires direct and honest conversation about differing points of view. It does not mean eliminating differences. Rather, it is about inviting dialogue to understand varying points of view.

Problem Solving

It is not your job as mentor to solve your mentees' problems. Rather, you should provide assistance in the problem-solving process by engaging mentees in finding solutions to the problem. By asking questions and holding up a mirror, you can help them define problems. Together you can discuss problem-solving strategies and alternative scenarios for working the problem through to a viable solution.

Feedback

Mentees rely on mentors as trusted sources of candid and direct feedback. Try to create an expectation for ongoing constructive (not corrective) feedback. Remember that most people are better at giving feedback than they are at asking for it, receiving it, and accepting it. As a mentor, you need to model good feedback practices and ask for feedback on your own feedback. Feedback creates momentum by keeping mentees on track and moving in the right direction.

Reflecting

If you personally engage in self-reflection, you are more likely to be adept at using reflection to facilitate learning in a mentoring relationship. By reflecting, mentors raise mentees' levels of awareness about how they frame their thoughts, the way they make meaning, and the way they translate ideas into action. Being comfortable with the process skill of reflection enables you to consistently model that skill for mentees.

Valuing Difference

One of the benefits of mentoring for both mentor and mentee is the exposure to different perspectives. During the course of a mentoring relationship, mentors are likely to hear views that are different from their own. These may be positional differences, generational differences, learning style differences, or gender or ethnic differences. Each individual has his or her own story: mentors need to be able to understand, learn from, and value differences.

SURVEYING YOUR MENTORING SKILLS

It is not unusual for first-time mentors (like first-time managers) to confidently overestimate their skills.[1] Self-preparation is a great opportunity for you to expand and deepen your own learning, hone your facilitation skills, and become a better mentor. Here is what Simone found when she completed the mentoring skills inventory in Exercise 4.4:

Simone's Story

When Simone completed the mentoring skills inventory, she didn't discover anything new. But the process did help to confirm her lack of comfort in managing conflict and reflecting. She generally tended to smooth things over and avoid conflict—taking time to reflect seemed like a luxury rather than a necessity.

As a result of taking the inventory, Simone became more conscious of these areas, and she was determined to work on strengthening them. She was also somewhat surprised when she looked at the skill list and saw that she was moderately comfortable in most areas but not very comfortable in any. Simone jokingly remarked, "I think I need a mentor to mentor me about mentoring!"

Exercise 4.4 will help you gauge your comfort with using the skills listed in the previous section and help you identify which of them you need to work on. From time to time, you may want to seek feedback from your mentee on how you are doing relative to each skill.

Prioritize the Skills You Need to Learn

Once you've inventoried your mentoring skills, the next step is to prioritize the skills you need to learn. In addition to realizing that she needed some mentoring herself, Simone targeted two mentoring skills she wanted to work on: managing conflict and reflecting. Of the two, managing conflict was the more pressing need because it would immediately help her challenge and support her mentee's learning.

The increase in self-awareness that comes with identifying your comfort with various mentoring skills may be just enough to help improve your effectiveness in a particular area. But the further step of developing and implementing a personal learning plan (Exercise 4.5 and Example 4.2) will provide the structure and discipline you may need to stay the course. The benefits of this approach enrich immediate and future mentoring relationships and potentially transcend the mentoring experience itself.

EXERCISE 4.4

Mentoring Skills Inventory

Review each skill in the first column and indicate your comfort level with it by circling V (very comfortable), M (moderately comfortable), or U (uncomfortable). In the next column, jot down a situation when you were either comfortable or uncomfortable using the skill. Put a checkmark in the final column for each skill that you feel you need to work on to develop a comfort level with it. Once you have completed the skills inventory, rank your overall comfort level with all of the skills on a scale of 1 to 5, with 5 being very comfortable, 3 being moderately comfortable, and 1 being uncomfortable.

Skill	Situation	Need to Work On?
Brokering relationships V M U		
Building and maintaining relationships V M U		
Coaching V M U		
Communicating V M U		
Encouraging V M U		
Facilitating V M U		
Goal setting V M U		
Guiding V M U		
Listening V M U		
Managing conflict V M U		
Problem solving V M U		
Feedback V M U		
Reflecting V M U		
Valuing difference V M U		

Overall comfort level:

1   2   3   4   5

EXERCISE 4.5

Establishing Learning Priorities, Measures of Success, and Milestones

First, identify the two or three skills from Exercise 4.4 that you need to work on that would most improve your effectiveness in a mentoring relationship. Write each one below. Then determine your measures for success for each skills goal, and jot them down. Finally, jot down the specific milestones that would indicate that you are making progress toward developing those skills.

Skill goal 1:

Measures of Success   **Milestones**

Skill goal 2:

Measures of Success   **Milestones**

Skill goal 3:

Measures of Success   **Milestones**

Develop a Personal Learning Plan

Simone decided that she needed to learn more about conflict management. She defined reasonable learning objectives for herself, and then identified the human and material resources and methods she needed to assess her progress. Her strategy was to talk with her coworkers and gather recommendations on what how-to books to read. In the process of gathering recommendations, she would also have the opportunity to talk with her peers about their preferred methods of managing conflict and get some ideas on ways to hone her skills.

EXAMPLE 4.2

Simone's Personal Learning Plan

Stretch Goal

Learn to be more comfortable and competent at conflict management.

Measures of Success

Getting positive feedback from colleagues. Feeling less anxious in situations that call for managing conflict. Using the skill regularly so that it comes naturally to me.

Objectives	Activities	Resources Needed	Time Frame	Next Step
Find out which books I should read.	Talk with good role models for this.	Various colleagues	Next month	Figure out whom I want to ask
Draw up a list based on interviews.	Read the top three recommended books.	Purchase books	Next month	Order books
Identify the most commonly used approaches.	Read the books.	Books and learning log	February–April	Keep at it regularly
Create a list of three techniques to master, and select one to work on.	Review coworkers' lists and learning logs.		By April 30	Compare and contrast lists
Practice using techniques.	Keep notes on what I am doing.	Learning log	May	Try it
Gather feedback.	Ask colleagues for specific feedback.	Time with colleagues and direct reports	May–June	Talk with mentor and manager
Work at getting better.	Continue to seek feedback.	Specific questions	Ongoing	Review learning log

Once she made her reading selection, she intended to read several books and apply the strategies as she learned them, gathering feedback from her colleagues. Part of the plan was to create a learning log to record what she was learning, as well as her successes in managing conflict. She decided that this would have the added benefit of helping her develop more comfort with the reflection process, her second objective.

Having defined her objectives and, identified resources and specific ways to assess her progress, Simone drafted a plan (Example 4.2), including a realistic timetable for accomplishing her objectives. She then sought out colleagues and asked for feedback on her plan. Once she revised it, Simone started implementing her plan.

Establish Your Stretch Goals

No matter how many times you have been a mentor, you can always get better at it. Stretch goals focus on the future—getting you out of your comfort zone and stretching you to be the best mentor you can be. These bold goals of possibility can help you bridge the distance between good and better.

Peer into the gap between where you are and where you want to be to find the learning you need to make that journey. Here's how Michael planned to bridge the gap between his being a new associate and eventually the founding partner in his own law firm:

Michael's Story

Michael, a new associate in a large law firm, dreamed about opening a private practice someday. He knew that in order to do so, he needed to learn the business of law. Every year, he identified three stretch goals that would move him closer to his dream. In year 1, he worked on developing his accounting skills. In year 2, he developed professional networks through attending bar association meetings and section meetings in his area of practice. In year 3, he developed skills in legal specialties outside his regular area of practice.

Identifying stretch goals is now part of his life. He encourages the partners and associates in his own firm to make stretch goals a regular part of how they conduct business.

Create an action plan that lays out your strategy for achieving each of your stretch goals. The key is to define reasonable goals, and no more than three, that take you beyond where you are now and raise the bar on your mentoring practice.

For each goal, define clear-cut objectives, outline activities that will help you achieve them, identify the resources you need (and where you can find them), lay out a time frame for accomplishing the objective, and identify the first step you will take toward achieving that stretch goal. Using the milestones you identified in Exercise 4.5 to evaluate your progress will provide momentum for your learning. Periodically review the measures of success you identify to keep yourself on track.

Clarify Your Role Assumptions

Expectations and assumptions about the mentor's role need to be clear to both partners from the outset. *Role* refers to the anticipated or expected functions a mentor might play—team builder, coach, confidant, teacher, guide, advocate, and so on. You and your mentee may have different ideas about this. Complicating matters, different roles may be required at different points in the relationship, blurring the mentor's role.

Because of this lack of clarity, it is crucial to keep revisiting both partners' understanding of their roles. The story of Fran and Cynthia illustrates what can happen when roles are not clearly defined:

Fran and Cynthia

Fran is a leader and political maverick. Articulate, bright, and energetic, she is a go-getter. Cynthia, a former journalist a decade younger, is every bit as bright and energetic. When introduced at work, they liked each other instinctively and immediately connected around similar interests and hobbies of volunteer work, writing, and hiking.

As they got to know each other, Cynthia came to respect Fran and admire everything about her: her drive for success, her individuality, and her leadership style. Fran was the role model of the successful woman leader she wanted to become. Fran viewed Cynthia as her younger counterpart, her earlier self revisited. She admired Cynthia's ideas and innovations, and especially Cynthia's eagerness to please and her palpable hunger for success. She decided to help Cynthia accelerate her development.

Cynthia was delighted that Fran wanted to mentor her and worked hard to earn her praise and approval. She gave her time and energy freely, without limit. The result of the collaboration between Cynthia and Fran was exciting to both of them. Their talents complemented each other, and the results they achieved together were impressive. Cynthia was learning new skills, and Fran was benefiting professionally and personally from Cynthia's efforts.

In time, Cynthia developed a reputation for innovation and high-quality performance. As she did, Fran became more and more possessive of Cynthia's time and effort. As Fran's demands escalated, Cynthia became increasingly overwhelmed, and a list of unaddressed topics grew, eroding the trust between them.

The relationship became clouded with emotion and mixed signals. Still, Cynthia remained loyal to Fran and continued to meet and even exceed her mentor's increasing demands, but she began to resent Fran. Because of her loyalty to Fran ("she owed her"), she did not want to hurt her, but, she said, "I felt as if she was extracting everything from me. I was giving her my best, and she was devouring it—and me. I felt conflicted and angry."

Mentors need to be cognizant of what happens when there is lack of clarity, and make sure that roles are clarified from the beginning of the relationship. Both Fran and Cynthia took their relationship for granted, never doing the work required to clarify assumptions about roles and responsibilities. As their relationship changed over time, this confusion led to ill feelings.

Partnerships that fail frequently fall victim to one of the following difficulties:

- *Role collusion* results from taking the role for granted. The mentoring partners unknowingly collude because they do not discuss role expectations. "We'll get to it later," they say, but never do. As a result, the relationship coasts along, never really getting to its destination.

- *Role diffusion* occurs when the mentor has the expectation of being all things to all people. The mentor assumes more roles than may be required or reasonable to expect and may end up being a caretaker. "Oh, I'll take care of that for you" is the typical response of this mentor.

- *Role confusion* occurs when lines of authority are blurred and there is lack of clarity about disparate (and sometimes overlapping) roles and responsibilities. The mentor is also the mentee's supervisor, evaluator, or relative.

- *Role protrusion* occurs when mentors inject themselves into situations in which they do not belong, as when a mentor intercedes on behalf of the mentee when it is inappropriate or unwarranted.

All four of these role challenges can be overcome when mentors set aside adequate time to engage in an open, frank, explicit, and direct conversation about roles. However, before you can do this in a good way, you need to be clear about your own role. That takes some self-reflection, as Andy discovered:

Andy and Myron

Andy and Myron worked together on several nonprofit board committees and naturally fell into a mentoring relationship. Both assumed that holding a specific discussion about their roles was unnecessary.

Myron relied on his mentor, Andy, for hints about how to delegate responsibility and to help him understand the political workings of nonprofit organizational life. Andy saw his role as preparing Myron, new to nonprofit work, to take on increasing responsibilities. Their amicable and friendly relationship shifted very quickly when Andy started pushing Myron to sit on the other task forces that he chaired.

Belatedly, Andy realized that if he had explored his assumptions and motivations (Exercises 4.1 and 4.2) and assessed his readiness for the role of mentor, he could have gotten his relationship started on the right foot.

Mentoring is a reflective practice. Reflection takes discipline and time to do well. Self-reflection on the part of the mentor prior to the mentoring relationship is the heart and soul of the preparatory work for the mentor and continues throughout the mentoring cycle.

In completing the exercises thus far in this chapter, you have begun the process that will help you get your relationship moving in a positive direction. Here's a quick refresher:

- Reflect on your motivation for becoming a mentor.
- Be clear about what you are looking for in a mentoring relationship.
- Get comfortable with the mentoring skills you may need to draw on.
- Identify two or three stretch goals.
- Establish criteria to measure success.
- Set milestones to keep up the momentum.
- Create a mentor development plan.
- Consider what you are willing to contribute to the relationship.
- Prepare for your role as mentor, understand it, and learn from it.

Once you have prepared yourself for the role of mentor, assessed your skill-comfort level, and considered your roles, it is time to prepare the relationship.

PREPARING YOUR MENTORING RELATIONSHIP

Building a sound relationship with your mentee is the most critical element in laying a strong foundation for a mentoring partnership. Without it, mentoring runs the risk of becoming merely transactional and superficial. When mentor and mentee have no real connection, they are simply going through the motions and not truly engaging with each other or with the process.

Connecting Through Conversation

Relationships take work, and they take time to develop. Building, establishing, and sustaining them begins with good conversation. According to poet David Whyte, "Any good conversation extends an implicit invitation to those who join it to meet at some as yet indefinable frontier, and through that joining to be part of the process of defining that new frontier."[2] This is a wonderful description of the goal of any mentoring relationship.

Mentoring conversations are conversations of connection. Recently I happened to overhear one of these conversations in a coffee shop. I hadn't intended to listen in, but the more I heard and observed, the more transfixed I became. I snapped a mental picture of a man and a woman, clearly (to me, at least) a mentor and mentee. She was talking about her current work situation and was wondering how and if it related to her future career path. He was asking clarifying questions and connecting her questions to the twists and turns of his own career path. He said, "That was then, and now is now. There are a number of ways you could go." Then he laid out some possible scenarios for her to consider and asked her how she felt about them. She responded with curiosity and asked lots of questions, which he guided into a mutual discussion of where their industry was headed and what it would mean for her company.

As I watched and listened, I was struck by the focus, intentionality, depth, and authenticity of the conversation. For them, no one else was present in the bustling coffee shop that morning.

Any observer would have seen what I saw: two individuals completely engaged in a robust dialogue that had real connection, learning, mutual commitment, and meaning. It was only because a foundation of trust and candor existed before that morning that the mentor could invite his mentee to explore her own frontier.

A mentoring relationship without this kind of connection clearly misses the mark. The old notion of mentoring was not concerned with connection as much as it was with the transfer of knowledge and know-how. Transfer of knowledge represents a more impersonal and autonomous way of knowing. We now know that for learning to be effectively sustained, two conditions need to occur: the learner needs to be engaged in the learning process, and the learning needs to be connected to the learner and to his or her life experiences. Connected knowing emerges out of a relationship between self and other. And as we saw in Chapter Two, connection comes as much through understanding and appreciation of abundant difference as it does through discovering commonality.

Staying in the Conversation

In our workshops, we frequently ask participants to think about a time when they had a really good conversation and to give us some descriptors for that conversation. What they tell us, time and time again, is that listening, trust, openness, honesty, respect, safety, optimism, integrity, engagement, reflection, and learning made it a high-quality experience for them. And yet when time and work pressures become an issue, as so often happens, conversation is the first thing that gets short-changed. To stay in the conversation, try the following exercise.

Think about a time when you had a really good conversation. What words would you use to describe that conversation? Make a list of whatever words come to mind. Then share your list with colleagues and friends and ask them for their input. Once you have a dozen items, stop and review your list. Make a chart for yourself, similar to the one in Example 4.3. After every mentoring session, look at that list to see if you and your mentoring partner engaged in good conversation. Example 4.3 shows my own conversation accountability list.

Engaging the Mentee

When you can engage your mentee in the mentoring process, you set a positive tone and level of expectation for the relationship. Use the following approaches to invite your mentees into conversation and keep them engaged throughout the mentoring relationship.

Satisfying Information Needs

A mentee may have information needs about the subtleties of a particular situation, organization, or office. He or she may want to know the ins and outs of how to scale the corporate walls, publish an article, establish academic credibility, or land a much-sought-after promotion.

EXAMPLE 4.3

Conversation Accountability List

Descriptor	Yes	No	What I Need to Work On
Listening			
Trusting			
Two-way			
Open			
Dialogue			
Honest			
Safe			
Optimistic			
Engaging			
Reflective			
Active learning			
Balance talking and listening			

Helpful Approaches

- Start with the mentee's questions.
- Identify the mentee's goals.
- Determine what the mentee wants to know.
- Present alternative approaches for reaching the goals.

Approaches That Are Not Helpful

- Telling the mentee everything there is to know about a subject
- Pontificating
- Talking about "how it was in my day"

Offering a Vision

Sometimes all it takes is another perspective to help a mentee reframe learning his or her goals and objectives. Sharing your own vision can broaden the mentee's understanding of what might be possible.

Helpful Approaches

- Ask the obvious and the not so obvious.

- Provide potential alternatives: for example, "Have you thought about . . . ?"

- Provide information about similar situations: for example, "In my experience . . ."

- Push the mentee's thinking and acting forward not by providing solutions but by helping in the problem-solving process.

- Encourage the exploration of options before pushing to action.

Approaches That Are Not Helpful

- Jumping in too soon without building trust

- Giving answers

- Demanding that the mentee do things your way

Lending an Ear

Hearing is easy. Really listening to what is being said is not. Yet both are necessary in any meaningful relationship. Sometimes we fixate on one particular aspect of what we listen to. It could be the words or what someone has said (thinking), the meaning assigned to it (emotion), or how the person is behaving (tone of voice, facial expressions) in your interaction. These affect not only what we listen for but also what it is we actually hear and learn. Hearing means listening for understanding and taking the time to check out what it is you think you heard.

Helpful Approaches

- Suspend judgment.

- Acknowledge emotion.

- Be empathetic.

- Provide feedback appropriately.

- Acknowledge what you hear, as well as what is missing.

Approaches That Are Not Helpful

- Playing therapist

- Concentrating primarily on the mentee's emotions

- Solving the problem for the mentee

Setting Realistic Expectations

When difficulties arise, mentees find someone whose experience and expertise they trust and respect to learn from. But sometimes they lean too hard and expect too much support. An open discussion of realistic expectations and roles can release tension and pressure in the relationship.

Helpful Approaches

- Discourage moaning, groaning, and bemoaning.
- Balance compassion with challenge.
- Ask questions.

Approaches That Are Not Helpful

- Becoming a permanent leaning post
- Thinking you are the only one who can help
- Interfering

Establishing the Big Picture

There are layers of complexity to solving business problems. Helping a mentee reach out from the immediate situation to embrace a larger context establishes a broader understanding of a problem, issue, or challenge. Establishing the big picture is often the first step to real understanding.

Helpful Approaches

- Encourage exploration of options before the mentee moves to action.
- Remember that the complex is often simple.

Approaches That Are Not Helpful

- Making seemingly impossible tasks too achievable
- Making it happen

Offering a Helping Hand

Sometimes a helping hand provided at just the right time becomes the catalyst to promoting a fuller discussion.

Helpful Approaches

- Provide encouragement in multiple and timely ways.
- Know when to ask the right question and how to convey the message, "You can do it."

- Tell your mentee what you are doing and why.
- Talk through possible strategies.
- Cocreate opportunities.

Approaches That Are Not Helpful

- Scripting for the mentee
- Talking for the mentee or about the mentee in the mentee's presence

Engaging the mentee begins before the relationship is formalized and continues throughout the relationship. Each of the strategies set out here is useful in preliminary and ongoing discussions with prospective mentees.

Building Trust

The potential for real learning in a mentoring relationship increases commensurate with the level of trust. When trust is high, mentoring partners can more honestly engage with one another. They can discuss issues, solve problems, and carry on genuine dialogue. This is where the significant learning action takes place.

In this anecdote, Judith had to work harder than usual to build trust with her mentee, Kari:

Judith and Kari

Kari, a new school principal, selected Elisa as a mentor. She knew Elisa from leadership team meetings and was very comfortable with her. But after three months of mentoring meetings, Kari received a call from the central district office announcing that a retired veteran principal, Judith, had been assigned to mentor her instead.

Kari was resentful and resistant. She was very standoffish when she and Judith met, and made up excuse after excuse as to why she couldn't meet with her mentor.

Judith had her work cut out for her. She needed to find a way to engage Kari in the conversation and connect with her on a meaningful level. It took time and considerable effort, and Judith had to remind herself to be patient—she understood how Kari felt and shared this with her. With each conversation they began to add a layer of trust between them. Rather than push forward when Kari wasn't ready, Judith took her time and kept Kari in the conversation.

If Judith had not worked to establish a connection with Kari, their relationship would have been a superficial one at best. This was a risky situation for Judith. She could have been angry and resentful that Kari didn't come to the table as a willing partner and showed her annoyance. Instead, she was respectful, managed her emotions, didn't take it personally, and listened to Kari's concerns. She had to demonstrate that she was trustworthy in order for Kari to be willing to learn from her and to make progress toward her learning goals.

Without shared understanding, trust quickly erodes. Authentic communication is challenging without trust; facilitating learning without it is impossible.

Assumption Awareness

We naturally base our assumptions on our experiences, and they determine how we see the world. After a while, they become truth, and we act on them. But our assumptions are just that; they are not necessarily the truth.

Mentors and mentees are human beings, and we each inevitably have assumptions about our role that guide our behavior. Mentoring partners who operate under differing assumptions have a very difficult time managing expectations. The process of checking out assumptions establishes the basis for candid communication, builds trust, and enables the partners to reach shared understanding, all necessary and vital components of a mentoring relationship.

It is important to be aware of the assumptions you have about mentoring and check regularly to make sure they are valid and accurate.[3] Brookfield coined the term "assumption hunting" to describe this process. Assumption hunting is one of the most formidable ethical and caring tasks that mentors carry out. "In many ways," he writes, "we are our assumptions. Assumptions give meaning and purpose to who we are and what we do. Becoming aware of the implicit assumptions that frame how we think and act is one of the most challenging intellectual puzzles we face in our lives."[4] He breaks the process into three interrelated phases: identifying assumptions, checking them out for accuracy, and acting in a more inclusive and integrative way.[5]

Assumption hunting is difficult and challenging work. As Bardwick notes, "When something is considered normal it is woven into our assumptions" and thus becomes difficult to challenge.[6] We all have our unique definition of what is normal in a mentoring relationship. Sharing those assumptions is a discipline that prepares us for mentoring in an honest, forthright way. Otherwise our existing assumptions guide our actions and get reinforced. A good place to start is with this question: "What is it I say to myself or to others to justify my actions?"

Assumption hunting is a three-step process:

Step 1: List your assumptions.

Step 2: Check their validity with others.

Step 3: Keep checking!

We'll follow the story of Meg and Claude to see how the process works.

Meg and Claude: Step 1

When Meg took on the role of mentor to Claude, a nurse practitioner, she made the following assumptions:

- That her role was to identify career and educational options that would move him out of his current job into one with more interesting challenges

- That she would need to coach, cheerlead, and help Claude evaluate options

- That her responsibilities would include meeting with Claude once a month, staying connected through e-mail, and making introductions for him

- That Claude would come to the relationship with some ideas about his career options, would follow up on the contacts she provided for him, and would do research between mentoring sessions

- That the mentoring relationship would take about an hour a month of face-to-face contact time

- That Claude could reach his goals within six months

Try step 1 now. Using the form provided in Exercise 4.6, identify the assumptions you hold about mentoring. Complete each question candidly.

In step 2, you will check your assumptions for validity by asking for feedback from others. If you are participating in a formal or organizational program, you might check with the coordinator and your mentee. If you are engaged in an informal relationship, you might invite your mentee to complete a parallel exercise and share your own responses, and then discuss the implications for your relationship. This is a helpful exercise for both new and seasoned mentors. The assumptions you made in previous relationships may not be consistent across all relationships. Meg had a surprise when she checked her assumptions with Claude:

EXERCISE 4.6

Assumption Hunting

What assumptions are you holding about your role as a mentor?

What assumptions are you holding about your mentee's role?

What assumptions might your mentee hold about your role as a mentor?

What assumptions is your mentee holding about her role in the relationship?

Meg and Claude: Step 2

Meg was surprised to find when she checked in with Claude that he held a different set of assumptions about his role. He had anticipated that Meg would play a more active role in the relationship: setting up interviews for him, coaching him through the interview process, and advocating for him. He was also surprised that Meg had assumed that they would meet so infrequently. Holding a discussion about the differences in their assumptions helped them both manage their expectations and forestall future problems.

In step 3, you make a habit of checking out your assumptions regularly. You can do this in conversation or by using the guidelines that Meg and Claude followed:

Meg and Claude: Step 3

Meg and Claude agreed on expectations, but later in their relationship, Claude became increasingly dependent on Meg for direction. Meg decided to facilitate a discussion about his assumptions using a similar but more structured approach than the one described in step 2.

She began by suggesting that both list their assumptions about how the relationship was going, share their responses without judging or analyzing them, and then discuss these points:

- What can we conclude based on these assumptions?

- Are our assumptions congruent? If so, on what items? If there is no agreement, why not?

- What are the implications for our mentoring relationship?

- Where are we likely to encounter choppy water? Smooth sailing?

Assumption hunting that is carried out consistently keeps the mentoring process flowing. It should be part of the beginning of a mentoring relationship and surface when you are evaluating progress in the relationship or when the relationship falls into a rut. Assumption hunting helps raise awareness about why we do things. Examining the congruence between our beliefs and actions helps build and maintain ethically strong mentoring relationships. No mentoring partner is well served by a mentoring relationship based on misunderstanding; that only adds additional layers of vulnerability to the relationship.

The Initial Conversation

Engaging the mentee in meaningful conversation from the very beginning starts building the connection, helps determine the compatibility of your goals, and helps the mentee decide whether the mentoring relationship is worth pursuing.

The natural tendency is to look for chemistry when meeting a new mentoring partner for the first time. Surely if you like one another, that's a good sign, right? But chemistry as a clue to the success of a mentoring relationship is overrated. So often, if the chemistry does not feel right in the first few minutes, mentors and mentees may shut down or foreclose the opportunity for further engagement—and miss a learning opportunity in the process. Mentoring is about learning. The critical question is not whether you have chemistry, but whether you can have a productive learning relationship.

Use the initial conversation to begin to get to know each other apart from titles and job descriptions. This conversation should be about the two of you—the individuals in the mentoring relationship—and what each of you brings to the relationship. That means sharing your history, context, culture, uniqueness, and so on.

You can also share your previous mentoring experiences and discuss what worked for you and what didn't (see Exercise 1.2). Ask your mentee to describe her career vision and articulate broad learning and development goals. Ask questions to clarify and determine how these goals align with her vision of the future.

You and your mentee should each communicate your own individual desires, needs, and expectations from the relationship. Together you can explore the assumptions that you hold about each other and the relationship and discuss what each of you is willing and capable of contributing to the relationships.

Finally, you can talk about your personal style and your learning style and how they might affect the learning and communication inherent in the relationship.

Table 4.1 presents an agenda for that initial conversation, along with strategies for conversation and questions for mentors to ponder.

It may take several conversations to address these items in a fully satisfactory way before you move on to the next phase. Use the checklist in Exercise 4.7 to decide when and if you are ready.

If you have not checked some items, it may mean one of a number of things: you have more to do to prepare yourself adequately for the partnership, you may need to have further conversations with your mentee and

TABLE 4.1

Getting Ready: Initial Conversation

Agenda	Strategies for Conversation	Questions to Ponder
1. Take time to get to know each other.	Obtain a copy of your mentee's bio in advance of the conversation. If one is not available, create one through conversation.	What kind of information might you exchange to get to know each other better? What points of connection have you discovered in your conversation? What else do you want to learn about each other?
2. Share mentoring stories.	Share your previous mentoring experiences with your mentoring partner.	What did you like about your experiences? What did you learn from those experiences? What would you like to carry forward into this relationship?
3. Talk to your mentee about his or her learning and development goals.	Ask your mentee to describe his or her career vision, hopes, and dreams, and articulate broad learning goals and the reasons they are important.	Why does your mentee want to engage in this relationship? What does he hope to learn? Do his learning goals align with his vision of the future?
4. Determine his or her relationship needs and expectations.	Ask your mentoring partner what he or she wants, needs, and expects out of the relationship.	Are you clear about each other's wants, needs, and expectations for this mentoring relationship?
5. Candidly share your personal assumptions and limitations.	Talk about the mentoring assumptions and limitations you each bring to the relationship. Discuss implications for your relationship.	What assumptions do you hold about each other and your relationship? What are you each willing and capable of contributing to the relationship? What limitations do you each bring to the relationship?
6. Discuss personal and learning styles.	Talk about your personal styles. You may have data from instruments such as the Learning Style Inventory, Myers-Briggs Type Indicator, Emotional-Social Intelligence, and DiSC	How might each other's styles affect the learning that goes on in the mentoring relationship?

Source: Zachary with Fischler (2009).

EXERCISE 4.7

Preparing: A Readiness Checklist

Review this list, and check all items that apply to you with respect to your prospective mentoring relationship:

❑ I have a sincere interest in helping this person succeed.

❑ There appears to be mutual interest and compatibility.

❑ Our assumptions about the process are congruent.

❑ I am clear about my role.

❑ I am the right person to help achieve these goals.

❑ I can enthusiastically engage in helping this person.

❑ I am willing to use my network of contacts to help this individual succeed.

❑ I can commit adequate time to mentoring this person.

❑ I have access to the kind of opportunities that can support this person's learning.

❑ I have the support that I need to be able to engage in this relationship in a meaningful way.

❑ I am committed to developing my own mentoring skills.

❑ I have a mentoring development plan in place.

perhaps delay your decision to mentor, this may not be a good learning fit for you, or you may decide that you are not ready for this relationship.

The preparation you do on your own behalf directly affects your own readiness to mentor and the quality of the mentoring relationship. Preparation of the relationship begins in earnest when the mentoring partners get to know one another and explore issues together. Getting to know a mentee does not mean knowing everything about that person. Rather, gaining a good sense about who the person is and what he or she brings to the relationship will help you make a strong connection and facilitate a more meaningful learning experience. Once the relationship preparation steps are complete, it is time to establish the agreements that build the foundation to support, guide, and nurture the relationship. The next chapter explores this important process.

CHAPTER 5

NEGOTIATING
ESTABLISHING AGREEMENTS

THE NEGOTIATING PHASE of a mentoring relationship builds consensus and commitment. You and your mentee are now concerned with the question, "How will we move our work forward?" The ground rules and agreements that grow out of this conversation will define your work together.

This free-flowing but focused discussion can take place over one or several sessions. Use this opportunity to consider together how each of you would like to see the mentoring process unfold; then add depth, specificity, and a framework to your broad mutual objectives. Your shared goal is to reach an understanding that you can express succinctly and concretely in written form: a mentoring partnership agreement and a mentoring work plan, both anchored in well-defined goals; measurements for success; delineation of mutual responsibility; and accountability assurances.

The negotiating phase is when you address time expectations and time constraints that might be problematic for the relationship. Discuss how much time each of you is willing and able to give the mentoring relationship. The words of this busy manager-mentor demonstrate the value of holding a frank discussion of how to deal with time-related problems: "We spent time discussing background and information and planning to make sure that we would be able to make this relationship work for us. We both have tight schedules, and wanted to use the windows of time we had."

Compounding the time issues idiosyncratic to mentoring are the time issues that relate to work, personal demands, and life in general. Mentoring is not something that can be done well on the fly or sandwiched between other appointments. Perhaps surprisingly, distance and virtual mentoring relationships (discussed in Chapter Three) take more time and energy, particularly in the early phases of the relationship. Dealing with time concerns now will help you and your mentee maintain perspective so that you can better focus on the learning goals and prevent later misunderstandings.

A good mentoring negotiation process will result in:

- Well-defined goals
- Success criteria and measurement
- Delineation of mutual responsibilities
- Accountability assurances
- A consensual mentoring agreement
- A work plan for achieving learning goals

A thoughtful negotiating conversation firmly sets boundaries. It also anticipates pitfalls, fosters the exploration of emerging possibilities and alternate pathways, and is flexible enough to accommodate renegotiations and closure. Table 5.1 lists each outcome and the big questions that need to be answered during your negotiating conversation.

DEVELOPING YOUR MENTORING PARTNERSHIP AGREEMENT

The mentoring partnership agreement is in essence a "learning contract."[1] It is a working agreement between you and your mentee that structures the mentoring engagement by setting boundaries and defining expectations so that learning can flourish.[2] Your partnership agreement will articulate specific components: objectives, evidence of accomplishment of objectives, learning resources and strategies, criteria, and the means for validating the learning.[3]

When you take the time to discuss the guidelines for your mentoring relationship and put them into writing, both partners know what to expect going forward. A mentoring agreement arrived at without sufficient conversation is a missed opportunity for connection. Take your time, and use this process to develop a relationship.

WELL-DEFINED GOALS

There is nothing quite as important as having well-defined learning goals in a mentoring relationship. A clear, compelling goal inspires action and is indispensable to the work of mentoring in enabling growth and evaluating the ongoing success of the relationship. That's why it's important for mentoring partners to pay attention to the goals they agree on and regularly revisit them throughout the mentoring relationship.

TABLE 5.1

Establishing Agreements

Outcomes	Questions Answered
Well-defined goals	What specific learning outcomes do we want to achieve?
Success criteria and measurement	What criteria will we use to evaluate the successful accomplishment of learning outcomes?
	What is the process for evaluating success?
Delineation of mutual responsibility	What are the roles and responsibilities of each mentoring partner?
Accountability assurances	How do we ensure that we will do what we say we are going to do?
Relationship ground rules	What norms and guidelines will we follow in the course of our relationship? What process should we have in place to deal with stumbling blocks as they occur? What can we do to ensure we engage in a positive closure conversation?
Confidentiality safeguards	What do we need to do to protect the confidentiality of this relationship?
Boundaries and hot buttons	What are the not-to-exceed limits of this relationship? What personal hot buttons might present barriers or boundaries?
Consensual mentoring agreement	What do we need to include in order to make this agreement work for us?
Work plan for achieving learning goals	What is our process for achieving learning goals?
	What action steps are necessary for achieving the goals?

The clearer a mentee's goals are, the stronger his or her motivation will be to accomplish them. High motivation combined with specific goals focuses energy, time, and attention. As you create your learning goals, strive to be specific. Specificity is an important part of clarity. As Heath and Heath so aptly point out, "*Some* is not a number: *soon* is not a time."[4]

Surprisingly, goals may not always be part of an inexperienced mentor's toolkit. Jackie works in a social service agency and was asked to mentor a colleague. But the relationship fell apart after a few weeks when both partners became confused and frustrated over what they were supposed to be doing. "I probably wasn't as clear as I should have been about insisting we have specific goals," she reflects. "We really didn't sit down and talk about goals. No one told me that goals were an important part of mentoring!"

Even when goals are discussed in the preparing phase, they are often broad and amorphous starter goals (that is, a glimmer of ideas about what they want to learn) that really aren't goals at all. When Rhoda first met with her mentor, she was all over the map when it came to trying to express her goals:

Nadia and Rhoda's Story

"Tell me something about what you think we need to accomplish," said Nadia to her mentee, Rhoda.

"Well," Rhoda said, "I've worked at trying to motivate change in my department—it's vital to customer service excellence, and I know that, and they know that, but it's hard to feel that I'm making any real progress. My team members don't really seem to want to change. They don't seem to care about implementing our new policies and practices. Meanwhile, I'm working until 9:00 P.M. half the time, just trying to cover my work and theirs." Her voice trailed off, and tears came to her eyes. "I can't really blame them, I guess."

"What do you mean?"

"Handling difficult coworkers has always been a challenge for me," said Rhoda. "During my whole career, I've had a hard time getting people on board with new ideas. I guess I feel intimidated when I'm confronted, and I don't speak up when I know I should."

Nadia, an experienced mentor, knew right away that Rhoda's starter goals begged for further specificity and exploration. They meandered and lacked coherence, and Nadia could see many different possible goal pathways. She immediately engaged Rhoda in a robust goal-setting conversation. That conversation eventually led to formulating well-defined goals, as we will see later in this chapter. But it took several sessions to get there. In the process, Rhoda began to feel understood by her mentor, who in turn was learning what Rhoda needed.

Goal setting is an evolutionary process that moves from general to specific. It usually begins with discussion of fairly broad starter goals like Rhoda's. As the mentor listens and asks clarifying questions that stimulate reflection, insight, self-awareness, and focus (see "What Mentors Do," Chapter One), the conversation moves to clarifying these goals.

When goals are left too broad, chances are that neither the mentor nor the mentee will be satisfied with the learning process, the learning outcome, or the mentoring relationship. Because the length of a mentoring relationship (particularly an informal relationship) is at least in part determined by the accomplishment of desired learning goals, establishing well-defined goals is critical.

Most mentees come to mentoring with a starter goal that becomes the starting point for the goal-setting process and robust conversation. Rhoda had multiple starter goals. Her mentor's challenge was to help her figure out which of these were the most "mentorable" and important. It took several conversations, some of which were especially challenging for Rhoda.

Even when your mentee comes to the mentoring relationship with well-defined goals, it is still important for you to talk about her learning goals to make sure you don't make assumptions about what your mentee is really saying. Test out your assumptions by asking clarifying questions—for example, "What do you mean when you say you want to get ahead?" or, "I am a little confused. Can you give me an example of what you mean by that?"[5] This focuses time and energy on what really matters. It is also a good opportunity for you to check to see if there is a good fit between your mentee's desired learning outcome and your own experience and expertise. For example, if your mentee's goals are to network with a wide range of people and your connections are limited, you may not be a good fit.

Whether your mentee's goals are vague or well defined, goal setting should be your first priority. This must be done before the work phase of the relationship begins.

You can help your mentee develop concrete, concise, and clear goals in a number of ways.

Write Down Your Goals

Encouraging mentees to put their goals in writing is a good way to encourage specificity. Once goals are defined in writing, they can be used as an accountability tool to benchmark progress.

Create SMART Goals

Well-defined goals are like the mission statement of the relationship: they maintain its focus and keep it on track. Smith identifies five criteria for creating SMART goals: goals must be specific (S), measurable (M), action oriented (A), realistic (R), and timely (T).[6] Other authors have used the same acronym and labeled the letters somewhat differently—attainable (A), relevant (R), and time oriented (T)—but the concept is a constant.

The conversation between mentoring partners that leads to formulating a SMART goal is critical to ensuring positive results. Formulating SMART goals is an iterative process that requires time and good conversation. It usually begins with a discussion of broad starter goals, like Rhoda's, and moves to more specific goals. Here are some pointers:

- A SMART goal should accelerate and enhance the mentee's professional or personal development.

- A SMART goal can be stated in one sentence or as multiple statements. Substance is more important than form. The goal should be clear, concise, specific, and comprehensive enough to capture the five requirements of a SMART goal: specific, measurable, action oriented, realistic, and timely.

- A SMART goal should represent a challenge or a stretch for the mentee. A not-so-SMART goal is just a quick fix or information acquisition.

- A SMART goal focuses on the mentee's future development. A not-so-SMART goal focuses on maintaining the status quo.

- A SMART goal is specific, concrete, and clear. A not-so-SMART goal is general and broad.

- A SMART goal seeks a quantitative or qualitative improvement that can be demonstrated or measured. A not-so-SMART goal is hard to measure.

- A SMART goal is directly linked to the question, "Why?"—for example, "Why is this goal important to your development and success?" A not-so-SMART goal focuses only on the how.

- A SMART goal requires more than one strategy in order to achieve it. A not-so-SMART goal is the strategy alone. Part of the work of the mentor and mentee is to choose the most effective strategies for accomplishing the goal.

Define Initial Goals

Best practice is to work on no more than two to three goals at a time.[7] As mentors and mentees work together, other goals will emerge. Sometimes, even though the goal is a SMART one, circumstances may change. You don't want to work on a goal that is no longer working for your mentee.

Rhoda and Nadia ultimately settled on two goals: Rhoda would (1) initiate and implement a highly visible customer service initiative by the end of the second quarter of the fiscal year and (2) develop a system for managing time and people better that would get her home by 6:00 P.M. at least three nights a week.

Use Exercise 5.1 to reflect on your mentee's goals and assess how well these goals are defined. You and your mentee may also choose to complete the worksheet together as a basis for formulating your mentoring partnership agreement.

Example 5.1 shows how one mentor completed this worksheet. This mentor quickly realized that the mentee's goals were not well defined and that there was more work to be done before moving forward.

EXAMPLE 5.1

Completed Mentor's Worksheet for Evaluating Mentee Goals

Stated goal: *To seek assistance in finding a job situation in the next twelve to eighteen months that will pay more, have opportunities for growth, and be closer to my family.*

Specific: What is the mentee trying to accomplish in this relationship? Are the mentee's goals specific, concrete, and clear?

Patsy states that she wants to find a situation where she can better balance work and family life. Her mother is becoming increasingly infirm, and she feels she needs to earn more money, take on more responsibility at work, and be closer to her mom.

Things I would like to know: What does "earn more" mean precisely? What kind of opportunities for growth is Patsy looking for? Is she talking about career advancement? Knowledge enhancement?

Measurable: Are the goals capable being of measured? In what ways can success be measured?

I will know more about this once I have a clearer idea of the answers to the previous question.

Success can be measured easily once she puts the dollar sign on. Distance is readily measured. In terms of career advancement, I need to know what Patsy's goals are and what her definition is for those terms.

Action oriented: Are the goals proactive? What results should you be able to see when the mentee's goals are accomplished? What concrete things will the mentee be able to do as a result of accomplishing the goals identified?

No problem here. I should be able to see a woman who is feeling more balanced, satisfied, and enthusiastic about her work and less guilty about the geographical distance. Eventually she will be ready to move. When she does, I hope she will learn how to think about career development from an ongoing growth perspective.

Realistic: Are goals achievable? Are there other resources that need to be available in order to achieve the goals?

I see my job as guiding her through the process. Initially our time will be spent in getting more clarity on this opportunity thing. She is going to have to find time to do a lot of the investigative work herself. I can set her on the right course, but she will have lots of decisions ahead of her. She is going to work on defining the career advancement piece. Patsy may need to go to a career placement agency, recruitment agency, or similar companies to get access to some of the resources she will need. She will need to get online and stay online, and do plenty of networking.

Timely: Is the time allocated for accomplishing learning goals reasonable? Will the mentee be able to achieve the learning goals within the time period of the mentoring relationship?

Yes, assuming she is willing to dedicate time and energy to the task. She has laid out a framework in broad brushstrokes. I will want to urge her to be more specific when we see how things develop.

EXERCISE 5.1

Mentor's Worksheet for Evaluating Mentee Goals

Answer the following questions to gauge the clarity of your mentee's goals.

Specific

What is the mentee trying to accomplish in this relationship?

Are the mentee's goals specific, concrete, and clear?

Measurable

Are the goals capable being of measured?

In what ways can success be measured?

Action Oriented

Are the goals proactive?

What results should you be able to see when the mentee's goals are accomplished?

What concrete things will the mentee be able to do as a result of accomplishing the goals identified?

Realistic

Are goals achievable?

Are there other resources that need to be available in order to achieve the goals?

Timely

Is the time allocated for accomplishing learning goals reasonable?

Will the mentee be able to achieve the learning goals within the duration of our mentoring relationship?

Source: Adapted from Smith (1995).

TABLE 5.2

Evaluating Mentee Learning Goals: Conversation Guide

1. Is your goal clearly anchored in the future? How do we know that?

2. Is the goal realistic? What evidence do we have to support that it is?

3. Will the goal be challenging? Is it a stretch goal rather than a maintenance goal? In what ways?

4. Will this goal help you grow personally or professionally? How?

5. Will this goal require you to make a personal investment of time, energy, and effort? Is this something you can manage?

6. Is this goal achievable within the time frame of our mentoring relationship? What makes you think that it is (or is not)?

7. Will you feel a sense of pride and satisfaction in accomplishing this goal? How will that manifest itself?

8. Is attaining the goal in your best professional or personal interest and in the best interest of your organization? In what ways?

You may also want to use the conversation guide in Table 5.2 to engage your mentees in analyzing the goals that you developed together.

SUCCESS CRITERIA AND MEASUREMENT

Once you've defined the goals, the next step is to figure out how you are going to know when the goal is achieved (your criteria or indicators of success) and how are you going to measure success (the scorecard). This means first identifying specific indicators that demonstrate that the learning outcomes have been accomplished—for example, "a 30 percent increase in personal sales by January 1" or "develop a strategy to free up 20 percent of my time so that I can spend more time meeting with each of my team members." Since these criteria flow directly from the goals, it's an easy conversation.

Once you've defined the criteria, the next step is to think about how success will be measured. What will be your process for evaluating success? Often the process is readily apparent. Sometimes, however, the answer to that question may need time to germinate. This is because learning often comes from application and integration, long after the mentoring relationship has concluded.

What are your benchmarks? In the first instance (personal sales increase of 30 percent by January 1), we see a date on the calendar and a specific numerical target. The second criterion suggests two indicators: the physical evidence of a plan and a log of meetings, before and after.

DELINEATION OF MUTUAL RESPONSIBILITIES

It's important to clarify your own responsibilities and those of your mentoring partners. If you are in a formal mentoring program, you can begin by reviewing the mentor's job description and discussing the implications for this particular relationship with your mentoring partner. In an informal mentoring situation, the outlines are less clear. Let's look at two examples.

Formal Mentoring Program: John

John's accounting firm has an internal mentoring program to orient its new employees to the firm's culture and business practices. The program also is intended to contribute to individual skill development and competency development.

John has learned that his responsibilities include providing support, guidance, and hands-on opportunities for the mentee to learn. It is also John's responsibility to provide specific feedback to his mentee and ongoing programmatic feedback to the mentoring program oversight committee.

As a mentor, John attends training sessions twice a year and meets regularly with his mentee—at least twice a week for the first month, once a week for the next five months, and twice monthly for one year after the date of hire.

John's mentee has a list of responsibilities as well. Among them are participating as an active learner in the relationship, attending a mentoring orientation program, agreeing to the protocols outlined in the mentoring program, honoring the confidentiality of their conversations, and providing feedback to John and to the program oversight committee.

John's mentoring relationship is very well defined: both partners have a good idea of what is expected from the outset. In addition, there are less visible partners involved in this mentoring relationship. The mentee's manager, the program supervisor, and the human resource specialist have responsibilities that affect the relationship directly or indirectly. Being aware of those responsibilities militates against the problem of role diffusion. Contrast this with Gerald and Linda's informal arrangement:

Informal Mentoring: Gerald and Linda

Linda is new to her job as managing editor for a monthly publication. Although she writes well and has good ideas, her job also involves scheduling and management capabilities. Linda has not previously been a managing editor, and she needs to learn quickly so that she can make a positive impression on subscribers, advertisers, her staff, and her boss. Her goal as a mentee is to learn everything she can about becoming a managing editor.

Linda chose to go outside the company for mentoring assistance, and Gerald, a retired managing editor, has agreed to be her mentor. Gerald asks Linda to schedule their meetings and keep them both on task. They agree that it is Linda's responsibility to bring the problems, situations, and questions. Gerald has accepted responsibility for getting her connected with some professional associations. They agree to accept mutual responsibility for evaluating Linda's progress every other month.

ACCOUNTABILITY ASSURANCES

Ensuring accountability means that both mentor and mentee must answer the question, "How are we going to hold ourselves and each other accountable in this mentoring relationship?" and then commit to those agreements. This process calls for clarity. As Patrick Lencioni writes in *The Five Temptations of a CEO*, "You can't hold people accountable for things that aren't clear."[8]

Accountability melds self-responsibility and rigor; people engaged in an informal mentoring relationship may view an imposed accountability procedure as cumbersome. Unless explicit accountability measures are built into the relationship, the temptation is to sidestep it altogether. Yet when the topic of accountability is squarely addressed, it becomes an ongoing part of the relationship and a shared frame of reference. Let's look at the elements of a reasonable framework for accountability.

Ground Rules for the Mentoring Relationship

We sometimes take partnering for granted and assume that it happens naturally. Too often, however, this erroneous assumption adversely affects the mentoring relationship:

Sara and Luis

When Luis received his mentor assignment he was very excited and couldn't wait to meet Sara, his mentor. After several weeks had gone by and he still hadn't heard from her, he sent her an e-mail expressing his excitement about getting started.

Sara immediately replied, inviting Luis to lunch the following week. Over the next several months, Sara and Luis met occasionally, when their schedules allowed. But even sticking to this loose schedule was difficult, and both had to cancel sessions. As a result, huge time gaps separated their meetings.

Luis was frustrated because Sara didn't remember what they had discussed at their prior meetings. He wondered if she wasn't really listening, was too preoccupied with her own issues, or simply didn't care enough about their relationship. Waiting until they could get something on the calendar wasn't working for him.

Sara, for her part, found too many of their meetings focused on solving Luis's day-to-day problems. Several times when she had suggested he read an article to discuss at their next session, he came unprepared. She was willing to commit her time working toward Luis's long-term development, but she didn't want to get involved in his crisis du jour.

Luis and Sara were paying the price for not setting ground rules for their relationship at the beginning. Each was stockpiling assumptions about the other, and the higher the pile grew, the more adversely it affected the relationship. Establishing ground rules at the beginning would have helped them keep lines of communication open and manage their expectations.

The most challenging part of the ground rule conversation is the discussion about what happens if and when agreements are not followed. What will happen if one partner dominates the relationship? What are the sanctions if one partner repeatedly does not honor appointment times? What happens when a partner compromises confidentiality? A formal mentoring situation may impose additional programmatic sanctions that will need to be taken into consideration.

It's a good bet that you and your mentee will eventually encounter a stumbling block in your relationship. Make these moments less of a problem by taking time together beforehand to anticipate what the stumbling blocks might be and discuss procedures to follow when and if they do occur.

You can begin by talking about internal and external factors that might affect the mentoring relationship—for example, the birth of a child, the imminent death of a loved one, pressures at work, a job change, or a sabbatical. Once these are identified, you can work together to determine how to deal with them when they do occur.

Some stumbling blocks are built into the mentoring relationship. If you don't consider them ahead of time, you may stumble right over them without seeing them and wonder what happened. Closure, for example, is a potential stumbling block for most relationships. You and your mentee must agree at the start how you will end the relationship when the time arrives. Successful closure depends on having well-defined goals, so that you both know when they have been met, as well as the opportunity for high-level conversation that engages both of you in processing the learning, the learning experience, and the accomplishments. It is important to predefine the terms of the closure to the extent that you can as part of your ground rules (see Table 5.1). If you are participating in a formal mentoring program, these will likely be defined in part for you.

Not all stumbling blocks are predictable. Mapping out what you will do when and if they occur keeps the lines of communication open.

Ground rules are the norms, acceptable behaviors, house rules, guidelines, or conventions that partners agree to abide by in a partnership. Rather than restrict the relationship, they serve to encourage and support accountability. Use the list of common mentoring ground rules in Table 5.3 to jump-start the discussion.

Checking in periodically to determine whether the ground rules are working effectively, particularly following the first several mentoring sessions, helps smooth the way and avoid difficulties later on. Whatever you and your mentoring partner ultimately decide about the ground rules of your mentoring partnership, you should consider establishing checkpoints to monitor the status of the relationship and agree in advance on what those will be.

TABLE 5.3
Common Mentoring Ground Rules

Issue	Ground Rules
Time	Our meetings begin and end on time. We will manage our time well and use agendas to keep us on track. We will put interruptions aside.
Feedback	We make regular feedback an expectation.
Role expectations	Each of us actively participates in the relationship. We will each keep a mentoring journal to reflect on our experiences. We will honor each other's expertise and experience.
Communication	Our communication is open, candid, and direct. We will respect our differences and learn from them.
Stumbling blocks	If we come up against a stumbling block, we will address it immediately and not wait until the next meeting.
Closure	In the event that our relationship doesn't work out, we will have a closure conversation and use it as a learning opportunity.

Confidentiality

Breach of confidentiality is a major stumbling block in mentoring relationships. Although mentors and mentees often confide in one another, people have differing assumptions about what confidentiality in a mentoring relationship actually means. Being a confidant does not always mean that the person you trust automatically safeguards confidentiality the way you would.

As a general rule, people shy away from talking about confidentiality; they just assume it. And because they assume it, those assumptions remain undisclosed and untested. They see confidentiality as a particularly difficult issue to discuss when there appears to be no immediate reason to do so. Mentees resist broaching the topic of confidentiality; they often fear reprisal or they worry that asking to talk about it will offend the mentor or make her think that her mentee doesn't trust her.

Assumptions about what confidentiality means in a mentoring relationship are myriad. Some view mentoring conversations as private, restricted, secret, undisclosed, and classified—forever. For others, confidentiality has a limited duration. It is important to talk candidly with mentees and agree on every aspect of confidentiality in a mentoring relationship.

If confidentiality is breached, address it immediately. Make sure that you put some agreements in place to safeguard confidentiality in the future so that such a situation doesn't happen again. Witness the following conversation between Carly and her mentor, Jorge:

Jorge and Carly

Jorge: Carly, the other day I got a call from Maryann Martin, head of billing. She was pretty upset with me. She said she had heard that I was bashing her department about delays in processing requisitions. I have to tell you, I was pretty embarrassed.

Carly: I can guess. What did you say to her? I know that you're upset with the way things get done down there.

Jorge: Well, that's actually a secondary issue for me. I told her that I did have issues with the speed at which things get turned around, but that I absolutely didn't bash her or her department in public. That's not my way. In fact, the only time I ever actually griped about it was with you in our last session.

Carly: We did talk about it. And I knew you had issues. Then I was having lunch with someone who was in billing and I thought I could help—so I mentioned it to her.

Jorge: Carly, when you and I talk about something during our mentoring time, I expect you to honor the confidence of our conversation. I don't share with others what you and I talk about, and I expect the same from you. I guess I just assumed that was understood as part of this relationship.

Carly: Well, I know things are confidential—but I thought it was when we were talking about personal issues or my boss or your boss. In this case, I thought I was helping you out with a problem. I really didn't mean to get you in trouble.

Jorge: It's not about being in trouble—I'm not in trouble. It's just not the way I handle problems. I was venting with you about the expediting of orders, but if I had a real issue with it, I would have called Maryann directly. That's how I do business—not behind anyone's back. It's what I would expect someone else to do with me if our department had problems.

Carly: I feel terrible! You're right; I just didn't think. I certainly didn't mean to break a confidence. I'm so sorry.

Jorge: I know, thanks. Let's just agree right now that what we talk about here stays here. If you think you want to share something that happens here with someone else, clear it with me first. And I'll do the same. Agreed?

Carly: Agreed!

Getting the conversation about confidentiality started is sometimes awkward, especially when it gets this far. Let's look at two possible approaches that can be used separately or in combination to frame the conversation: perception identification and assumption testing.

In *perception identification*, the mentor and mentee begin the discussion of confidentiality using a free association exercise. They individually write down words associated with the word *confidentiality*, thereby generating a list that can serve as a basis for discussion. Ultimately the partners will come to mutual agreement about what confidentiality will mean in their relationship.

Assumption testing can be accomplished using Exercise 5.2, which lists eight common assumptions about confidentiality. The mentor and mentee review the list independently to establish a framework for candidly discussing their own assumptions about confidentiality. This discussion encourages additional assumptions to emerge. Working from this prepared list focuses the conversation and makes discussion of this slippery concept much less threatening.

EXERCISE 5.2

Checklist for Assumption Testing About Confidentiality

Make copies of this checklist before you complete it: one for you to complete and the other for your mentee to complete. With your mentee, look at the assumptions and decide whether either of you holds assumptions that should be added. Write these in the bottom box.

Answer each question with a check in the "yes," "no," or "not sure" box. When you have completed the checklist, review and discuss each item with your mentee. Then come to consensus about what confidentiality will mean in the context of your agreement.

Which of the following assumptions about confidentiality do you hold?	Yes	No	Not Sure
What we discuss stays between us for as long as we are engaged in our mentoring relationship.			
We can freely disclose what we talk about in our conversations with other people.			
After our mentoring relationship has ended, it is okay to talk with others about what we discussed or how we related.			
If there is a demonstrated need for someone else to know, we can appropriately disclose our conversations and impressions with that person.			
What we say between us stays here unless you give me specific permission to talk about it with others.			
Some issues will be kept confidential, while others will not.			
It is okay to discuss with others how we relate to one another but not the content of our discussions.			
It is okay to talk about what we talk about as long as it is positive.			
Other assumptions I hold that should be added to this list:			

As a mentor, you may have more than one mentee. This means that you must have clarity about what confidentiality means to both partners within each mentoring relationship. This can be tricky. The object is to create consensus about what should remain confidential without getting so specific that conversation becomes restricted, unnatural, and guarded. The underlying goal of agreements about confidentiality is to allow both partners to feel comfortable. Whatever you decide, make sure that your understandings promote open and candid communication that is authentic and flows freely.

Boundary Setting

A frank discussion about the limits of the mentoring relationship enables mentoring partners to sustain their focus on learning, manage expectations, and ensure mutual accountability. Undefined boundaries frequently undermine the relationship by deflecting energy away from the learning focus of the relationship. When boundaries are too loose, they may be misinterpreted, and when they are too rigid, they constrain the relationship.

Boundaries vary according to circumstance, and individuals vary in their ideas about what is acceptable and what is boundary crossing. When you set boundaries with your mentee, you will need to maintain a delicate balance between meeting your own needs and your mentee's needs. An explicit discussion about boundaries—both before and during the mentoring process, if necessary—is crucial. Here's an example:

Dora and Theo

Dora saw great promise in her mentee, Theo, and wanted to see him succeed as quickly as possible. She encouraged him to stop by her office whenever he had a question. Before long, however, responding to Theo's interruptions was taking up a significant portion of Dora's work time, and she fell behind in meeting the demands of her own job. The push and pull she was experiencing was the result of not having set and communicated personal boundaries with her mentee.

The most overlooked aspect of boundary setting has to do with access, which directly relates to managing expectations. Consider the following questions. Figure out what you are willing to do and unwilling to do in the mentoring relationship, and communicate that to your mentee:

- Does being a mentor mean the mentee has unlimited access to you?

- Will your mentee need to go through a gatekeeper to get to you?

- Will your mentee need an appointment with you?
- What kind of access does the mentee have to you (e-mail, Facebook, and so forth)?
- What kind of access do you have to the mentee?
- What is the limit?

Mentees also need to set their own boundaries. Here's an example:

Maria

Maria was so anxious to please that she volunteered time to help her mentor and did whatever was asked of her to perfection. Soon her mentor came to expect that level of performance from her. The ante had been raised, and Maria felt there was nothing she could do, even though she was letting other things slide in her personal affairs. She had allowed her mentoring relationship to encroach on the rest of her life.

Boundary setting requires a frank and open discussion about the "not-to-go" places in the relationship. Getting issues out in the open at the beginning of a mentoring relationship keeps the relationship and the learning moving forward.

Mentors can guide the boundary-setting conversation by facilitating discussion of the following questions:

- What sorts of boundary issues might we face in our mentoring relationship?
- Are any topics, issues, or discussions out of bounds?
- What is our process if either of us crosses the boundaries we have agreed to?
- What strategies can we put in place that would help prevent us from crossing boundaries?

Despite the best of intentions, mentoring partners do cross boundaries and limits are tested or exceeded. This can harm the mentoring relationship and negatively affect the learning taking place within it. The best way to handle crossed boundaries is to have a strategy in place to deal with the situation when it occurs. Table 5.4 presents some potential strategies to consider when boundaries are crossed.

To ensure flexibility in the relationship and make sure it continues, mentoring partners might agree to the following procedures when boundaries are crossed:

TABLE 5.4

Responses to Crossed Boundaries

Boundary Crossed	What to Do
Mentee demands more time than the mentor is willing to give	Mentees should not "demand" anything. This is a partnership. If more time is needed, the mentoring partnership agreement should be revisited.
Mentee misses scheduled meetings and does not call to explain	Mentoring is a partnership built on respect for the individual. This includes respect for the mentor's time. You may need to renegotiate the mentoring agreement.
Mentee starts confiding serious personal problems	Avoid playing therapist. The mentor-mentee relationship focuses on fulfilling learning needs, not psychological needs.
Mentee calls too frequently for advice	Mentor and mentee need to talk about why this is happening and review the mentoring partnership agreement.

- Let your mentoring partner know that she has crossed a boundary.

- Refer to the ground rules outlined in your mentoring agreement.

- Describe the behaviors that clearly demonstrate how the boundary was crossed.

- Request that the behaviors stop.

- If your mentoring partner acknowledges she has crossed a boundary, let her know you appreciate the understanding.

- If boundaries go unacknowledged and continue to be crossed, ask your mentoring partner to stop crossing the line. If the behavior continues, insist that it be stopped. And, if that fails, walk away from the relationship.

Hot Buttons

We all have hot buttons—things that consistently irk us. When someone's behavior pushes our buttons, it triggers an emotional response in us. We become annoyed or even angry, make assumptions about that person's behavior and intentions, and react accordingly. Here's what happened to Jon and Matt:

Matt and Jon

Jon was driving his mentor, Matt, crazy. Every one of their mentoring sessions seemed to start with Jon's venting—usually a full-blown description of his current crisis or his shaky relationship with his girlfriend. Jon was obsessed with his crises and called Matt at home one night to get his advice. Jon even took a call from his girlfriend during their mentoring session at their last meeting. In addition to being rude and distracting, it added to Matt's increasing frustration. Having to hear about other people's dramas was one of Matt's hot buttons.

Matt was impatient and more than a little uncomfortable. Jon came to most mentoring meetings with his papers and notes in a jumble. He frequently bashed his peers and especially his immediate supervisor, a colleague whom Matt respected and liked very much. Matt couldn't keep it in much longer. He grew to dislike Jon, which he knew wasn't helping their relationship.

Jon just kept pushing Matt's buttons and crossing his boundaries. Matt had zero tolerance for disorganization and small talk. One day, he blew up. He told Jon to get out and not come back. He felt terrible afterward and wished he could have handled the whole situation better.

Much conflict and emotional upset can be avoided if mentoring partners spend some time telling each other what pushes their buttons. A mentee who knows that a mentor has zero tolerance for interruptions, for example, can avoid dropping in to chat. A mentor who knows that a particular mentee needs time to gather his thoughts won't push with unnecessary questions. Both partners should share the things that annoy them. If either mentor or mentee crosses that agreed-on boundary, the issue needs to be addressed.

Encouraging Accountability

Mutual accountability begins with a candid and open conversation about the softer issues in a mentoring relationship: ground rules, confidentiality, boundary setting, and hot buttons. Discussing these four topics builds trust and avoids stumbling blocks later. As you think about meeting the challenge of mutual accountability in a mentoring relationship, consider how best to encourage and support accountability.

Table 5.5 summarizes the discussion of accountability assurance.

A CONSENSUAL MENTORING AGREEMENT

Putting shared understandings about a partnership in writing facilitates the learning process. The form a mentoring agreement takes is not as important as its content. The agreement might consist of a series of bulleted notes that resulted from the negotiating conversation, a written

TABLE 5.5

Accountability Assurance: A Summary

Ground rules	Establish norms or guidelines to manage mutual expectations and minimize the likelihood of problems developing. *Examples:* how often you will meet, when and where; dealing with interruptions; how meeting cancellations will be handled; meeting notes and documentation; how to raise concerns and give feedback to each other; how and when to end the relationship.
Confidentiality	Mentoring partners should hold a frank conversation about confidentiality even though this is often an uncomfortable topic. Once breached, trust is hard to restore. Discuss what confidentiality means to you. *Examples:* what we talk about stays between us; we can share good things with others; the mentor won't speak to the mentee's supervisor without advanced notice or permission.
Boundary setting	Mentoring partners talk about the limits of the relationship and what they are willing to commit to do. *Examples:* the availability of the mentor, the degree of advocacy, discussion of personal issues and problems, evening and weekend contact.
Hot buttons	Mentoring partners talk about things that personally irk them. By sharing hot buttons early in the relationship, they avoid pushing them. *Examples:* being late, canceling at the last minute, coming unprepared, not following through with a commitment, multitasking during a mentoring meeting.

contract, a memo of understanding, or a learning contract. When you mutually choose a form or format, the agreement becomes meaningful to both partners. You and your mentoring partner may want to use Exercise 5.3 as a template, with the answers to the questions serving as the basis of a mentoring agreement. Example 5.2 illustrates a completed mentoring partnership agreement.

This template may suggest other forms and formats. Whatever the ultimate form the agreement takes, it must be clear to all mentoring partners and emerge from shared understandings. The very process of constructing the agreement together builds trust and creates shared accountability.

Use the following guidelines in developing your partnership agreement:

- Agree on the goals.

- Determine the criteria for success.

- Articulate the relationship ground rules.

- Spell out the "what-ifs"—for example: what to do in case time availability becomes an issue, or in case of incompatibility.

EXERCISE 5.3

Mentoring Partnership Agreement Template

We have agreed on the following goals and objectives as the focus of this mentoring relationship:

1.

2.

3.

   We have discussed the protocols by which we will work together, develop, and, in that same spirit of partnership, collaborate on the development of a work plan. In order to ensure that our relationship is a mutually rewarding and satisfying experience for both of us, we agree to:

1. Meet regularly. Our specific schedule of contact and meetings, including additional meetings, is as follows:

2. Look for multiple opportunities and experiences to enhance the mentee's learning. We have identified, and will commit to, the following specific opportunities and venues for learning:

3. Maintain confidentiality of our relationship. Confidentiality for us means:

4. Honor the ground rules we have developed for the relationship. Our ground rules are:

5. Provide regular feedback to each other and evaluate progress. We will accomplish this by:

   We agree to meet regularly until we accomplish our predefined goals or for a maximum of [specify time frame]. At the end of this period of time, we will review this agreement, evaluate our progress, and reach a learning conclusion. The relationship will then be considered complete. If we choose to continue our mentoring partnership, we may negotiate a basis for continuation, so long as we have stipulated mutually agreed on goals.

   In the event one of us believes it is no longer productive for us to continue or the learning situation is compromised, we may decide to seek outside intervention or conclude the relationship. In this event, we agree to use closure as a learning opportunity.

Mentor's signature and date _____

Mentee's signature and date _____

EXAMPLE 5.2

Sample Mentoring Partnership Agreement

We have agreed on the following goals and objectives as the focus of this mentoring relationship:

- *To develop a leadership career pathway to prepare the mentee to assume a significant high-profile leadership position within the community*

- *To assist the mentee in depth analysis of leadership strengths and weaknesses*

- *To create a leadership development plan for the mentee*

- *To introduce the mentee to best-practice leadership experiences*

We have discussed the protocols by which we will work together, develop, and, in that same spirit of partnership, collaborate on the development of a work plan. In order to ensure that our relationship is a mutually rewarding and satisfying experience for both of us, we agree to:

1. Meet regularly. Our specific schedule of contact and meetings, including additional meetings, is as follows:

   - *We will meet twice a month and be in contact by telephone or e-mail at least once a week.*

2. Look for multiple opportunities and experiences to enhance the mentee's learning. We have identified, and will commit to, the following specific opportunities and venues for learning:

   - *Mentee will attend board meetings as mentor's guest. We will meet prior to each meeting and debrief following each meeting.*

   - *Mentee will attend a nonprofit institute with mentor.*

   - *Mentee and mentor will attend community leadership forum meetings.*

3. Maintain the confidentiality of our relationship. Confidentiality for us means that what we discuss remains between us.

   - *Mentor and mentee will agree ahead of time if specific information is to be shared with anyone else.*

4. Honor the ground rules we have developed for the relationship. Our ground rules will be:

   - *We will meet after business hours.*

   - *Mentee will assume responsibility for confirming meetings.*

   - *Mentee will pay own expenses.*

   - *Mentee will maintain an ongoing journal of mentoring experience.*

   - *At the conclusion of each meeting, we will target topics for discussion at the next session.*

(Continued)

5. Provide regular feedback to each other and evaluate progress. We will accomplish this by:

- *Reviewing learning goals once a month, discussing progress, and checking in with each other regularly for the first month to make sure our individual needs are being met in the relationship, and periodically thereafter.*

- *We agree to meet regularly until we have accomplished our predefined goals or for a maximum of eighteen months. At the end of this period of time, we will review this agreement, evaluate our progress, and reach a learning conclusion. The relationship then will be considered complete. If we choose to continue our mentoring partnership, we may negotiate a basis for continuation, so long as we have stipulated the mutually agreed-on goals.*

- *In the event one of us believes it is no longer productive for us to continue or the learning situation is compromised, we may decide to seek outside intervention or conclude the relationship. In this event we agree to use closure as a learning opportunity.*

Mentor's signature and date _____

Mentee's signature and date _____

- Decide how to come to closure if the relationship terminates by mutual consent (or not).

- Establish how to process learnings and bring the relationship to a productive conclusion.

Whether the result is a formal or informal agreement, a contract, or a written set of goals and operating procedures depends entirely on the partners. It may be that a written document is more than you need; in this situation, a dedicated conversation, with something in writing—say, notes or a journal entry—is highly recommended. "In the final analysis," says Owen, "what is right will be what works for you. It must be appropriate to your style, circumstances and way of doing things."[9] Arriving at a mentoring partnership agreement together is as important as the agreement itself.

Once the agreement is negotiated, both mentor and mentee should be clear about the following issues:

- The goals of the relationship

- What the mentee needs from the relationship

- How often the mentor and mentee need to meet

- What kind of learning supports the mentee's needs

- How much time the mentee has committed to achieving the learning goals

- How the mentee prefers to learn

- How the mentoring partners plan to monitor their progress and keep the relationship on track

- How the mentor plans to encourage and support accountability

A WORK PLAN FOR ACHIEVING LEARNING GOALS

A mentoring agreement is just the beginning; you will need a work plan to get the relationship moving. Once you and your mentoring partner have come to agreement, the next step is to develop a strategy to achieve each of the goals and objectives. The following five steps will take you through this process:

1. *Identifying the learning goals and success criteria.* Remember that this will take time and good conversation. You will need to check out assumptions, make sure the goals really matter,[10] and that they meet all SMART goal criteria. A goal might be, "Strengthen and leverage my leadership capabilities by developing three new strategic partnerships in the next twelve months."

2. *Lay out the objectives.* These will describe how to achieve the goals. Objectives must be specific and measurable, with visible results. For example, an objective would be, "Determining which three new assignments I can take on that would give me the exposure and experience I need."

3. *Identify the learning tasks.* These are the specific steps that need to be *taken* to meet the objectives. For example, in order to "determine new assignments," what will the mentee have to do? Attend a conference? Take on a project? Shadow the mentor? Make presentations? It is helpful to know something about the mentee's learning style when designing this part of the work plan.

4. *List potential resources.* These can be both human and material. For example, will the mentee be interviewing specific individuals, reading briefing documents, or participating in a community of practice?

5. *Set a target date.* People are more likely to make progress if they have a deadline to work toward. Setting a date designates a specific time to evaluate progress, assess where the partners are, and determine how the relationship is going to proceed. You can always renegotiate this deadline if necessary.

Use the form in Exercise 5.4 to develop a partnership work plan.

EXERCISE 5.4

Mentoring Work Plan

Learning Goal(s)		Success Criteria	
Objectives	**Learning Tasks and Processes**	**Resources**	**Target Date**

MOVING ON

When learning permeates the negotiating phase, it is often quite liberating: you and your partner have created a map and a compass to guide you through the remaining phases. Your mutual commitment to fulfilling the mentee's goals enriches the partnership and gives you a better chance of holding each other accountable. Remember that having a formalized mentoring agreement does not preclude having an informal mentoring relationship. Articulating the commitment simply ensures accountability and increases the likelihood of success.

Once you come to agreement and articulate a work plan, it is time to begin implementing the plan. The items in Exercise 5.5 provide a checklist to see whether the work of the negotiating phase is complete.

If you could not check every item in the checklist in Exercise 5.5 as complete, you may need to seek clarification and talk further with your mentee until you feel comfortable enough to check all these items yes. If you were able to complete the checklist, you are ready to move on to the next phase: implementing the mentoring partnership agreement as you facilitate your mentee's learning in the enabling growth phase. We explore this phase in Chapters Six and Seven.

EXERCISE 5.5

Negotiating: A Readiness Checklist for Moving Forward

Complete the following checklist to determine if you have completed the negotiating phase:

Check yes, if complete

❑ Goals are well defined and SMART.

❑ Ground rules have been developed and agreed to.

❑ Expectations and responsibilities are clear.

❑ Protocols for dealing with stumbling blocks and obstacles are in place.

❑ Operating assumptions about confidentiality have been clarified.

❑ Boundaries and limits of the relationship have been established.

❑ Mutual responsibilities have been defined.

❑ A meeting schedule has been created.

❑ A plan for when and how to connect outside regularly scheduled meetings is set.

❑ Criteria for success have been laid out.

❑ A work plan has been designed that allows flexibility and midcourse correction.

❑ Agreements for how to bring the relationship to closure have been articulated.

CHAPTER 6

ENABLING GROWTH, PART ONE
SUPPORT, CHALLENGE, AND VISION

THE REAL WORK, the heart of the mentoring process, begins here, in the enabling growth phase. Now that your agreements are made and your work plan is in place, you and your mentee are ready to implement the plan you've developed together. It is time to create a climate that enables your mentee to learn and grow by keeping the learning fresh, your mentee engaged, and the relationship on track.

The work of this phase falls into three broad categories: managing the process, maintaining momentum, and encouraging movement. I've found connecting these efforts with Daloz's three core conditions for facilitating learning—support, challenge, and vision—to be an especially good model:

- *Manage the relationship* and support learning by creating a learning environment and building, maintaining, and strengthening the relationship.

- *Maintain momentum* by providing appropriate levels of challenge, monitoring the process, and evaluating progress.

- *Encourage movement* by providing a vision, fostering reflection, and encouraging personal benchmarking against desired learning outcomes.

Ruth and Lorraine's story provides an overview of this phase:

Ruth and Lorraine

Ruth, a graduate student and research fellow in her mid-fifties, and Lorraine, a stay-at-home mother with a master's degree, met by chance at a coffee bar. Before long, they struck up a conversation and discovered many shared interests and professional connections. As she listened to Ruth talk about her work, Lorraine was suddenly transported into a world she had not realized she missed. Ruth sensed Lorraine's interest and invited her to attend a university seminar she was conducting. Just two days later, Lorraine was back in a graduate school classroom—fascinated, mesmerized, and totally immersed.

A month later, Ruth asked Lorraine to participate as a team member in a research project. Lorraine was not sure she was ready for the challenge, but with Ruth's support, Lorraine exceeded even her own expectations.

Ruth facilitated Lorraine's learning by managing the learning process and providing appropriate support, maintaining the momentum as Lorraine faced challenges, and encouraging movement, which continued to enable her growth and learning. Ruth's adeptness at providing continuous feedback effectively accelerated the learning curve.

Ruth patiently listened as Lorraine shared stories about her new experiences and daily challenges, and offered regular feedback (managing the process). She coached Lorraine on how to use a variety of research tools and methodologies and provided ongoing support (maintaining momentum). When Lorraine had moments of doubt about how to apply her new knowledge, Ruth suggested that she experiment (encouraging movement). After several years, Lorraine became project team leader.

Enabling growth—ensuring support, challenge, and vision—is where you will be spending most of your mentoring time. This means that you must be adept at giving (and receiving) feedback and overcoming (or preventing) obstacles. In order to give all of these areas their due, we consider the first three topics in this chapter and feedback and obstacles in the next. There is much to take in during this exciting phase. I encourage you to take your time, and use Table 6.1 as reference for the ongoing work of both chapters.

MANAGING THE PROCESS: SUPPORT

Managing the mentoring process effectively means consistently supporting your mentees in their efforts: providing a safety net, holding a place for connection, and offering a wellspring of trust.[1] Jeff, who made a successful transition during the midpoint of his career, describes his mentor's support

TABLE 6.1

Facilitating Growth and Development

Conditions That Facilitate Growth and Development[a]	Enabling Process[b]	Mentor's Key Tasks
Support	Managing the process Listening Providing structure Expressing positive expectations Serving as advocate Sharing yourself Making it special	Creating a learning environment Building, maintaining, and strengthening the relationship
Challenge	Maintaining momentum Setting tasks Engaging in discussion Setting up dichotomies Constructing hypotheses Setting high standards	Monitoring the process Evaluating progress
Vision	Encouraging movement Modeling Keeping tradition Offering a map Suggesting new language Providing a mirror	Fostering reflection Assessing learning outcomes

[a]For a full description of the facilitative behaviors, see Chapter Eight in Daloz (1999).

[b]The functions listed here are discussed extensively in Daloz (1999) and are not directly explained in this chapter. They are listed here to illustrate processes a mentor might use to enable mentee learning.

in this way: "Since the start of our mentor-mentee relationship, Tom has always made time to discuss my career aspirations and has been very supportive during my times of uncertainty. His guidance has had a significant influence over my approach to learn the business outside of the financial field."

Support can take many forms, especially when deep or uncomfortable emotions surface. One mentee commented, "The ugliest parts of me were exposed, accepted and relabeled with positive words. At times I ran from [my mentor], yet I felt drawn to her because she helped me see that I neither had to be perfect or positive . . . only real."[2]

Most mentees will tell you that the most important way that a mentor can support them is to listen. When you are able to genuinely listen to what your mentee is saying, and prove it by reflecting back that understanding, your mentee will feel heard and cared for.

Nina's conversation with her mentee, Marc, demonstrates what can happen when a mentor intends to listen, fully concentrates, checks for understanding, and pays attention to the underlying meaning of what is being said:

Nina and Marc

Nina: Marc, catch me up. What's been going on for you in the last month?

Marc: Nothing really. Just the same old stuff.

Nina: Sounds like you might be bored.

Marc: Yes, as a matter of fact. I always seem to be bogged down in all the operations stuff, and it's really not what I'd rather be doing.

Nina: What would you rather be doing?

Marc: Well, I'm an ideas type of person. I get really excited when I am in a creativity mode. I think the company needs new ideas, and that could be a really good use of my talent.

Nina: What is it about being creative that energizes you so much?

Marc: I'll give you an example. I was at a meeting last week, and everyone there was stuck for ideas. I stepped up and put an idea out there that everybody just grabbed right onto. Before I knew it, we had a time line, a strategy, and implementation teams. I was so excited, and it felt great.

Nina: So I just want to make sure that I understand. What was it that excited you most: generating the idea, the fact that people ran with it, or that it was being done so quickly?

Marc: You know, first of all, I really felt valued—like I was a contributor, like I was making a difference. I was finally getting credit for something around here. I felt respected, and it gave me confidence. I also felt a little sad in the sense that other people had taken my idea, tweaked it, and came out with something different from what I had originally thought.

Nina: So I'm hearing several things. One, you felt a sense of loss that the idea was no longer yours. Two is something very exciting—your idea generated excitement among others and they took it to the next level. Three, you did something nobody else could do. You broke the logjam!

Marc: I never thought about it that way. I guess I created value for myself in creating value for everyone else. Maybe I need to speak up more and look for other opportunities to light a spark. Maybe I can make that carry over into operations. What do you think?

Nina: I think you're on to something. I sense more energy and excitement in you than I've seen in a long time.

Marc: Awesome!

This is a great example of how listening can work to gain new understandings. Nina and Marc were both fully engaged in the conversation. Nina heard not only what Marc was saying, but what he was not saying. She asked good, thoughtful, and well-timed questions that showed that she was listening and thinking about the meaning and emotions that lay beneath what Marc was saying. She consistently checked for understanding and made sure her assumptions were valid. Marc was supported by her reflections, which gave him the space to make a leap of understanding about himself.

Referring back to your own mentoring experiences (perhaps the ones you identified in Exercise 1.2) can help you deepen your understanding about the critical role a mentor plays in providing support. Take the opportunity to do this in Exercise 6.1.

The key tasks in providing support are creating a learning environment, and building, maintaining and strengthening the relationship. As Daloz notes, mentees are most likely to feel support when mentors listen, provide structure, express positive expectations, serve as advocates, share themselves, and make the relationship special.[3]

Creating a Learning Environment

One of the best ways to keep the mentoring relationship fresh is to take advantage of all the learning opportunities it offers, even expanding them beyond your established agreement. In this way, you will create a dynamic environment that encourages and enables learning.

By now, you and your mentee have gotten to know each other better; you should also have a much clearer understanding about his or her context and learning needs. If you think your mentee could benefit by exposure to additional knowledge, skills, and experience, reach out to colleagues and professional networks to find out what kinds of learning opportunities they would recommend. You will need to take learning style, context, individuality, goals, and timing into account as you and your mentee brainstorm possibilities. Don't be surprised if your mentee comes up with ideas you've never considered as you work through Exercise 6.2 together.

EXERCISE 6.1

Facilitating Learning Through Support: Self-Reflection

Take a moment to reflect on your previous mentoring relationships, particularly when you were the mentee. Then ask yourself the following questions and write down the answers. Be sure to cite specific examples.

What support did you need?

Were there times in your career when you needed more support? Less support?

What did your mentor do or say to support you as a learner?

What more would you have wished that your mentor had done to support you?

Which of the support functions in Table 6.1 is likely to be the most difficult for you?

What do you need to do to increase your skill at providing support?

EXERCISE 6.2

Identifying Learning Opportunities

Use this worksheet in one of the following ways:

- Jot down ideas about possible learning opportunities, and then discuss them with your mentee.

- Brainstorm a list of learning opportunities together.

- Complete this worksheet yourself and ask your mentee to do the same (seeking input from others, such as experts and colleagues). Bring your completed worksheets to the next mentoring session, compare your results, and come to consensus.

Learning Opportunities	Within the Organization	Outside the Organization
Gain exposure to new learning		
Reinforce learning		
Accelerate learning		

The learning that surrounds a particular occasion can be as important as what happens during the event. For example, when Marc mentioned to Nina that he was going to attend an off-site team meeting with his manager's manager, Nina went beyond simply wishing him well:

Nina and Marc

"That's a great opportunity," said Nina. "Let's talk about what you might see and experience so that you don't miss anything. I want you to take full advantage of this opportunity."

"I was hoping you'd say that," replied Marc. "I have no idea what goes on at these things."

Marc and Nina discussed the purpose of the meeting, who would be attending from their organization and from other organizations, the key players, and specific things he should look for during the meeting and at the trade show. Nina also encouraged Marc to keep a journal of what he observed, including his questions and his insights.

Marc found that the discipline of noting his observations helped him pay attention. He made another note to thank Nina for preparing him—he was taking in much more information than he would have if he had gone to the meeting cold.

Several days later, Nina met with Marc to talk about what he had seen and learned, and especially how this new input might relate to his learning goals. Out of their discussion they generated a new list of learning opportunities, shown here in Example 6.1.

Building, Maintaining, and Strengthening the Relationship

Building, maintaining, and strengthening the relationship requires respect, trust, and effective communication. Let's look more closely at each of these important elements.

Respect helps individuals engage effectively and learn from one another. Taking respect for granted eventually hampers the partners' ability to build rapport and earn each other's trust.

Sometimes we equate respect with trust, but you can respect another person even if you don't fully trust him or her. Respect without trust, however, is not enough to build a strong mentoring relationship, and respect lost because trust has also been lost will undermine the relationship.

EXAMPLE 6.1

Marc and Nina's List of Possible Learning Opportunities

Learning Opportunities	Within the Organization	Outside the Organization
Gain exposure to new learning	*Journal club* *Annual operations meeting*	*Conferences* *Trade shows* *Site visits to other facilities*
Reinforce learning	*Project committee* *Prepare a presentation together* *Attend office meetings* *Check-in conversations*	*Present at a conference*
Accelerate learning	*Stretch assignments* *Shadowing* *Making presentations to managers*	*Attend regional operations* *Advance training sessions*

Even if you and your mentee do not immediately respect each other, it is important to act as if you do. When you begin by treating one another with respect, even if it is not authentic, real respect has a chance to grow.

Trust can grow, but it cannot be maintained automatically, and once it is lost, it is not easily regained. Attitude and intention, as Wells points out, are both important to creating it.[4]

Mentoring partners have to work at holding on to the bond of trust between them. The authenticity of the relationship depends on it, and so does effective communication. The potential for mistrust and miscommunication in a mentoring relationship should not be taken lightly. That is precisely why establishing and then honoring ground rules for communication is so important.

Differences in learning and communication styles can often lead to misunderstandings and conflict. It is important to be aware of your own and your mentee's communication style, and shape your communication and responses accordingly. Chad and his mentee, Nate, serve as an example:

Chad and Nate

Chad is personable, friendly, energetic, and enthusiastic. He loves to be with people. His mentee, Nate, appears reserved and shy. Where Chad uses broad brushstrokes to paint the big picture, Nate is practical, orderly, and realistic. Chad is a quick decision maker; Nate takes time to process information. In style, the two could not be diametrically more opposed.

Their first meeting was awkward: Nate felt that Chad was racing ahead and not making sense, and Chad was frustrated that Nate seemed to chew over every little thing and say nothing. But that didn't last long, mostly because Chad had had some experience mentoring different sorts of people. He suggested that they begin over by talking about their opposite styles. Chad knew that he would need to be more specific in his interactions with Nate. Nate, for his part, realized that he would need to be more open and outgoing in order to get his needs met. Together they set up some ground rules that allowed them to talk openly without misconstruing style for conflict.

If you consciously behave in ways that build trust, your mentees will feel comfortable acting in ways that are consistent with the level of trust you demonstrate and desire. Review this list to identify ways in which you demonstrate each of these trust-building behaviors:

- Listen in ways that show you respect your mentee and that you value his or her ideas.
- Practice openness when sharing information.
- Speak authentically about your feelings.
- Explain what you understand and admit what you do not understand.
- Explain why you shift the level of your support according to the situation.
- Follow through. Do what you say you will do.
- Continuously work at safeguarding confidentiality.
- Be open to feedback.
- Be truthful.
- Be consistent.
- Be supportive publicly and privately.

MAINTAINING MOMENTUM: CHALLENGE

Moving mentees from their current reality to their desired future requires momentum. You can maintain momentum by challenging mentees to keep moving forward. Daloz suggests setting tasks, engaging in discussion, setting up dichotomies, constructing hypotheses, and establishing high standards.[5] Brookfield suggests challenging your mentees by asking questions that offer other ways they might interpret their experience, as illustrated by the following example:[6]

Frank and Zoey

"I just got promoted from customer service representative to supervisor, which is awesome," said Gen Y Zoey. "But the idea of having people report to me makes me really nervous." Her mentor, Gen X Frank, could see that she would need his support. After their first meeting, Zoey called Frank several times a day to ask if she was doing the right thing and to get his advice about how to handle almost every problem that came up. Frank's first thought was, *Uh-oh, this could be high maintenance.* The degree of affirmation she needed seemed extreme.

Frank didn't want to create a dependent relationship. He had his own work, and as Zoey's mentor, his goal was to help her learn to do her work. But he also realized that for Zoey to get launched successfully, he would need to make himself available to her.

Frank made a point of being encouraging and supportive, but rather than tell her what to do, he first asked how she thought she might approach the problem. He then gently offered Zoey alternative points of view so that she wouldn't feel intimidated. He facilitated discussions with her on the pros and cons of different approaches so she could begin to think through things on her own. He frequently engaged in "what if" conversations to get her thinking about the possible ramifications of a particular course of action.

To help her change her habit of thinking that she had to react immediately to each challenge, they developed a task list that encouraged her to plan ahead for problems. Frank encouraged Zoey to seek feedback from her manager, peer group, and direct reports to check that she was on the right path. They set three stretch goals to help Zoey develop in her role and set times to evaluate her progress. But Frank didn't stop with advice and verbal support; he went a step further and offered himself as a model of the behavior they were trying to achieve.

One of Zoey's goals was to lead more effective, productive staff meetings, so Frank invited her to sit in on several of his own meetings to get a sense of how productive meetings were run. He was pleased to see that she was not only paying attention but taking notes. "Thanks," she said later. "I learned a lot." Then he went a step further. "I know this might take you out of your comfort zone," he said with a smile, "but I think I could get a good sense of your style if you allowed me to observe one of your team meetings."

"You're right," said Zoey, "that does make me nervous. But I think it might speed things up, so let's do it."

The experience of watching her lead a meeting and then sitting together and assessing the outcome proved to be positive for them both. Frank was surprised that she exhibited so much presence and confidence in front of her team; it was not at all what he'd expected from her comments about her insecurities.

In their next meeting, Frank began his feedback by telling her how impressed he was with her ability and offered specific observations to help build her confidence. When he addressed areas for improvement, he focused on issues and took care not to make his comments personal. Zoey listened attentively and stayed engaged. Frank was relieved to see that the fear and defensiveness she had shown in the past was gone. He attributed that to the support he provided as he challenged her thinking. Although his mentoring relationship had once felt as if it was going to require high maintenance, he saw that as Zoey grew more confident, she would become less dependent on him.

Frank's work with Zoey shows two major tasks in action: monitoring the mentoring process and evaluating progress. Both are key components of challenging mentees and keeping the momentum going.

Monitoring the Mentoring Process

A vibrant mentoring relationship requires regular care and attention. Monitoring your partnership regularly—in person, on the phone, or online—gives you the opportunity to make midcourse corrections, address mentoring stumbling blocks before they become obstacles, and keep your communication on track. Most important, touching base regularly with your mentee about how the process is going maintains the momentum of the relationship, contributes value to the learning of each mentoring partner, and strengthens the relationship.

Monitoring should be done on a regular basis, whether it is once a month or every quarter. Use Exercise 6.3 to guide conversation about meetings, relationships, and learning. This worksheet is particularly helpful when each partner completes it independently and then both partners discuss their results.

EXERCISE 6.3

Mentoring Partnership Accountability Discussion Guide

You can use this worksheet in three ways: (1) each mentoring partner completes this form independently, and then partners discuss individual responses together; (2) mentoring partners discuss each item and complete the form together; or (3) each time you complete a mentoring partnership reflection, save it and use it as a starting point for conversation.

Meetings

1. When and under what circumstances did we get together?

2. Generally when we got together, what did we talk about? (List subjects or topics.)

3. What are we working on right now?

4. What is our progress to date in achieving our goals and objectives?

Relationship

1. What is going particularly well in our mentoring relationship right now?

2. What has been our greatest challenge in our mentoring relationship thus far?

3. What do we need to work on to improve our mentoring relationship?

4. What assistance could we use?

Learning

1. What are we learning about ourselves? Each other? The relationship?

2. What has the mentee learned?

3. What are some of the conditions that promote that learning?

4. What are some personal insights? Hunches? Things to watch for?

EXERCISE 6.4

Monitoring the Quality of the Mentoring Interaction

Answer the following questions to monitor the quality of the mentoring interaction and prepare for a mentoring session. You may want to encourage your mentee to fill out a version of this as well and then use it as a basis for discussion. When entries are collated, the tool can become a useful developmental log for evaluating progress with respect to interaction in the relationship.

1. What are some words or phrases I might use to describe our current interaction?

2. Describe our interaction more fully.

3. Where is my mentee on the continuum from dependent to interdependent learner?

   |———————————————|———————————————|
   Dependent   **Independent**   **Interdependent**

4. To what extent are our interactions authentic and genuine?

5. Are the frequency and duration of interactions adequate? If not, what needs to be done to correct the situation?

6. How would my mentee characterize our relationship?

7. Does my interaction reflect interest and caring?

8. Am I balancing talking and listening?

9. Am I being too forceful or not forceful enough?

10. What action strategies do I need to take to improve the quality of the mentoring interaction?

Monitoring Mentoring Interaction

Monitoring the quality of the mentoring interaction (Exercise 6.4) affords an opportunity to reflect and prepare for mentoring conversations.

Although it may seem that taking the time to actively reflect on the quality of your mentoring relationship would add work to your already busy schedule, it can actually save time and strengthen the partnership. Look at Rachel's experience:

Rachel and Annie

Rachel had been meeting with her mentee, Annie, for several years, and both would have assessed the relationship as "fine." But as she completed Exercise 6.4, Rachel suddenly saw that the quality of interaction in her mentoring relationship was no longer satisfactory—something she had known on a visceral level but hadn't wanted to think about. She realized that she needed to pump new life into the relationship or end it.

Rachel began to think about what she had contributed to the current situation and decided that her desire to meet at 6:00 A.M. every Tuesday was not productive. Neither was the small talk that diverted their conversation from the real purpose of the relationship. When she apologized to Annie for letting the relationship coast for so long, Annie confessed that she had been having similar thoughts. Both wanted to continue the relationship. In fact, this conversation made it clear that over the past three years, both had accomplished more than they had originally believed possible. Now they were able to talk about what each could do to strengthen the relationship in the future and agreed to monitor it more regularly.

Regular Check-In

Even if the relationship seems to be going well, checking on its health (Exercise 6.5) ensures that the needs of the mentoring partners are being met.

Use any of the following conversation starters to provide a framework for beginning discussion about the learning process:

- Check in at the beginning of your meeting. Regularly ask, "How is it going?" Probe your mentee's response, and take it to a deeper level.

- Share your observations about how things are going and what concerns you have about the learning process—for example, "I've noticed

EXERCISE 6.5

Mentoring Partnership Check-In

Complete this check-in periodically throughout your relationship to make sure your relationship stays on track and the trust level remains high. Discuss your results, and decide what you can do to improve your relationship.

Today's Date:	Never	Sometimes	Most of the Time	Always
We meet regularly.				
We do a good job of communicating schedule changes that may affect mentoring meetings.				
We notify one another if we cannot follow up or honor our commitments to each other.				
We eliminate outside influences and distractions when we meet.				
We check out our assumptions.				
Our communication is clear, and misunderstandings are infrequent.				
We check in with each other to make sure that we stay on track with the learning goals.				
We provide feedback regularly and make sure it is two-way.				
Our meetings are relevant, focused, and meaningful.				
We respectfully acknowledge and address conflict when it occurs.				
We are conscientious about safeguarding confidentiality.				

that our discussions are very general and theoretical. Are you finding them helpful?"

- Take a step back before you go forward—for example, "Let's take a look at how we are doing. What is particularly helpful to you in your learning? What has been least helpful? What do you think is going well? What do we need to improve? What kind of additional assistance do you need?"

Evaluating Progress

Your mentee's goals—including the objectives outlined on the mentoring work plan form (Exercise 5.4) and the goal statement articulated in your mentoring partnership agreement—are benchmarks for measuring the progress and achievement of learning goals. Be sure to refer to them frequently. Evaluating progress regularly helps maintain momentum, keeps learning goals at the forefront of the relationship, and holds partners accountable for achieving the goals.

Use your mentoring planning form as the yardstick for measuring progress and to alert you to when it is time to consider bringing the relationship to closure. Make copies, and refer to it at each mentoring session. If your mentee is not making good progress toward achieving goals, consider whether these goals are still relevant. You may need to revisit the goals and reformulate them.

ENCOURAGING MOVEMENT: VISION

"Good mentors," says Sharon Daloz Parks, "help to anchor the promise of the future."[7] They inspire, motivate, inform, and even empower a mentee to step boldly into the future. By inviting conversation that releases imagination, creativity, and energy, mentors can keep their mentees moving steadily to higher ground to give them a vision of their future. By sharing your unique story, modeling behavior, and holding up a mirror, you create possibility.

Mentors encourage movement and momentum during (and after completion of) the relationship by facilitating continuous reflection and assessing learning outcomes. Karen's mentor, Vicki, was a successful account manager. Karen was eager to learn everything about how Vicki got started, what she had to learn, what the career path ahead looked like, and what it took for a woman to succeed in a male-dominated industry. Their story has a lot to say about encouraging momentum:

Vicki and Karen

Vicki told Karen about her own journey, her struggles, and her successes. She reflected on trends in the industry and where she saw it headed in the next five to ten years. Karen was intrigued and had lots of questions. Instead of answering every question herself, Vicki suggested that Karen talk with other female account managers about their careers. Together Karen and Vicki narrowed down the list of questions so that they focused specifically on skills, competencies, talents, and behaviors that led to career success. Vicki then made a few calls, and Karen set up interview appointments.

At their next meeting, Karen reported on her findings. With this information in hand, Vicki was able to deepen the conversation. Now they could begin talking in earnest about how to create a path for Karen's future development and growth.

Vicki had just completed reading *The Art of Possibility*, a book in which the authors described an interesting exercise called "Getting an A," which she thought might be helpful in the situation.[8] She asked Karen to write her a letter entitled, "I got my A as a successful account manager because . . ." She gave her the following guidelines: "Write in the past tense as if it has already happened; don't use phrases like 'I hope,' 'I intend,' or 'I will.'"

Karen found that doing the exercise pushed her thinking forward and created momentum. Now she was able to conceptualize some concrete ideas about what her future might look like.

Fostering Reflection

As we have seen throughout this book, reflection—on both the past and the future—is instrumental in the facilitation process. Help your mentees to step back and use hindsight to make sense of their experience. Ask questions that bring past actions into consciousness and promote insights about change. You can also inspire a vision of possibility by encouraging foresight about what might be.[9] The right questions asked at the right time can stimulate mentees to reflect on their experiences and frame their interpretations into suitable actions.[10] In this way, reflection on experience becomes the text for learning.

Mentees are often better able to focus and accomplish more when they have engaged in reflection before coming to a mentoring session. This preparation saves an incredible amount of time, and promotes richer, more focused discussion and discovery learning. You can help the process along by reflecting about where you are in the mentoring relationship and what the next steps might be.

For example, you might call your mentee and ask him to think about feedback he received on a previous performance review and reflect on what reinforced what you and he already knew, what was a surprise, and what he is now doing differently. Your mentee arrives at the mentoring session primed for conversation, having already reflected on his experience. This allows you, as his mentor, to focus mentoring time more on building for the future than reflecting on the past.

Assessing Learning Outcomes

Assessing learning outcomes is a natural outgrowth of ongoing monitoring and evaluation. It is appropriate when a mentee completes a particular learning goal or cluster of objectives and is especially important in deciding when the time has come to end a mentoring relationship. Assessing outcomes prepares the mentee for the transition out of the relationship and helps to create the vision for the future that follows closure of the relationship. It also places accountability squarely back on the mentee's shoulders.

Assessing learning outcomes is connected to the mentee's specific SMART learning goals. It is not a matter of checking items off a list, but of getting accurate feedback that forces continuous improvement and ongoing learning.

Because this is more than a check-in conversation, feel free to invite feedback from a variety of sources. Your mentee may choose to seek objective feedback from coworkers, colleagues, family, and friends, in addition to subjective evaluation with the mentoring partner.

MANAGING MENTORING TIME

Time is a major challenge for mentoring relationships in general and specifically during this phase, the longest of the mentoring relationship. Effectively managing and monitoring your time keeps the relationship on track. You can begin to manage your time effectively by following these simple guidelines:

- Schedule mentoring sessions wisely. Avoid the pitfalls of mentoring on the run, such as sandwiching mentoring between meetings, multitasking, and giving advice without taking time to explain the context.[11]

- Encourage your mentee to use the available time constructively.

- Maximize time spent together by coming to the meeting prepared.

- Start each session with a progress review or update to help you regain focus. Consider e-mail as a way to jump-start the discussion.

It takes time to sustain a learning relationship and to keep it fresh and vibrant. Time becomes an issue when the partners cannot find enough of it or do not use the time they do have wisely. Here are some pointers:

- *Finding time.* You may be procrastinating because you begrudge the time spent on the mentoring relationship. Step back and ask yourself why it is you cannot get started or continually postpone. Perhaps you are assuming too much—or too little. You may be seeing your mentoring obligation as bigger than it is.

- *Calling time-out.* The importance of the pause as a transforming moment should not be overlooked.[12] If you need to give the relationship space, call a time-out from mentoring sessions. Reflection and contemplation are necessary for real learning. You may find that you need to build in time to let new learnings sink in, gel, and come together or to let new ideas emerge.

- *Using time consciously.* Finding the time is one thing; using it well is another. Use Exercise 6.6 to reflect on how you use your mentoring time and changes you might make.

Martin and Irene

Irene's goal is to become an entrepreneur, and she is delighted that Martin, who has a reputation as the entrepreneur's entrepreneur, has agreed to mentor her. But after three months of meeting together, something in their relationship seemed to be amiss.

Martin completed the mentoring time pie in Exercise 6.6 and discovered two things that surprised him: he and Irene have not spent enough time on exploring topics that would help her meet her goals, and he has not really let Irene participate actively in the relationship. He realized that he has been grandstanding and she has been the passive listener.

At their next meeting, Martin shared his circle with Irene and asked for her thoughts. As they discussed ways to strengthen their relationship, Martin had several new ideas about how he could facilitate Irene's learning more effectively—and how he might make better use of his mentoring time in general.

EXERCISE 6.6

Reflection: How You Use Your Mentoring Time

Use the circle here to represent the totality of your mentoring relationship time. Divide it into slices based on how much time you spend on various activities and topics.

Check out your perceptions with your mentee's perceptions, and then answer these questions:

1. What does this circle say about the quantity and quality of time you spend in your mentoring relationship?

2. What would you like to do less of?

3. What would you like to do more of?

4. Look at the circle again from the perspective of the percentage of time you spend talking and the amount of time your mentee is speaking. What do you learn from that analysis?

5. Identify three ways you can improve the quality of the time you spend on this mentoring relationship.

The dynamics of time involved in a mentoring relationship are not always straightforward. The following strategies promote successful time management in a mentoring relationship:

1. *Schedule time in advance.* Always try to get a date on the calendar. If you need to postpone a mentoring session, do it, but make sure you schedule your next one when you do. Used wisely, a calendar reminder is a point of contact for communication. Just a few minutes spent in talking about how you will spend your mentoring time can make all the difference in the world. E-mail ahead of time or at the end of a meeting.

2. *Monitor your time.* Be aware of the amount of time you are spending on mentoring (also in proportion to your other tasks). Acknowledge when you are pressed for time, but do not put mentoring on the back burner.

3. *Spend quality time.* Make the most of your time together. How you spend your time in the relationship is far more important than the quantity of time you spend together. Be fully present, and plan to use the time well.

4. *Pay attention to personal time zones.* One person's morning is another person's night, both figuratively and literally. Knowing whether your mentee is a night person or a day person is important when planning when and how to meet.

5. *Take care of yourself.* Make time to work on your own growth and development. We often think about what we can do for others through mentoring, but this is an opportunity to optimize personal development too. Consider the time you will need to receive training, hone skills, and get feedback from your mentee.

In the next chapter, we'll continue our exploration of the enabling growth phase with a look at two very important strategic enabling processes: engaging in feedback and overcoming obstacles. Feedback is a critical aspect of managing the process, maintaining momentum, and encouraging movement. It helps facilitate learning, anticipate stumbling blocks, overcome hurdles, and deal with obstacles.

CHAPTER 7

ENABLING GROWTH, PART TWO

ENGAGING IN FEEDBACK AND OVERCOMING OBSTACLES

ENGAGING IN FEEDBACK—asking for it, giving it, receiving it, accepting it, and acting on it—is a vital part of enabling growth for your mentee. Feedback given and received in the right way nurtures the growth of the mentoring relationship; feedback given or received in the wrong way can upend a relationship—but doesn't need to end it altogether.

Every relationship faces obstacles, and the mentoring relationship is no exception. The challenge is to overcome them and learn from the experience. A mentor who understands how to support, challenge, and provide vision can facilitate mentee growth and development despite obstacles that present themselves. Mentoring partners who are prepared to engage in a meaningful feedback process have a much easier time overcoming obstacles.

ENGAGING IN FEEDBACK

Feedback is a powerful vehicle for learning. Your role as mentor is to provide thoughtful, candid, and constructive feedback in a manner that supports individual learning and development while encouraging the mentee's authorship and expression. As Fairly and Zipp point out, feedback must be both safe and sound: "Being safe is creating the context for effective feedback by controlling our emotions and attending to the needs of the relationship in being careful how we say things. Being sound is delivering the content of effective feedback by focusing on the issue at hand and making sure that what we say is honest and truthful."[1]

Providing feedback without having first established a climate of readiness and expectation can create a frustrating and negative experience for both of you. As a mentor, you need to set the stage for success by creating the expectation early on that feedback will be an ongoing part of the mentoring process. For example, you might relate your own personal story about someone who provided feedback that had a significant impact on you.

When you and your mentoring partner are setting up the ground rules for your relationship, spend time talking about the feedback process itself. Ask about the areas in which your mentee expects or needs to receive feedback. And be sure to explore your mentee's personal challenges in receiving it. I might ask my mentee, for example, "When you receive feedback from someone else, how would you prefer to receive it?" My mentee might say, "Be gentle," or, "Be direct," or, "Tell me how I can improve." Just to make sure we continue to agree on this, I would add, "Write me an e-mail to give me a heads-up if I am off track with the way in which I am delivering feedback."

It's very important to make sure both partners have the same understanding of what feedback is. Sue thought she had set up a climate for feedback, but found that she needed to take a step back to help her mentee understand what feedback really looks like:

Sue and Cathy

Sue: Cathy, this is our third month into our mentoring relationship, and we said we were going to build in some regular feedback during the year. I think this is a good time to do it. What do you think?

Cathy: Okay, I guess I'm ready. Okay, give it to me.

Sue: Hold on! First of all, I'm not here to "give it to you." I want us both to be able to give each other feedback about how it's going and what we could do better—both you and me.

Cathy: Yeah, you're right. Sure, I agree. Do you want to go first?

Sue: Okay. Let me start by saying that even though we got off to a rocky start at the beginning with the problem of—

Cathy: Wait. I told you that the scheduling screw-up wasn't my fault. My manager—

Sue: Hold on a minute, Cathy. It wasn't my intention to focus on that issue. I actually wanted to comment on how well I think the mentoring is going since that difficult beginning. And I wanted—

Cathy: Oh, I'm sorry. I just get upset about how my manager tends to throw new things at me, no matter what I have on my plate. It happened when we were trying to find time to meet, and it happens all the time. In fact, even yesterday, she did it again. I almost couldn't make this meeting because she dumped this big assignment on me yesterday and she wants it done tomorrow. I get so—

Sue: Cathy, I have to interrupt. Your manager's way of doling out assignments is not the subject that I wanted to talk about now. Let's get back to what we were focusing on, which was giving each other feedback. But you know, in fact, what just happened is a good example of something that I think is a problem in the way we use our time. I think you frequently get off track in the middle of our conversations.

Giving Feedback

Giving feedback is not as simple as offering advice or constructive criticism. Your goal in providing feedback is to facilitate learning, so feedback must be relevant, practical, and specific to your mentee's needs. It is an act of caring that requires knowing what you need to do and how to do it meaningfully. Table 7.1 offers some practical tips and examples.

Timing of feedback is also important. A good rule of thumb is to wait until rapport has been built and trust has been established before giving feedback. In the example, Sue was able to give feedback using a situation that was occurring at the time. It was a teachable moment.

Asking for Feedback

Be sure that you model all aspects of good feedback practice. When you regularly ask for feedback, your personal performance as a mentor improves. It also sets the bar for the mentee, who may not be comfortable asking for feedback. The more specific you can be, the better the quality of the feedback and, ultimately, the more effective you will be as a mentor. For example, you might ask questions such as these:

- Was my feedback helpful in improving your performance in that situation?
- What else might I have done to make that feedback even more useful to you?
- What specific support do you need from me right now?
- Am I offering learning challenges that are pushing you in the direction you want to go?
- Are they challenging you enough?

TABLE 7.1

Tips for Giving Feedback

What to Do	How to Do It	Examples
Align your feedback with your mentee's needs and learning goals.	Provide real-time feedback. Make it usable and realistic. Offer concrete, practical steps and options.	"I have a few ideas that might help." "What works for me is …"
Provide feedback about behavior that the mentee can do something about.	Stay with the mentee's behavior, and try to walk in his or her shoes.	"Tell me about the impact of the behavior …" "How might someone else see that behavior?"
When you talk from your perspective, remember that your reality may not be the mentee's reality.	When you talk about your own experience, set the context and be descriptive so the mentee can see the parallels.	"In my experience, which was …, I found that … I know that's not your situation, but maybe there's something to learn here."
Check out your understanding of what is being said.	Listen actively. Clarify and summarize.	"If I understand what you are saying …" " Help me understand what you mean by …"
Use a tone of respect, especially when you and your mentee see things differently.	Take care not to undermine your mentee's self-esteem.	"I appreciate that you are trying to give me another point of view." "I am curious about …" "I wonder …" "Have you ever considered …"
Be aware of your communication and learning styles and how they work with your mentee's style.	Acknowledge different styles, and speak to both.	"I find that I get defensive when …" "I react positively to …"
Avoid giving feedback when you lack adequate information.	Ask for time to get the information you need.	"To be honest with you, I need to think about that a little more."
Encourage the mentee to experience feedback as a movement forward rather than an interruption in the journey.	Keep linking progress and learning to the big picture, the journey, and the learning goals.	"When we started out … And then … And now …"

Table 7.2 summarizes the key components in each of these feedback processes and offers some questions and issues for you to discuss with your mentoring partner.

Dynamics of the Feedback Process

The "asking for feedback-receiving feedback" model is linear. A more helpful approach is to see feedback as a dynamic process: asking for feedback, giving feedback, receiving feedback, accepting feedback, and acting on feedback.

Asking for Feedback

Encouraging mentees to take the initiative in asking for feedback facilitates self-direction. In the same way, learners who invite feedback are able to accomplish more than those who do not. Sometimes, however, a mentee's lack of experience, lack of power, feelings of intimidation or inadequacy, or fear of revealing personal vulnerabilities may get in the way. Here's an example:

> **Marcus and Roger**
>
> Roger is studying for the clergy and has been paired with a mentor, Marcus, who holds a senior clergy position in a large, urban congregation. Marcus is easygoing and a great conversationalist who is always open to questions. Roger knows that he is lucky to have Marcus as a mentor, but feels that his mentor is leaving too much up to him in the relationship. He feels that Marcus never initiates, directs, or guides him and lets him talk about whatever he wants to in their sessions. Roger doesn't know what to do, and Marcus is irritated that Roger never asks for feedback.

Roger is not getting the support he needs because he does not know enough to ask the right questions. Sometimes mentors need to coach mentees like Roger in how to ask for feedback, what to expect from feedback, and the importance of feedback in the mentoring relationship (setting the stage). When and if this happens, it is helpful to find out what the mentee's experience has been with asking for feedback and what, if any, hesitation he or she might have. Encourage your mentee to:

- Be specific and descriptive in asking for feedback.

- Confirm that what you are asking for is clear and understandable.

- Stay focused.

- Avoid being defensive.

TABLE 7.2

Feedback Processes, Components, and Discussion Points

Process	Key Components	Questions or Issues for Your Mentee
Setting the stage	Talk about the value of feedback for the mentee. Early on, create the expectation that feedback will be part of the process. Ask for and provide feedback on a regular basis.	What are your personal challenges? What kind of feedback works best for you? What areas do you expect or need to receive feedback in?
Giving feedback	Wait until the relationship and trust have been established. Allow sufficient time to provide effective feedback. Ensure privacy. Address positives as well as specific areas for improvement. Think about the individual needs of your mentee. Link to the mentee's goals, organizational imperatives, and areas of mentee self-development. Allow opportunities for your mentee to respond.	Is it the right time to give feedback? Set a context by identifying the areas you want to focus on. Direct your feedback toward something that is changeable. Be specific and descriptive. Be nonjudgmental. Be authentic. Keep the feedback two-way, allowing the mentee to respond. Be respectful of different perspectives. Check to ensure the mentee understands. Make eye contact. Balance candor and compassion.
Asking for feedback	Be specific and descriptive in asking for feedback. Confirm that what you are asking for is clear and understandable. Consider the timing of the request for you and your mentee. Avoid being defensive when asking for feedback. Listen and stay focused. Make sure you are getting what you need. Ask for feedback regularly.	Was my feedback helpful toward improving your performance? What else might I have done to help make the feedback more useful for you? What specific support do you need from me to help you grow and develop? What can I do more of? Less of? Am I helping you see and realize a sense of the possible—a professional vision? What kinds of challenges have I provided that are most helpful? Are they challenging enough? What can I do more of? Less of?

- Seek alternatives, not answers.

- Check for understanding.

- Make sure your mentee is getting what he or she needs.

- Ask for feedback on a regular basis.

Giving Feedback

Giving feedback may be one of the most valuable and challenging aspects of the mentor's role. Daloz cautions that "balancing the imperative of providing 'honest feedback' with the equally compelling need to let them [learners] know that they 'can do it' is enough to strain the best of us."[2] Three factors are potential barriers to providing effective feedback to a mentee: your own attitude and comfort level, feedback requests, and organizational situations.

If you are hesitant to provide the feedback your mentee requests, ask yourself:

- How comfortable am I with providing feedback? (Refer to the mentoring skills inventory in Exercise 4.4.)

- Is my personal reaction to getting feedback affecting my attitude?

- How can I best provide the information in ways that promote learning?

Before responding to a request for specific feedback, you should be able to answer yes to each of the following questions:

- Is the request for feedback clear?

- Do I have adequate information in order to understand the reason for the request?

- Is the request or inquiry an appropriate or reasonable one?

- Is there enough time to respond to the request adequately?

- Is what the person is asking really what he or she wants to know?

Be aware that particular practices and procedures in a mentee's organization may discourage candid feedback. For example, some organizational cultures make an effort to avoid conflict, so employees submerge their honest feelings. There may also be some situations in which it may not be appropriate to give feedback. If you suspect that this is the case, consider the following questions:

- Am I the right person in this organization to provide this feedback?

- Am I compromising another person's role by giving feedback?

- Is this the right time in this person's career (and in this organization or institution) to provide the feedback being requested?

- What opportunities are available within the organization that will allow the mentee to apply this knowledge?

- How would others within the organization react to the advice I have given?

- Is the feedback going to be consistent with the policies of the organization and aligned with the organization's mission?

Receiving Feedback

Receiving feedback is not a passive activity. It is an open, interactive, clarifying, and confirming conversation.

One mentor, engaged in a distance mentoring relationship with an aspiring writer, concluded an e-mail note by saying, "Anyway, I hope this is somewhat helpful. Let's stay in touch with all this. Let me know what is helpful and what is not. We'll stay on this." With these four short sentences, he invited feedback, left the door open for further conversation, and stated a desire to be helpful and supportive. The mentee who received this comment, along with written feedback, felt validated. Her mentor had reinforced the fact that it would be the mentee's responsibility to continue the conversation.

When receiving feedback, both mentoring partners need to keep an open mind so that what is being said is also being heard. Remaining open to the experience avoids creating a situation where the mentor or mentee is fighting negative feedback. One way to make sure that feedback has been heard as it was intended is to encourage the mentee to summarize understandings and feelings when feedback is received. Taking this time provides an opportunity for further clarification:

Kamala and Andrew

Andrew, a middle school language teacher, was experiencing difficulty in managing his students. With each passing day, the challenge of teaching rambunctious seventh and eighth graders was becoming more than he could handle. He tried being more directive, showing his displeasure, and even setting up some classroom ground rules—better late than never, he thought—but nothing seemed to be working.

Andrew shared his concerns with his mentor, Kamala. "Kamala, I am really having a problem. I've tried just about everything I can think of. I know you've had tons more experience than me. Tell me what to do."

Kamala listened and then turned to him and said, "Andrew, help me out here. What exactly is troubling you? Is it the kids themselves? Are you feeling out of control?"

Andrew shrugged and replied, "I guess it's a bit of both."

"Okay, Andrew. Let's start at the beginning. I know you're discouraged, but if I am going to help you, I am going to need more to go on. Let's focus on what is going on before the students start acting out. What are you doing? What are they doing?"

After Andrew described a couple of situations that had come up, Kamala asked, "Do you think that there might be some correlation between the time of day the incidents occur and the work you are asking the students to perform?"

"Whoa," said Andrew. "You're right. "The worst is 11:15 in the morning and around 2:15 in the afternoon. Low blood sugar time." He smiled. "I can't believe I didn't realize that myself."

"Okay, so we have something to work with. I always have a couple of high-energy activities in my back pocket for times like that, and I'd be happy to share those with you. I'm also wondering how you are feeling around that time of day. Could that be contributing to the situation?"

"Oh yeah. I really want coffee around then. Why couldn't I see this? It's so obvious!"

Kamala started to laugh. "And along those lines, there's one more thing we might talk about: how you set expectations. Shall we take them one by one?"

As they reviewed these possibilities and talked about how to address them, Andrew began to relax. Kamala encouraged him to respond, ask questions, and check for understanding. The experience of checking for understanding (as opposed to just listening) provided new insights for Andrew and also suggested to him that perhaps he needed to check for understanding with his students in the same way.

Accepting Feedback

Strong reactions to feedback are natural. Sometimes the recipient of the feedback reacts with denial or resistance. A mentee may seem surprised, even shocked, perhaps stating outright, "That's not my problem!" In this situation, you should present information linking the past to the present and future outcomes and then present a strategy or suggestion that demonstrates the benefits of the particular strategy (the answer to the question, "What's in it for me?").

If a mentee appears to be resisting feedback, it could be that the mentee doubts his or her ability, feels hurt, or blames others for the situation. Be supportive by letting your mentee vent—in the session, or later, if necessary—before you begin to offer suggestions.

When receiving feedback, we need to let go of reaction and resistance in order to integrate new learning. Once they are able to receive feedback, some individuals are filled with energy to start making changes. If you find yourself in this situation, you can help rein in your mentee by asking him or her to think about setting priorities. The point is not to do everything possible but to consider new possibilities and identify a new course of action.

Acting on Feedback

Action, not reaction, is the ultimate goal of feedback. Encourage your mentee to move forward to meet new challenges. As the feedback cycle begins again, be ready to provide feedback, ask challenging questions, and help integrate new learnings. This is truly an opportunity for reflection-in-action.[3] It may be helpful to encourage the mentee to develop a step-by-step action plan (and perhaps a contingency plan) with follow-up and accountability mechanisms and ask for feedback on that plan. Table 7.3 offers some ways to help your mentee engage more meaningfully in the feedback process.

The Gift of Feedback

There is no greater contribution to mentee learning than the gift a mentor provides by giving and receiving ongoing, honest, constructive feedback. Expanding the capacity of a mentee to do the same promotes competence, inspires confidence, and enriches the learning experience.

Building personal capacity not only improves your effectiveness as a mentoring partner but strengthens the mentoring experience. Use the feedback checklist in Exercise 7.1 to gauge your personal effectiveness and identify strategies for improvement.

OVERCOMING OBSTACLES

Lurking dangers—potential obstacles and stumbling blocks—threaten to affect the dynamics of every relationship. The enabling growth phase,

TABLE 7.3

How to Help Your Mentee Get Better at Feedback

Feedback Component	Suggestions for Mentees
Ask for feedback	Be proactive about getting feedback from you. Be specific and descriptive in asking for feedback. Make sure that the request for feedback is clear and understandable.
Receive feedback	Be focused. Listen and really hear. Ask questions for clarification. Acknowledge differing points of view.
Accept feedback	Take time to digest the feedback. Think about the positive messages heard. Reflect on surprising messages. Catch yourself being defensive. Discuss your insights.
Act on feedback	Focus on your goals and priorities. Develop an action plan. Communicate your plan. Check in with yourself periodically to determine how you are doing. Continuously look for ways to integrate what you've learned from the feedback you received. Catch yourself moving forward.

where mentoring partners spend the bulk of their mentoring time, is the phase in which these difficulties are likely to crop up.

Mutual Accountability

Either party can be the cause when relationships fail, and such failure can have long-lasting impact.[4] Eby describes a continuum of relational problems ranging from minor to serious.[5] Here's one example:

Ron and Paul

Ron and Paul never seemed to do more than exchange pleasantries during their session. Ron felt that he had been dragged into his role as mentor and resented it. Without taking the time to learn more about his mentee, he discounted Paul as someone who didn't have much potential. In this way, he gave himself permission to slide through his mentoring with the minimum exertion of effort.

EXERCISE 7.1

Feedback Checklist for Mentors

Use this list to give yourself feedback on your feedback effectiveness and consider how to improve.

Feedback Techniques	Yes	Strategies for Improvement
I pay attention to and build on my mentee's unique experiences.		
I encourage my mentee to reflect on experience and use it as a learning opportunity.		
I allow enough time for my mentee to integrate and reflect on the feedback I give.		
I regularly check in with my mentee to confirm that the learning process is effective.		
My feedback focuses on behavior that the mentee can actually act on.		
I regularly check my understanding about what is said.		
I use a tone of respect in providing feedback.		
I am sensitive to my mentee's learning style when giving feedback.		
I avoid giving feedback when I lack adequate information or the timing is inappropriate.		
I encourage my mentee to welcome feedback and see its value in making progress.		
What feedback does your mentee need right now?		

Paul had initially been excited about having a mentor, but Ron's detached attitude quickly dashed his hopes. The combination of low expectations (on Ron's part) and unmet expectations (on Paul's part) minimized the possibility of personal and professional growth. As Ron and Paul became increasingly disengaged, their interactions became more hostile.

The decision to end mentoring was the first thing they agreed on, and the last. Neither Ron nor Paul ever thought to take the other to task for not living up to expectations, and both vowed they would never again have anything to do with mentoring.

Mutual accountability is an essential part of mentoring success. The best way to foster mutually accountability in your mentoring relationship is to hold regular accountability conversations. The exercises provided in this chapter and the previous one can facilitate the process for you and your mentoring partner. Some mentors encourage their mentees to use journals, or to summarize the learning and next steps at the conclusion of each mentoring session. This ensures continuity and sets a common point of reference for jump-starting the next mentoring session. Exercise 7.2 offers ideas.

During the enabling growth stage, it is particularly important to acknowledge lurking dangers and potential obstacles and deal with them as they occur. Purposeful discussion can dispel tension by bringing topics out in the open that might later become impossible to talk about—for example, breach of confidentiality. Addressing the situation immediately rather than letting it fester keeps mentoring partners in conversation where they can reevaluate and renegotiate the relationship and still move forward.

When It Is Not Working

Every so often, a relationship encounters an obstacle, takes a wrong turn, and is not salvageable. Let's see what happened with Elaine and Diane:

Elaine and Diane

Elaine, forty-three, is a concerned, compassionate, and resourceful mentor. She raised two children alone while working full time and earning a master's degree, and she is committed to helping other women do the same. Darlene, ten years younger, is the divorced mother of a twelve-year-old daughter and a six-year-old son. She has a history of family dysfunction—parental abuse, neglect, and alcoholism. When she relocated to a new community to start over, she was offered the opportunity of working with a mentor.

EXERCISE 7.2

Journaling for Mentors and Mentees

Journaling for Mentors

Journaling is particularly helpful for mentors during this phase of the mentoring relationship. It is useful to summarize the session and make notes about insights, and it also helps you remember and stay on track. The track you want to stay on is facilitating learning and, in particular, the functions of support, challenge, and vision. To that end, after each mentoring session, you might reflect on these questions:

1. What did I do to support my mentee's learning?

2. In what ways did I challenge my mentee to learn and to grow?

3. Did I effectively balance support and challenge?

4. How did I assist my mentee in envisioning and moving toward a possible or desired future?

   Take care with your answers. This is an opportunity for you to deepen your own mentoring practice.

Journaling for Mentees

You might want to ask your mentee to reflect on these questions. Then you can follow up with a candid discussion.

1. In what ways is my mentor supporting me? What do I need more of? What do I need less of?

2. Is my mentor challenging me appropriately? What do I need more of? What do I need less of?

3. Do I feel that I am making progress in defining and moving toward a future vision? What additional assistance do I need from my mentor?

Elaine's motivation to become a mentor was connected to her work as a counselor. She was excited about working with Darlene and felt she could offer direction and motivation for her to grow socially and professionally. Elaine and Darlene had chemistry. They liked each other immediately, and both looked forward to the new learning that the mentoring relationship would bring them. Soon both experienced dissatisfaction, and their excitement was short-lived.

Elaine told her mentoring coordinator she was angry. "Darlene seems to have issues of entitlement," she said. "When I try to move her toward personal and professional growth, she just says, 'I don't think so,' or 'I tried that already.'" The few goals Darlene did set she soon discarded.

Despite these setbacks, Elaine remained committed to helping Darlene become self-sufficient and attain a better quality of life. She remembered her own difficulties as a single parent without support. Elaine even researched a scholarship to summer camp for Darlene's son and provided a list of agencies that could assist her in relocating to a better neighborhood. But the longer they worked together, the more Darlene met Elaine's efforts with excuses, resistance, and reasons not to follow through.

As time wore on, Darlene either failed to show up for scheduled appointments or would bring her son, who was often disruptive. Darlene's negativism increased. She insisted she was simply "a victim once again" and "not understood." She regularly complained about her mother's negative influence on her, her children's fighting, and the problems in her housing complex. Still, Darlene refused to consider making any change.

After four months, Elaine had had enough. She met with her coordinator and blurted out, "I feel burned out and used. I worked very hard to get Darlene the free tuition to summer camp for her son. I cannot understand why she turned down the offer. I raised two boys alone. I know how hard it is to be a single mother. If someone offered me the help I offered Darlene, I would have been grateful and accepting. I really do not think she wants to be helped. I don't think I am able to motivate Darlene to make meaningful changes in her life."

What's going on here? Among other things, we see a mentee who is sabotaging the relationship (not showing up, being disruptive) and passively participating in this relationship (her attitude of entitlement, resistance to help). Elaine was projecting her own needs on her mentee. She had assumed that she was standing in Darlene's shoes but had not taken time to discover if her assumptions were correct.

The relationship also suffered from lack of goals, trust, and inauthentic communication. Elaine may have been in denial about where the relationship was headed; Darlene was clearly in resistance. The wall that had built up was too tall for either of them to scale. The relationship did not work because each had contributed to the toxic situation they found themselves in.

Potential obstacles like these are ever-present in a mentoring relationship and can easily alter its dynamics. By recognizing the sorts of obstacles that mentees can bring to the relationship, as well as the obstacles that mentors bring on themselves, both partners can anticipate problems and preserve productive relationships.

Mentoring Challenging Mentees

Some mentees present unique obstacles and particularly challenging situations for mentors. It's helpful to become familiar with some of the possibilities in advance so you can consider your best options for working with them. Here are some strategies for overcoming obstacles with particularly challenging mentees:

• *User mentees*. Mentees who assume entitlement often have a user mentality and are exploitative of mentor knowledge and time. *Strategy*: Avoid becoming your mentee's 411 (for all information) or 911 (emergency road and rescue service). If you let that happen, you become codependent and a possible victim of mentor abuse.

• *Jealous mentees*. When mentees grow or advance beyond their mentors, resentment often builds up, and they perceive their mentor as holding them back. *Strategy*: This is a signal for closure. Be sure to focus on learning conclusions and appropriate celebration. Then move on.

• *Unfocused mentees*. Unfocused mentees are all over the place. They ask for advice but show little follow-through or commitment. *Strategy*: At each mentoring session, focus on the goals of the relationship and preplanned agenda. At the end of the session, review how much progress there has been against the goals and agenda.

• *Manipulative mentees*. These mentees seek favors, opportunities, and control in the relationship. Mentors in this situation can feel used and resentful. *Strategy*: This is the time to revisit boundaries and roles in the mentoring partnership agreement.

• *Submissive mentees*. These mentees are sponges and rely too much on their mentors, accepting everything that they say without question. They are passive and look to the mentor as the source of all truth. *Strategy*: This is a signal that it is time to review relationship roles and expectations.

- *Apathetic mentees.* Some mentees lack candor, good intentions, and follow-through. They are not prepared or committed to the relationship and only seek to satisfy their immediate needs. *Strategy*: A mentee who lacks internal motivation sees little reason to follow through. The goal is to get commitment by clarifying goals and roles. The mentee may not have a clear understanding of roles and responsibilities or may lack commitment to goals that are not specific and clear enough.

- *Saboteur mentees.* These mentees can damage a mentor's career. They may blame their mentors for failing to win a promotion or make false accusations. Some people just do not belong in a mentoring relationship. *Strategy*: Give yourself permission to reset boundaries and limits, or bring the relationship to closure immediately.

Overcoming Your Own Obstacles

Sometimes it's the mentor who has the obstacle. Here are some strategies you can use to get past whatever obstacles you have put in your own path:

- *Impostership.* This notion, introduced by Brookfield, has to do with the expectation that a mentor needs to be all things to a mentee.[6] *Strategy*: Mentors who do not manage their self-expectations set themselves up for failure. Be clear about what you do not know. Do not expect to be able to do it all or provide it all.

- *Burnout.* Mentors who take on too much in the relationship or let themselves be manipulated may burn out. *Strategy*: When mentoring becomes a burden, try to figure out why, and then do something about it. Perhaps you need to rethink your time commitments or other stressors in your life.

- *Stress.* Mentoring is one of many other commitments and situations in life going on at the same time. And there are always situations beyond a mentor's control. *Strategy*: Call time-out if you need to lessen stress. Mentoring should not be stressful.

- *Lack of disclosure.* Being unwilling to share information and feelings may create a situation where mentees read more into communication than is intended. *Strategy*: Be straightforward, firm, and upfront in your communication.

- *Ethical dilemmas.* Mentors sometimes get pushed where they do not want to go. In the desire to meet a mentee's learning needs, mentors may find themselves in a situation where they need to make ethical decisions. *Strategy*: Be on the alert, and stay true to yourself.

- *Crossing boundaries*: Mentors need to let mentees know when a boundary has been crossed. *Strategy*: Don't make it personal. Use the mentoring partnership agreement as a point of reference, and begin the conversation there.

- *Prejudice and bias*. Prejudice of any kind (gender, racial, ethnic) has no place in a mentoring relationship. *Strategy*: If you find that you are exhibiting prejudice or your biases are getting in the way, it is time to consider closure.

- *Procrastination*. When mentors find themselves rescheduling mentoring meetings or putting off mentoring conversations, it is time to consider why this is happening. *Strategy*: It may be a time crunch issue or a signal for closure.

- *Jealousy*. Mentors may experience jealousy if a mentee advances beyond them. *Strategy*: Express pride in your mentee's accomplishments. Then decide if it is time for you to move on. If it is, help the mentee set new goals or find a new mentor.

- *Chain of command*. When the mentor also signs the paycheck, the intimidation factor comes into play. *Strategy*: Mentors can have a productive mentoring relationship with someone in their chain of command if they are clear about the boundaries of the relationship. Keep lines of communication open, and focus on the learner's questions and needs.

- *Mentee neglect*. Intended or not, when you neglect your mentee and don't show an active interest, your mentee begins to make assumptions. *Strategy*: If you take on the role of mentoring, be committed to it. Stay in conversation with your mentee.

MOVING THROUGH

It is easy to see why the enabling growth phase is so challenging. Its unexpected delights, vast opportunities, learning challenges, and lurking dangers present relationship peaks and valleys. Readiness, in this phase, is about moving through rather than moving on.

The readiness checklist in Exercise 7.3 will help you determine where you are in your learning journey. You may find it helpful to come back to this exercise periodically to make sure that you stay on track. From time to time, you may find that you answer some of the items negatively. When that is the case, the checklist is useful as an indicator that you need to work on strengthening the support, challenge, and vision you are providing.

You will know you are ready to move on to closure when the mentee's learning goals have been completed.

EXERCISE 7.3

A Readiness Checklist

Answer each of the questions below, adding examples after each yes or no response.

❑ Am I providing enough balance of support, challenge, and vision to effectively facilitate learning?

❑ Have we identified sufficient and varied opportunities and venues for learning?

❑ Is the learning still fresh?

❑ Are we continuing to build and maintain a productive relationship?

❑ Is our mentoring interaction satisfactory?

❑ Are we continuously working on improving the quality of the mentoring interaction?

❑ Are we continuing to work at maintaining the trust in this relationship?

❑ Have we put in place a variety of mechanisms to ensure continuous feedback?

❑ Is the feedback I am giving thoughtful, candid, and constructive?

❑ Do we make time to reflect on our partnership regularly?

❑ Are there lurking dangers or subjects that seem too difficult to discuss in the mentoring relationship?

Finally, the list of ways to support mentees in the enabling growth phase is a long one. This phase is fluid: there is no beginning, middle, or end to the process tasks within in it. These processes continue throughout the duration of the relationship:

- Meet with your mentee on a regular basis.
- Establish a regular pattern of contact.
- Keep focused on achieving goals and not just day-to-day challenges.
- Follow through on your commitments.
- Be open to new learning opportunities.
- Periodically reflect on what you and your mentee are learning.
- Hold your mentee accountable for his or her growth and development.
- Provide regular feedback.
- Invite and welcome feedback from your mentee.
- Use your time well.
- Expect to make midcourse corrections.
- Check in and check things out.
- Be consistent in your participation.

The process of bringing a mentoring relationship to closure offers a developmental opportunity for you and your mentee to look back on the learning, celebrate it, and move forward. Regardless of whether the relationship has been positive, it always presents an opportunity for growth and reflection. It is this experience that we explore in the next chapter.

CHAPTER 8

COMING TO CLOSURE
LOOKING BACK, MOVING FORWARD

COMING TO CLOSURE should be a mutually satisfying learning experience. For this to happen, however, mentoring partners must be prepared for it and be mindful of it throughout the mentoring process. This means building in closure protocols and processes from the beginning and letting them evolve with the relationship—hence, the term *coming to closure*.

Jesse and Felipe brought their mentoring relationship to closure well. They talked about the good times and the not-so-good times and celebrated their triumphs.

Jesse and Felipe

Jesse and Felipe's relationship had gotten off to a rocky start because Jesse had never been a mentor before. At first, he treated it as simply another item on his to-do list. But Felipe was very serious about the relationship and was determined to make it work. He pushed hard to build the relationship and get the time he needed from Jesse. Over the months of their mentoring relationship, they had established a real bond. Now, both of them knew it was time to come to closure.

Felipe suggested that instead of meeting at the office, they meet for drinks at one of Jesse's favorite restaurants not too far from work (he checked out the location first with Jesse's assistant). On the appointed day, Filipe walked into the restaurant with a package under his arm and plopped down in the chair next to Jesse, who had already ordered drinks for both of them.

"Hey, Felipe, how are you?" said Jesse. "I'm in my element here. Thanks for suggesting it."

"No problem," Felipe said, smiling. "It's my way of saying thank you for your time and support this last year."

"Well," said Jesse, shaking his head, "I have to say even though I was your mentor, you taught me a few things about mentoring. I couldn't have asked for a better first mentee. You're doing great. Even if the program weren't ending now, I don't think you need me anymore. You've nailed every learning goal we agreed on."

"You know what really helped?" said Felipe. "Getting the numbers thing under my belt. Before, I couldn't make sense of them. I didn't know what they meant or how to use them to make decisions. You taught me that numbers were my friend, not my enemy. I don't know why I was fighting it so long—maybe it was the math thing. You've given me the language to ask the right questions. Oh—do you remember the time we sat down and I asked you for advice about firing my direct report?"

"How could I forget it?"

"Well, you were right on. Letting George go was not a good idea. What you said stuck with me, even though I didn't follow your advice. I needed to learn how to delegate and to listen better. And I'm on it."

"We may as well learn from our mistakes; we make enough of them! I can't believe I didn't want to do this mentoring thing in the beginning. That's a mistake I won't make again." Jesse looked Felipe right in the eye. "I really do want to thank you for making my first go at mentoring such a great experience. I've enjoyed getting to know you. And by the way, that ball game was great. I took my son, and we had a great time. Thanks for the tickets."

"My pleasure," said Felipe. "Hey, Jesse," he said, handing him the box, "this is for you—just a way of saying thanks. I hope we can stay in touch."

"Definitely," said Jessie. "It's been a pleasure."

THE CASE FOR CLOSURE

Sometimes, as was the case for Jesse and Felipe, closure is a graceful process. But it can also present significant challenges for mentoring partners.

The end of any relationship is often beset with anxiety, sadness, resentment, or surprise. Sometimes partners hang on indefinitely, not wanting to let go of the emotional and personal ties; inertia or a sense of comfort often sustains a mentoring relationship long after it should end.

Closure sometimes evokes an emotional reaction from mentoring partners. Acknowledging these emotions and moving on is an expected part of the process. But dealing with them takes more time than most people anticipate, and it is often tempting to avoid the conversation altogether.

Avoiding Closure

Sometimes mentoring partners prefer to avoid closure because they fear hurting the feelings of their mentor partner or are otherwise anxious about terminating the relationship. Let's look at two examples:

Betsy and Helen

Helen felt obligated to Betsy, who had been her mentor for over a year. Although she was not satisfied with their mentoring relationship, Helen did not want to hurt Betsy's feelings, so closure was not an option. Helen preferred to let her mentoring relationship run its course and live with the discomfort of obligatory niceness. As a result, she was stuck and unable to move on.

Greg and Art

Greg never felt connected to his mentee, Art. He had agreed to be part of the staff mentoring program because he felt that it made him look good to have a mentee. As time went on, however, maintaining the relationship became a chore. Greg felt that he had no choice in the matter; he thought it would look bad if he asked for another mentee. He kept his feelings to himself and lived with the pretense until the program came to its natural end.

Things were not going well in Helen's or Greg's mentoring relationships. No one wanted to take action. No one was comfortable discussing closure, although each participant knew that their relationship had already ended. If they had each held a negotiating conversation early in their relationship, they would have had a preestablished process in place to bring the relationship to closure comfortably.

Unanticipated Ending Without Closure

Many mentoring relationships end because one of the partners has a shift in personal priorities that changes the balance of the relationship. If closure is not planned for, this kind of change can leave mentees feeling bitter about the process:

Sam and Gretchen

One day Gretchen received a telephone call from her mentor, Sam, telling her that he was being promoted to another division of the company—a promotion that meant immediate relocation to another city. Sam assured Gretchen that he would be in touch "when everything settled down."

Gretchen waited two months for Sam to call; finally, she called Sam and left a message. He never called her back. Gretchen had shared personal vulnerabilities about her work issues with Sam, and his inability to even call her back left her feeling betrayed and hurt.

Mark and Ken

Life circumstances caused Mark to pull back from everything but the basics at work. His spouse had developed a life-threatening illness, and it was all he could do to take care of her and their children and still do his job. Their conversation was brief: Mark called Ken and told him that he was sorry, but he had his hands full and hoped Ken would understand.

Ken, his mentee, was disappointed in Mark, but chose not to push. He let Mark off the hook by finding another mentor, but he felt as if he was starting all over again and that his time with Mark had been wasted.

In these examples, both Gretchen and Ken had previously articulated their learning goals with their mentors, but the unanticipated closure caught them off guard. The lack of formal closure for Gretchen and Ken foreclosed an opportunity to process what they had accomplished and learned and to celebrate their mentoring relationship.

When mentoring partners become friends and drift into a more informal relationship based on the growing familiarity, it is particularly difficult to let go of the mentoring component of the relationship. In such a situation, it is important to mark the transition out of the mentoring relationship and into friendship and use it as an opportunity for learning.

Caren and Juanita

Caren and Juanita had a lively and engaged mentoring relationship and enjoyed their meetings immensely. After several months, Juanita had accomplished her learning objectives—much more quickly than she had thought possible.

"Well," said Caren, looking at her notes, "I think you've done it! It's been a real pleasure. We should definitely get together next month, when we both have some time, maybe get some dinner." Then she rose, gave Juanita a brief hug, watched her leave, and went back to work. That afternoon, however, she found herself feeling sad and even guilty, as if she'd forgotten something very important.

Juanita left Caren's office feeling confused. Were they friends or mentoring partners? Was the mentoring part of their relationship really over?

Caren and Juanita had never discussed closure and drifted from mentoring partnership to friendship without celebrating their own good work together. Although both felt that they had accomplished much together, they had missed out on an opportunity to learn even more.

The intimate nature of the relationship makes the transition from mentor to friend a common occurrence. It happens imperceptibly. With the new relationship, attention to accountability may wane, and closure with respect to learning goals may appear to be superfluous because the relationship is continuing through friendship.

In all these examples, the mentoring partners lacked prior agreement about how to come to closure. If they had planned for this phase, they could have preempted some of the emotional after-effects of not coming to closure and instead would have optimized the positive learning outcomes of the relationship.

When closure does not happen, the transition to the next stage of the relationship (post-relationship or reengagement) is often attenuated and awkward. Because there is a particular point when the relationship is ready for closure, timing is critical. Drawing out the separation process serves neither the mentor nor mentee well and can turn a positive mentoring experience into a negative one.

Closure is also a demarcation between what is (the mentoring relationship) and what will be (perhaps friend, manager, or colleague). Closure helps prevent situations where a mentee might continue to expect access and advice when it is no longer appropriate.

As long as one of the mentoring partners continues to view the relationship as a learning opportunity, ending that relationship can be a valuable source for learning. If there is no other choice but to terminate the relationship, it may be better to make a clean break and discuss what went right and what went wrong. In both situations, the mentor and mentee can learn something from the experience.

Even when mentoring partners discuss the inevitability of closure or establish a no-fault learning conclusion agreement early on in the negotiating phase of their relationship, most rarely revisit that agreement when closure is at hand.

Unanticipated Ending with Closure

Most healthy mentoring relationships end at some point. Planned closure is often the easiest way to deal with this ending, but it nevertheless presents its own set of challenges.

Unanticipated endings occur even in the healthiest mentoring relationships. Whether the change is forced by an external event or a shift in personal circumstances, planning for how to deal with such unanticipated obstacles ahead of time helps mentoring partners know what to do when circumstances change.

Liam and Tricia, Marie, and Tom

Tricia, Marie, and Tom had been group mentoring partners with Liam, their mentor, for nearly eight months. When Liam was suddenly pulled into a new project that would require increasing amounts of his time over the next six months, he felt terrible about leaving them in the lurch. Rather than putting off telling his mentoring partners about the change in his work responsibilities, Liam scheduled a meeting with all of them and confronted the issue head-on.

"Wow," said Tricia. "That's kind of a shock—but congratulations. Your project actually sounds pretty interesting. Does this mean you won't have any time for our group?"

"I have no idea how this is going to affect our relationship," he said. "I just know that it will. Any ideas about how we can work with this?"

Tom looked at his partners and said, "I don't know what your time line is, Liam, but I think we'd like to continue. Maybe we can still be in touch with you, but on your schedule and for shorter periods of time. Would that work?"

Liam thought that might be workable, and the group also agreed to set up regular online get-togethers in the interim. They planned to review the situation in a month's time; if the new setup was not satisfactory, they would bring the relationship to a formal close.

Everyone left the meeting feeling positive. Liam was relieved that he didn't have to leave his mentees in the lurch, and his mentoring partners felt empowered, supported, and respected. By squarely facing foreseeable obstacles, these mentoring partners were able to anticipate closure and develop a contingency plan for dealing with it.

RECOGNIZING THE NEED FOR CLOSURE

A number of telltale signs and signals can suggest that it is time to consider coming to closure (see Table 8.1). When such signals are ignored or overlooked, they can eat away at even a good relationship. Learn to recognize these signals when they first appear, and then try to validate your perceptions and assumptions.

TABLE 8.1

Signals That It Might Be Time to Come to Closure

Signals	Possible Indications
I am bored, uninterested, and thinking about other things when I meet with my mentee.	I am just going through the motions, and this relationship is not meaningful or important to me.
My mentee shows up on the scheduled date, and we meet whether or not there is an agenda.	We are meeting just to meet, and there is no real purpose to our meeting.
I begrudge the time I must spend to maintain this relationship. There are more important and pressing matters I must attend to.	Mentoring is not a high priority for me right now. I am no longer engaged in the relationship.
It feels as if my mentee is hanging on and will not let go.	My mentee has accomplished her learning goals and is ready to move on, but she does not see it that way.
I have run out of things to talk about with my mentee.	We are wasting each other's time.
There has been a consistent breach of confidence.	I do not trust my mentee and need to be selective about what I choose to share.
My mentee listens to my advice or counsel but does not follow through.	I am spinning my wheels and wasting my time.
We have been meeting for many months and do not seem to be making progress.	Someone else could better fill my mentee's needs.
After most meetings, I feel wrung out, as if my mentee has drained all my energy.	This is not a healthy relationship.
This appears to be a one-way relationship.	I get little, if any, satisfaction from contributing to this mentee's growth.
Being with my mentee is unpleasant and painful.	I do not like or respect my mentee.
My mentee is high maintenance.	My mentee requires a lot more support than I can or want to provide. It may be that I no longer want to continue this relationship.

Sometimes there are no overt signals that indicate mentoring partners should come to closure, yet a mentee or mentor may decide to end the relationship. When this happens, it is important for the other person to respect that decision. At other times, a mentee wants to end a mentoring relationship and the mentor does not feel that that decision is a logical or well-reasoned choice. Nevertheless, a wise mentor respects that choice and knows when, and how, to leave the door open in case the mentee's circumstances change. Here are two approaches from mentors who have kept the door open:

1. Even though we need to end the formal mentoring relationship now, I want you to know that I am very interested in continuing to know how you are progressing in applying your learning. Please stay in touch, and let me know how you're doing. In fact, how about if we put a date on the calendar now?

2. I know that you're going through a hard time personally right now, and I understand why continuing to meet is no longer feasible. I've enjoyed our relationship, and I'd be glad to work with you again. Hang on to my phone number and e-mail, and please let me know when you're ready to pursue your learning goals again.

Both of these mentors have signaled that they are not hurt because the mentee decided to end the relationship. They remain interested and supportive, and leave the door open for their mentees to return.

PLANNING FOR CLOSURE

Most mentoring relationships don't have the kind of closure we are talking about here. Certainly the mentee may have achieved his or her learning goals, and the mentoring partners may feel they have ended on a high note, but because they did not plan for closure from the beginning, they have lost the opportunity to capitalize on learning and enrich the entire experience. As we discussed in Chapter Five, the time to agree on the closure process is when you are negotiating the mentoring partnership agreement as part of the relationship ground rules.

It is essential to plan the process of coming to closure, taking into consideration how it will play out both when closure is anticipated and when it is not. Using the learning goals of the mentoring relationship as a focal point provides a basis for discussing best-case and worst-case closure scenarios. Identifying potential stumbling blocks such as avoidance of closure or continuation of the relationship when one or both partners are unhappy makes it easier to plan how to overcome them.

Formal mentoring programs help facilitate the process of coming to closure because structures for reviews and end dates are usually specified. Mentors in informal mentoring relationships have to be more conscientious about bringing a mentoring relationship to closure because there is no proscribed end date.

It is helpful to establish a process to acknowledge the need for closure that helps you both end on a positive note and identifies a framework for organizing a "learning conclusion" conversation—a highly focused conversation about learning outcomes that have resulted from the mentoring relationship. Let's look at two examples of what can happen when closure is planned for:

Frank and Minh

Frank and Minh's mentoring relationship came to closure when their company's mentoring program cycle ended. "I'm sorry to see it end," said Frank, "but it looks as if you really did achieve the goals you set out to achieve."

"Yes," said Minh with a laugh. "If the company hadn't set up this deadline, I don't know how long it would have taken to accomplish all this."

Frank and Minh attended the company's formal mentoring luncheon and received congratulations and certificates acknowledging their participation in the program.

Without that formal event, they might not have brought the relationship to closure or acknowledged their accomplishment and mutual appreciation. But knowing that closure was expected triggered a conversation about this phase and provided a rallying point for the transition that was to follow. Because their relationship was part of a formal program, Frank and Minh were able to tailor Minh's learning goals according to the time frame that his company had set. By the time the final luncheon rolled around, Frank and Minh had met these articulated goals and had held their closure conversation:

Frank and Minh, continued

"You know, I've learned a heck of a lot from this experience," said Frank. "I've never thought of myself as a mentor before, but working with you has shown me that I've got a few more skills than I was giving myself credit for. I was telling my wife the other day that if the company ever lets me retire, I might want to put more time into helping out people who are just getting into the business."

Minh laughed. "You've definitely got the chops for mentoring, Frank. For me, maybe not so much, but I make a much better mentee than I would have thought going into this. I would never have done this if the company hadn't made it part of my job requirements. To tell you the truth, I didn't even get what mentoring was."

"Well, you took to it like a natural," said Frank. "You accomplished your goals in nothing flat. I've been really impressed with your energy and dedication."

"Okay, okay, that's enough of sharing the love," said Minh. "Let's eat!"

Yvonne and Raj

Yvonne and Raj's informal mentoring relationship resulted in meeting only three of the five learning objectives they had set out to accomplish for the year. When they met to process the learning at the end of the year, they realized that it would be advantageous to continue their mentoring relationship.

They talked about what went well for them and what might improve their relationship, and then they renegotiated a time line for accomplishing the remaining learning goals. Despite the initial time frame they had set, they realized they were not yet ready to end the relationship.

In this case, reaching closure meant renegotiating rather than ending the relationship. It still required engaging in a meaningful closure conversation.

REACHING A LEARNING CONCLUSION

An indispensable part of the experience of coming to closure is bringing the relationship to a learning conclusion: a highly focused conversation about specific learning that has taken place during and as a result of the mentoring relationship. It is a blameless, no-fault, reflective conversation about both the process and content of the learning.[1] As the following example shows, even when the relationship has been problematic, this conversation can be constructive:

Jim and Carol

Jim and his mentee, Carol, had not had a productive mentoring experience. In fact, in just a few months, they had placed so many demands on one another that they wore themselves out trying to maintain the relationship. When Jim finally said, "I hate to say it, but I think we need to end this relationship," Carol breathed a deep sigh of relief. They agreed in advance to hold a learning conclusion conversation, and both actually looked forward to it.

They began by reviewing Carol's learning goals. Using that as a personal benchmark, they focused on the specifics of what Carol had learned and what else she would need to reach the remaining learning outcomes. They talked about what went well for them in the relationship—they did like each other—and what did not, and why.

In the course of the conversation, Jim realized that he had not focused well on Carol's needs. He hated to admit it, but a mentoring relationship might require more patience than he had. Carol saw that she needed to take more responsibility for her own learning; she had kept waiting for Jim. She decided to work on being more focused on her own needs and taking some risks. "I think I've learned more in this one conversation than I have in the last few months," she said, laughing.

"Yeah," said Jim. "Live and learn, I guess. But listen, I think I can help connect you with a couple of other mentors who have the expertise and background you need and who are good at mentoring." Carol was pleased and agreed to contact them. She really did want to further her learning.

It is important to remember that mistakes, failures, and missteps offer rich experience for learning. Because they had a blameless conversation focused on the learning, both partners were able to take something positive away from the mentoring experience. The negative aspects of Jim and Carol's relationship were softened by focusing the conversation on what each had learned and how they might apply that knowledge in the future.

When mentoring partners prepare and plan for closure, it can be a mutually satisfying and meaningful learning experience. Exercise 8.1 offers step-by-step guidance in planning for closure. Ideally this conversation takes place as part of the negotiating conversation and is revisited again toward the end of the enabling phase in preparation for the closure conversation.

When a mentoring relationship disintegrates or fizzles out, the mentor and mentee miss an opportunity to learn from the relationship. Routinely reviewing goals and objectives throughout the relationship keeps the relationship focused on mentee goals and enables mentoring partners to take stock of their progress. This process builds momentum and helps to identify the appropriate time for closure.

EXERCISE 8.1

Closure Preparation: Steps and Questions

Follow the steps in column 1 by asking the related questions in column 2.

Closure Preparation Step	Related Questions
1. Revisit your purpose	What was our goal in working together?
2. Envision a best-case scenario for closure.	What would we ideally like to see happen when this mentoring relationships ends? How can we ensure the relationship reaches a positive learning conclusion? If the ideal isn't possible, how can we still ensure a positive learning outcome?
3. Envision a worst-case scenario for closure.	What might get in the way of a positive learning conclusion? What might a positive learning conclusion look like under these circumstances?
4. Plan for mutual accountability.	What will we do to overcome any factors that get in the way of reaching a learning conclusion?
5. Establish a process for acknowledging the time for closure.	How will we know when it is the right time to bring the relationship to closure?
6. Establish ground rules for the learning conclusion conversation.	What will the agenda be for our learning conclusion conversation?

As soon as goals and objectives have been met, it is time to reflect on what has been learned, celebrate, and move on. If you agree to continue the mentoring relationship, it is necessary to articulate new goals, renegotiate the terms of engagement, and review what has worked well in the past and what has gotten in the way.

INTEGRATING LEARNING

Closure gives mentoring partners the opportunity to apply and integrate what they have learned as a result of the relationship. Without closure, that opportunity is lost. Your questions and thoughtful analysis can help mentees evaluate learning outcomes and identify how to maximize and build on that learning. Here's how Neal and Elliott handled the opportunity to learn from closure:

Neal and Elliott

For over a year, Neal and his mentee, Elliott, have been engaged in a mentoring relationship that came about as a result of a corporate mentoring initiative. In a recent memo from the company's training and development department, Neal was reminded that the year's mentoring cycle was almost through, and he realized that it was time to bring closure to the mentoring relationship.

Neal began the process by sending an e-mail asking Elliott to come to the next mentoring session prepared to review the learning plan they had laid out when they started meeting. When they met, Neal focused the conversation on each of the original learning goals and then asked Elliott for his assessment in relation to each of them. Elliott responded that his goal had been to learn how to position himself for new opportunities within the department and felt he had made considerable progress.

Neal then asked Elliott to describe the progress he felt he had made and to identify how he had specifically applied what he had learned. Once Elliott articulated his response, he and Neal explored other questions: What were the implications of that learning? In what ways could Elliott apply learning to other situations? What other learning would be helpful for Elliott?

Once they addressed these questions, Elliott focused on the process of learning, asking questions such as: What did we learn as a partnership? What did we learn as individuals about ourselves? How can we integrate that learning?

Let's look at a more detailed mentoring closure scenario that addresses Elliott's questions, and illustrates how this conversation can be handled:

Mentor: As we bring our mentoring relationship to a close, it's time to reflect on what we've each taken away from our mentoring experience. You know, I've really been impressed with how far you've come. I have seen you grow into your role as a leader, and it's obvious that you now have a better understanding of what is required for you to take the next step. I've watched you learn to handle yourself much more competently, particularly when it comes to managing conflicts with your staff. You seem to be so much more comfortable and confident than you were when we first met.

Mentee: Now that you mention it, I do feel more comfortable. You've really helped me with that. Plus, I see that by improving my own skills in managing conflict how much it has positively impacted my team and helped them grow and learn—which was not really something I considered before.

Mentor: Speaking of learning, you're not the only one! You've been really helpful to me in my growth as a mentor.

Mentee: Really? Thanks. Like what?

Mentor: Well, I could have done some things differently to support you better. I've been so involved in my own department projects that I don't think I gave you enough time sometimes, and I really apologize for that. So I've learned that I need to commit my time as well as my intention! And my advice to you is that if you are going to be a mentor, be prepared to commit the time.

Mentee: You know, initially, when it was hard to meet with you because you had work to do, I took it personally. But that also taught me that I have to fight for the time I need. I also realized that our styles are different, and sometimes I let those differences get in the way. At first I just wanted you to be like me, but over the months I saw that difference was really an opportunity for me to figure out how to interact with someone who thinks and processes differently than I do—which, basically, will be true of most of the people I interact with!

Mentor: Well, I guess this process has been good for both of us. But it's not over yet! As you move forward, there are some next steps to consider. I was thinking that you may want to focus your time and attention on developing your strategic thinking and on being able to align what you do on a daily basis with your own long-term goals and the challenges your department is facing right now.

Mentee: Your suggestion about strategic thinking is really right on for me. So many times this year you pointed out how easily I get trapped in the day-to-day. I have come to see how that focus holds me back from getting to the next level. But listen—is that a goal that you and I can continue with, even though our time is up? Or do you think I should get another mentor to help me with that?

Mentor: It's a possibility, and I'd be open to it, although you may want to get another mentor's perspective. Let's talk about it again in another month. How about the twenty-fifth?

Mentee: Excellent. I'll let you know if that needs to change, but for now it sounds good. I want you to know that I have learned so much from you about what it takes to be successful. You have truly been a great role model for me. I especially appreciate getting to know you better. Your insights have given me a lot to think about. Thank you so much.

As this scenario suggests, mentors can also learn about themselves and how to improve their personal mentoring practice from engaging in a mentoring relationship. To turn the closure experience into a learning experience will take some self-reflection.

If you have been keeping a learning journal, now is the time to take it out and review it and reflect on your development as a mentor. Exercise 8.2 provides a worksheet to stimulate self-reflection before your actual closure conversation with your mentee. You might use the sentence stems as a journal entry or separately. The important thing is that you use this as a personal and professional learning opportunity.

Even when a mentoring relationship has been beset with a problem, reaching a learning conclusion can turn it into a positive experience. In such a situation, mentoring partners should use the following approach:

1. Acknowledge the problem or difficulty encountered without casting blame or passing judgment—for example, "It looks as if we've come to an impasse."

2. If the decision is to end the mentoring relationship, make a clean break of it and end on an upbeat note. Consider what went right with the relationship as well as what went wrong—for example, "Let's look at the pluses and minuses of our relationship so that we can each learn something from the relationship."

3. Express mutual appreciation. Acknowledge the progress and accomplishments that did result from the relationship—for example, "Although we haven't been able to accomplish all of your objectives,

EXERCISE 8.2

Self-Reflection: Turning Closure into Learning

Use the following sentence stems to reflect on what you have learned from your mentoring relationship:

1. What I have learned about myself:

2. My mentoring gifts and strengths:

3. What I wish I could learn to do better:

4. How I will apply what I have learned:

5. Specific steps for applying what I have learned:

we were successful in one area. I attribute our success to your persistence and determination; those are the very characteristics you will need in your new job."

CELEBRATING LEARNING

We are more likely to celebrate success in our personal lives than in our workday life, where celebration is viewed as appropriate only within limits. In fact, celebration is a fundamental part of concluding a mentoring relationship because it reinforces learning and signals the transition process.

If celebration is to have any value, it must be genuine. Authentic celebration engenders enthusiasm, builds a sense of community, and creates venues for communication. Terrence Deal and M. M. Key, in *Corporate Celebration: Play, Purpose and Profit at Work*, speak to the value of celebrating: "Celebrations infuse life with passion and purpose. They summon the human purpose. They attach us to our human roots and help us soar toward new visions. They touch our hearts and fire our imaginations."[2]

Celebrating Learning Together

Mentoring relationships can be celebrated in a variety of settings, from formal events to informal meetings. Here are some suggestions for incorporating celebration into the closure of a mentoring relationship:

- *Collaborate on the planning.* Don't take on all the work of celebration yourself. Engaging the mentee in the planning process will heighten the sense of individual contribution and foster the sense of partnership that permeates a mentoring relationship.

- *Elevate and expand knowledge.* The celebration can be a vehicle to continue to educate about the past, present, and future of the organization; use it as a context for growth. Ask your mentee to relate her or his perspectives, experiences, and challenges.

- *Leverage learning.* The opportunity to leverage and maximize learning is the very essence of a mentoring relationship. By sharing your own development stories with your mentee, you create a sense of momentum that extends beyond the celebration.

- *Expand your thinking.* When considering how to celebrate, look for permanent mementos or meaningful ways to remember the partnership. Formal mentoring programs, for example, often give partners certificates of completion.

- *Brag about accomplishments.* Boast about your mutual mentoring accomplishments with your mentee. Celebrate the triumphs and big wins with big celebrations. And while you're at it, make connections with the mentee's personal mission (and, if you are mentoring in an organizational context, with the organization's mission).

- *Rekindle memory.* Revisit the journey. There is an old saying, "If you don't have a sense of where you come from, going backward looks like progress." Look to create a shared sense of progress and purpose with your mentee. You may find that it will reawaken your own sense of purpose and keep the focus on learning.

- *Appreciate.* Honor achievement. Let mentees know what it is that you appreciate about them. Tell them they matter and why, and be honest when you do. Leave space and opportunity for mentees to express their appreciation to you. This allows them to feel that they are giving something of themselves to you.

- *Talk about transitions.* Talk about changes before they take place. Celebration is an opportunity to create self-awareness, educate for change, and prepare for next steps.

- *Espouse the vision.* Articulating personal (and organizational) vision harnesses energy and engages the spirit. Linkages to vision help leverage learning. Create consistent thought and action by helping your mentee keep the vision out front.

Ways to Celebrate

Celebration is nurturing; it engages people through connection. Challenge yourself and your mentee to create ways to celebrate. Celebrate the mini-miles, mile markers, and finish lines. Here are some ideas you can use to get started:

- *Gift giving.* Gifts—meaningful tokens or souvenirs related to the purpose of the mentoring relationship—should be kept to a minimum and be modest in cost. For example, you might choose a book relating to your mentee's area of interest, inspirational or motivational books you think your mentee will enjoy, or a blank journal for reflection which your mentee can use going forward.

- *Written expressions.* Written notes offer a permanent record of support and encouragement as well as a memento. You might write your mentee a note about what you learned from him or her, a simple message wishing good luck in the future, or a motivational message for the future.

- *Face-to-face conversations.* Sometimes the right words uttered at just the right moment are the best and most remembered gifts in the long term.

In expressing appreciation, be specific and focus on behaviors. You will remind the person of their value—for example, "I admire your . . .," "You have a real knack for . . .," "I especially appreciated it when you . . ."

Deal and Key describe effective celebrations as "well-crafted processes that embrace and honor participants."[3] And it was Kahlil Gibran who spoke so eloquently about the value of personalism in gift giving: "You give but little when you give of your possessions. It is when you give of yourself that you truly give."[4] Personalism should be part of mentoring celebrations.

REDEFINING THE RELATIONSHIP

Before you and your mentee engage in a conversation about how your relationship will be different once this phase of it ends, you need to decide if you want to continue to be in contact with your mentee and, if so, on what basis. Consider if you want to continue the relationship on an ad hoc basis or informally. Perhaps you will want to reengage and work on a new set of goals or work on goals that you were not able to complete. Here's what Greta and Marina did:

Greta and Marina

Greta and Marina had had a wonderful year together. Although it had taken them considerable time to identify the goals they wanted to focus on, they made steady progress once that was done. The year flew by fast, and at the end, they met together over a good meal to celebrate and talk about what they learned.

Both admitted they would have liked the relationship to continue the way it was, but the intensity of the work and the time it required to fully engage with one another precluded another year of mentoring. Marina put down her fork and asked, "Couldn't we just touch base occasionally? It seems a shame to stop now that we've built such a good rapport." Greta agreed. They decided the best plan was to continue to stay in touch by e-mail and phone from time to time.

During one of their phone calls, they decided to reengage as mentor and mentee, but to do it on a much more informal basis. It meant having different ground rules, expectations, and goals for the relationship, and they scheduled a meeting to discuss what these would be.

Moving On

Once you have redefined your relationship, it is time to let go of it as it was and embrace it as it will be as you move forward. Moving on is often difficult for mentees and mentors. Mentors often experience a sense of loss; their mentoring conversations have stopped, yet their commitment to their mentee's growth and success remains. They often worry about how their mentees will fare without them. For mentees, the sense of loss is often greater. They no longer have the continuity of regular mentoring sessions they have come to depend on for support, feedback, and safety.

Even after the mentor and mentee have come to closure, there may be times when the mentee reappears in the mentor's life. It could be by way of a personal visit some years later, a letter, an e-mail, or a telephone call. At these mostly unpredictable times, the mentee will likely report on her accomplishments and wait for the mentor's approval. In this way, mentors become a bellwether in mentees' lives for measuring progress and receiving validation and kudos for their accomplishments. The exchange is a satisfying but very different one from the relationship that spawned the initial learning experience.

Table 8.2 summarizes the closure steps and action strategies that lead to a successful closure experience.

Coming to Closure About Closure

Good closure should elevate a mentee's learning and catapult it forward, raising the learning to another level. Unsatisfactory closure can block

---

TABLE 8.2

Summary of Closure Steps and Action Strategies

Steps	Action Strategies
1. Planning	Discuss the best- and worst-case scenarios.
2. Learning conclusion	Decide how to structure the closure conversation.
	Reflect on lessons learned.
3. Integrating learning	Focus on the application of learning and next steps.
4. Celebrating success	Identify meaningful ways to celebrate the learning and express appreciation.
5. Redefining the relationship	Decide whether or how to reengage and what will happen after the mentoring relationship ends.
6. Moving on	Let go and move forward.

growth by minimizing the desire to achieve learning goals. Although individual needs for closure vary, at least some closure is essential for growth. When mentoring partners do not come to closure, they forfeit the potential for future learning.

Effective mentoring comes from learning throughout the mentoring relationship. The process of coming to closure is not just for the benefit of the mentee or the mentoring relationship. It presents a development opportunity for the mentor as well. After closure of the relationship, mentors should take time to focus on their own learning and consider how they can apply what they have learned to their advantage in future mentoring relationships. Exercise 8.3 provides a worksheet for mentor self-reflection.

Coming to closure in mentoring is an important part of learning, development, satisfaction, and promise. It frees you and your mentee to move on and helps ensure that your mentee comes away with significantly deeper learning that will lead down the road of possibility.

To be sure it is time to move on, answer the questions in Exercise 8.4. If you cannot answer all the questions affirmatively, you may need to do more work on your own mentoring partnership to come to closure successfully. Refer to items 1 through 6 with your partner at the end of the closure conversation to make sure that you have covered all the necessary bases.

EXERCISE 8.3

Mentor Self-Reflection on Learning

This diagram represents the time line of your mentoring relationship from when you started in this relationship to the present day. Use the time line to indicate the highlights of your journey and its successes and challenges.

Preparing	Negotiating	Enabling Growth	Coming to Closure

As you complete each grid, you will begin to see your mentoring relationship from a larger perspective. As you analyze it further, common themes and patterns will emerge. Reviewing them should reveal some powerful insights about your own developmental journey as a mentor. The questions that follow will assist you in identifying your next steps.

1. What are your mentoring gifts and strengths?

2. In what ways have you grown and developed as a mentor?

3. What have you learned about yourself?

4. How has that learning contributed to your own professional development?

5. What do you want to work on to further your development as a mentor?

6. How will you hold yourself accountable for your development?

7. What action steps will you take, and when?

EXERCISE 8.4

Coming to Closure: A Readiness Checklist

Answer each of the questions, adding examples after each response. The first six questions by themselves provide a checklist for concluding the closure conversation.

❑ Did we use the protocols we established to bring closure to the relationship effectively?

❑ Did we hold a meaningful learning conclusion conversation?

❑ Did we adequately evaluate learning outcomes?

❑ Did we discuss the application and integration of new learning?

❑ Did we acknowledge our accomplishments?

❑ Did we celebrate milestones?

❑ Did I identify the signals when it was time for closure?

❑ Did I personally evaluate my own learning as a result of this experience?

❑ Have I identified ways to apply and integrate my new learning?

❑ Have I decided what I would do differently as a mentor the next time?

CHAPTER 9

DIGGING DEEPER

REENGAGEMENT AND RESOURCES FOR LEARNING

YOUR MENTORING RELATIONSHIP has come full cycle. Along the way, you've challenged your mentee to think about who and what he or she might become, and you've set your mentee on a path. You've supported, challenged, and encouraged him or her to envision new possibilities. You've engaged in reflective conversations so that he or she might learn from experience.

As mentors, we hope the lessons our mentees have learned continue to light their path. But these lessons can also continue to light *your* path. One of the gifts of mentoring is the gift of reengagement. It is a gift that keeps giving if you are open to receiving it.

REENGAGEMENT

Mentoring can be a life-changing experience that offers opportunities to engage with life in new and powerful ways. Many mentors, attuned to the habit of critical reflection with their mentees, find that they are more focused in their mentoring relationships. They bring expanded energy, take more informed action, and are generally more satisfied with their mentoring relationships. They also experience a carryover to their personal and professional relationships and become reengaged in new ways as the habit of critical reflection becomes internalized. Here are some stories of real mentors who have connected with life in a new way as a direct outcome of mentoring.

Cyril: A Sense of Purpose

Cyril was in a high-pressure job and always on the run, whether he was on the road or in the office. Still, he continued to connect regularly with his two mentees. He enjoyed the intellectual and emotional stimulation each provided, and he made the relationships a priority. Cyril's mentoring experience ultimately reconnected him with his sense of purpose and made him rethink his priorities.

Dana: A New Perspective

Before her mentoring relationship with Clark, Dana had had no interest in sports. But her mentee Clark was a sports enthusiast whose spirited descriptions about games and events were contagious. As a result, her curiosity was piqued, and she began to listen more closely to the conversations her coworkers were having about sports, to which she had previously turned a deaf ear.

As Dana learned more, she began to make connections between sports metaphors and her work as a leader. She became a keen observer of the team process. Dana became fascinated with observing how coaches did their jobs on the field. She learned skills that she could apply as a mentor at work—and negative behaviors to stay away from. Dana began seeing ordinary things from a whole new perspective and was having fun in the process.

Bertrand: Staying Fresh

Bertrand, a retired interior designer, discovered that mentoring reenergizes him. It adds to his sense of purpose, keeps him abreast of what is current in the furniture industry, and makes him feel useful. By mentoring young people, which he has done for the past seven years, he is always engaged in doing something new.

Marna: Reengaging with Ideas in New Ways

Marna holds a chair of distinction at her university. She is a renowned and respected scholar and has been mentoring students for three decades. Students flock to her classes just to be in her presence. One of the greatest joys and pleasures of her career is mentoring the next generation of scholars. She derives enormous personal satisfaction from sharing her expertise and experience.

As her mentees begin their academic journeys and grow and then distinguish themselves in their careers, she keeps a watchful eye. Mentees continue to share insights with her for many years after their mentoring relationships have come to closure. These insights allow her to reengage with concepts and ideas in new ways. Mentoring has prolonged and energized her six-decade career.

Leslie: Exposure to New Ways of Thinking

Leslie, a career counselor and pastor, looks forward to mentoring relationships because of the constant exposure to new ways of thinking, perspectives, and views they bring. What he learns from his mentoring relationships stimulates new ideas and pinpoints areas for his personal growth and development. He feels that he learns as much from his mentees as they learn from him.

Elisha: Developing Relationship Skills

Elisha, an attorney in a large law firm, has mentored many mentees, some more successfully than others. She attributes the development of her relationship skills to the feedback she has received from them. She takes their comments very seriously and has worked diligently to develop the interpersonal skills to which she attributes her career success.

Martha: Becoming a More Effective Mentor

Martha had been a mentor several times during her fifteen-year career as a public service employee. In one formal mentoring relationship, the focus was on orienting a new employee. In another, an informal mentoring relationship, she was mentoring a friend who was working on rebuilding her image. She also mentored a man who had moved to the United States from Argentina and wanted to set up a home-based business. She enjoyed each of these relationships and received a good deal of satisfaction from watching each of her mentees succeed.

Only recently, when she reflected on the quality of her mentoring interaction, did she realize that her previous relationships had been more about transfer of knowledge than self-directed learning. This was a real opening for her in terms of reflecting on who she was as a mentor and how she was able to enrich a mentoring relationship.

As a result, she started reading about mentoring and learning all she could about the process. The more she read, the more she realized that mentoring was about her own growth and that reflection needed to become a regular part of her mentoring practice.

What You Can Do

As you've worked your way through the phases of the mentoring relationship, you've probably gained some new insights about yourself, about mentoring, and about how you can apply what you've learned to other situations. Make the time now, in Exercise 9.1, to reflect on your experience and capture your learning while it is fresh in your mind.

EXERCISE 9.1

Self-Reflection: What You Learned from Mentoring

Think for a moment about your most recent mentoring relationship. In your journal, answer these questions:

1. What insights did you gain about yourself?

2. What did you do well in the relationship?

3. What could you have done better?

4. What commitment are you willing to make to raise the bar on your performance as a mentor?

5. How are you going to measure the success of your improvement goal?

6. What did you learn that can carry over to other situations?

Lessons Learned

My goal in writing *The Mentor's Guide* is to encourage reflective mentoring practice and thus raise the bar on the practice of mentoring. By working through the exercises and reflecting on your own mentoring experiences after each of your relationships is completed, you will find that you will become an even more effective mentor and enhance your personal mentoring practice.

Here are some final dos and don'ts for facilitating your mentees' learning and for nurturing your own growth and development.

- *Heighten awareness*. This book is a guide to facilitating effective mentoring relationships. Heightened awareness leads to more informed action. Use the concepts presented in this book to heighten your awareness, but do not be a slave to its forms and format.

- *Stay in the conversation*. This book is about the engagement of mentoring partners. Be present when you are meeting with a mentee. Keep communication open, authentic, and flowing. Don't let mentoring become another to-do list item or a transaction.

- *Capture the learning*. This book advocates reflective practice. Capturing the action and taking time to learn from it as it happens empowers the mentor and facilitates the relationship. Take time after each relationship to recapture the learning. If you wait until tomorrow, you will lose the advantage of being in the moment.

- *Partner*. This book presents partnership as a relationship of commitment and care that can be nurtured with the mentor's purposeful preparation. Partner with the learner. Do not let yourself become a dispenser of knowledge. Seek to promote self-directed learning.

RESOURCES FOR MENTORS

Mentor was the consummate teacher: he faithfully educated Telemachus in the ways of the world and gave him the requisite knowledge to live in that world. When Telemachus grew up and Odysseus returned, his responsibilities as a mentor were complete. But that was then, and this is now—mentors, as we have seen, have evolved far beyond this model. Today's mentor is a facilitator, a partner in an evolving learning relationship focused on meeting mentee goals and objectives. Today's mentor is an active learner and reflective practitioner in pursuit of continuous improvement.

And that brings us back to you. What's next? Are you willing to continue to hone your mentoring skills and grow in the role? If you are, consider this an invitation to keep learning about mentoring. To help you in that effort, I've put together a list of books to help you dig deeper into the key concepts presented throughout the book.

Larry Daloz's *Mentor: Guiding the Journey of Adult Learners* (San Francisco: Jossey-Bass, 1999) is required reading for any mentor concerned with adult development and learning. Daloz uses the metaphor of the guide to describe the mentor's role in accompanying the learner on a journey. His depth perspective expands the current understanding of mentoring as a developmental journey. He offers rich examples and practical approaches to transform the learning and the learner.

Learning: Grounding the Work of Mentoring

Women's Ways of Knowing: The Development of Self, Voice, and Mind, by M. Belenky, B. Clinchy, N. Goldberger, and J. Tarule. New York: Basic Books, 1986.

This book provides five approaches to understanding cognitive development based on qualitative research with women. The authors' findings about how individuals receive and process knowledge are applicable to both men and women. Connected knowing (in contrast to separate knowing) is congruent with the type of effective mentoring practice I've described in this book. Knowledge about ways of knowing helps explain behavior and develop the mentor's ability to understand how mentees process knowledge.

Understanding and Facilitating Adult Learning: A Comprehensive Analysis of Principles and Effective Practices, by S. D. Brookfield. San Francisco: Jossey-Bass, 1986.

Effective facilitation is a basic process skill in the mentor's toolkit. Stephen Brookfield offers an in-depth description of the facilitation process. Using six principles of effective practice, he outlines ways to keep the learning relationship on track in order to stimulate reflection and assist mentors in helping mentees reflect on their learning processes.

Big Questions, Worthy Dreams: Mentoring Young Adults in Their Search for Meaning, Purpose, and Faith, by S. Daloz Parks. San Francisco: Jossey-Bass, 2000.

Sharon Parks affirms the purpose, promise, and possibility of mentoring for mentor and mentee. You will immediately (and always) become aware of the awesome responsibility of the mentor in supporting meaning making at each stage of the mentee's developmental journey. Parks solidly anchors mentoring in the rich dynamic of developmental theory. At the same time, she challenges us to heightened levels of accountability. The examples she offers are inspiring. Most important, she raises big questions and worthy dreams for mentors and mentees alike.

Student Development in College: Theory, Research and Practice, Second Edition, by N. J. Evans and others. San Francisco: Jossey-Bass, 2010.

> If you want to explore the theories presented in Chapters One through Three in more depth, this is the book for you. Simply go to the table of contents, and find the theory you want to know more about. Although the book is set in the context of postsecondary education, the theories and models presented are universal.

"Examining and Expanding Mentoring Practice." *Adult Learning*, 2009, *20* (entire issue 1–2).

> This issue of *Adult Learning* draws on the rich experience of researchers and practitioners who present personal and organizational stories in a variety of mentoring practice contexts. In it, my colleagues and I examine the shifting role of the mentee and the dynamics of the relationship, shift to an in-depth look at two popular mentoring processes (peer mentoring and e-mentoring), and finally focus on expanding theory to practice in two institutional examples of mentoring programs in different educational settings.

Emotional Intelligence: Why It Can Matter More Than IQ (10th anniversary ed.), by D. Goleman. New York: Bantam, 2006.

> When Goleman, a writer for the *New York Times*, published this book in 1995, it became an instant classic. He introduced and popularized the concept of emotional intelligence as a predictor of success. This book describes the origin of the concept, its foundational principles, and the research that substantiates it. In this newest edition, Goleman updates the research on how and where it is being applied.

Perspectives on Mentoring: Trends and Issues, ed. C. A. Hansman. Columbus, Ohio: ERIC Clearinghouse on Adult, Career, and Vocational Education, 2002.

> In this jam-packed, multiauthor publication, Catherine Hansman melds her knowledge, expertise, and experience with those of her colleagues, Vivian Mott, Andrea Ellinger, and Talmadge Guy, to present a variegated and critical review of the mentoring literature. They address the broad definitional landscape of mentoring, its institutional context, telementoring, diversity, and power, as well as the realities of mentoring practice today and in the future.

Learning in Adulthood: A Comprehensive Guide, by S. B. Merriam, R. S. Caffarella, and L. M. Baumgartner (3rd ed.). San Francisco: Jossey-Bass, 2006.

> The title of this treasure trove gives the contents away. It is, in fact, a comprehensive in-depth approach to understanding adult learning.

It explores the context of adult learning, theories and models, new approaches to adult learning, and the links between learning and development. It provides many of the theoretical underpinnings of the theories presented in *The Mentor's Guide* and firmly embeds mentoring in context.

Transformative Learning in Practice: Insights from Community, Workplace, and Higher Education, by J. Mezirow and E. W. Taylor and Associates. San Francisco: Jossey-Bass, 2009.

It is important that we as mentors understand the nature of transformative learning. It is equally essential that we build our capacity to facilitate it in a variety of contexts. This book will help you do just that. It describes transformative learning theory and includes chapters on how reflection on practice (an essential part of transformative learning) gets translated into different settings. The final part of the book is a distillation of the common themes and implications for practice.

The Language of Emotional Intelligence, by J. Segal. New York: McGraw-Hill, 2008.

Emotional intelligence is essential in building relationships. Segal's book provides five tools and multiple strategies to help assess and improve relationships. She outlines how to recognize a low emotional quotient, how to replace negative behaviors with constructive behaviors, and how to have less stressful, more honest, and more effective communication, all of them essential in a mentoring relationship.

Considering Context

The Blackwell Handbook of Mentoring: A Multiple Perspectives Approach, ed. T. D. Allen and L. T. Eby. London: Blackwell, 2007.

This compendium of scholarly mentoring work contains articles drawn from the multiple perspectives of thirty-eight contributors (academicians and practitioners). It offers an in-depth look at mentoring models, methods, and theoretical approaches. The last part integrates the multiple perspectives into a coherent framework for understanding mentoring practice today and its implications for the future.

Relevance: Hitting Your Goals by Knowing What Matters, by D. Apgar. San Francisco: Jossey-Bass, 2008.

This is a technical resource on how to strengthen strategies for hitting your development targets. Apgar, an experienced business consultant, suggests that failure to develop testable strategies and the difficulty of identifying relevant experience often lead to disappointing results. His four rules for developing workable strategies with relevant experience offer intriguing possibilities for dynamic mentoring conversations.

Surviving the Baby Boomer Exodus: Capturing Knowledge for Gen X and Y Employees, by K. Ball and G. Gotsill. Boston: Cengage Learning, 2011.

Ball and Gotsill argue that as more and more organizations employ multigenerational workforces, it is imperative (as never before) to capture explicit, implicit, and tacit organizational knowledge. Each generation has its own way of communicating, learning, and working that challenges an organization's ability to capture and share knowledge. Mentors need to be aware of these differences in order to facilitate learning.

Planning Responsibly for Adult Education: A Guide to Negotiating Power and Interests, by R. M. Cervero, A. L. Wilson, and Associates. San Francisco: Jossey-Bass, 1994.

Power is a topic that is often alluded to but not discussed when it comes to mentoring, and yet it is ever present in this relationship. The authors bring it front and center and offer examples and perspectives on the topic that transcend higher education and are relevant when it comes to mentoring, particularly transforming boundaries of power and the power of race and gender.

Teaching Strategies in the Online Environment, ed. S.C.O. Conceição. New Directions for Adult and Continuing Education, no. 113. San Francisco: Jossey-Bass, 2007.

The strategies and tools offered in this volume will be helpful to mentors who spend significant time engaging with their mentees online. The contributors to this volume offer practical tips and guidelines that address the cognitive, affective, and managerial roles that facilitate learning online.

Reverse Mentoring: How Young Leaders Can Transform the Church and Why We Should Let Them, by E. Creps. San Francisco: Jossey-Bass, 2008.

Reverse mentoring presents an opportunity to learn from the younger generation. This is not always a comfortable process for those who are older and presumably wiser. The fear of embarrassment and being exposed for what they don't know is very real. However, there is a great advantage to allowing yourself to be mentored by someone younger. It reduces the risk of becoming obsolescent and builds community for the future.

Mentoring Millennials: Shaping the Next Generation, by D. Egeler. Colorado Springs: NavPress, 2003.

Although this book is couched in Christian evangelism, many of Egeler's points are universal in application. He examines the needs of his young millennial parishioners who are hungry for mentors and ways of grounding themselves socially and in faith. Egeler explores how their needs can be met and the opportunities for mentoring them.

What's Next Gen X? Keeping Up, Moving Ahead and Getting the Career You Want, by T. Erickson. Boston: Harvard Business School Press, 2009.

Gen Xers often face a disconnect with their boomer superiors, who, they think, just don't understand them. As a result, many get caught up in doing something because they think it is "going to lead to something else even though they don't enjoy or it or think it is worthwhile." Erickson suggests ways that mentors can help define expectations, provide a longer-term perspective, recalibrate a career path, and better manage both superiors and direct reports.

Diversity and Motivation: Culturally Responsive Teaching in College (2nd ed.), by M. B. Ginsberg and R. J. Wlodkowski. San Francisco: Jossey-Bass, 2009.

Ginsburg and Wlodkowski articulate the need for a more culturally responsive pedagogy that supports student motivation across diverse student groups. Culturally responsive pedagogy is important to mentoring relationships as well. A successful mentoring relationship is built on respect for diversity, recognition of individualized motivation, and creation of a safe and inclusive, blame-free, and respectful learning environment. The authors include case studies, step-by-step guides to constructing motivational frameworks, lesson plans, and resources to aid in facilitating discussion.

EPowerment: Achieving Empowerment in the E World, by I. Justice. Bloomington, Ind.: iUniverse, 2010.

This book explores the workplace and the workforce over the next five to ten years. It brings together an amalgam of ideas–empowerment, emotional intelligence, and leveraging the e-world—to introduce five learning principles (extended learning model, emotional safety, mentoring, multimode learning, and outcome-based learning) that position working professionals and corporations to be competitive in the upcoming decade.

Creating a Sense of Presence in Online Teaching: How to "Be There" for Distance Learners, by R. M. Lehman and S.C.O. Conceição. San Francisco: Jossey-Bass, 2010.

Online presence is an important component of most mentoring relationships today. Knowing how to create that presence can spell the difference between success and failure. When you are not there even though you are physically present, your mentee can sense your distance. This book explains the methods that work and provides tools for creating, maintaining, and evaluating your online presence.

White Privilege and Racism: Perceptions and Actions, ed. C. L. Lund and S.A.J. Colin III. New Directions for Adult and Continuing Education. no. 125. San Francisco: Jossey-Bass, 2010.

This collection of eight essays focuses on a discussion of white privilege and racism and how they manifest themselves in adult and continuing education. The authors collectively note the continuing prevalence of racism in a nominally postracist society on both an individual and institutional level. Mentors need to be aware of their own biases and stereotypes and how they can have a negative impact on a mentoring relationship.

The Essential Guide to Training Global Audiences, by R. McClay and L. Irwin. San Francisco: Jossey-Bass/Pfeiffer, 2008.

This is a guide for trainers who are presenting to global audiences, and it has some wonderful tips and strategies that will be useful for those who are mentoring someone from a country other than their own. For example, it makes the point that international mentoring can be enhanced by using written documents. Short outlines or discussions should be sent to mentees before mentoring meetings so that parties can review them. It also discusses face-to-face interaction versus online interaction.

Building Online Learning Communities (2nd ed.), by R. M. Palloff and K. Pratt. San Francisco: Jossey-Bass, 2007.

This book's approach to online learning is refreshing and thought provoking. The authors focus on how to use technology to enhance learning experiences and offer concrete strategies for creating a collaborative learning environment. They blend adult learning theory and practice in a way that aligns well with mentoring, addressing topics such as connection, timing, facilitation, and transformation. Whether you are engaged in a virtual one-to-one or group mentoring relationship, you will find their nuggets, such as creating virtual presence, stimulating as well as practical.

The Handbook of Mentoring at Work: Theory, Research and Practice, ed. B. R. Ragins and K. E. Kram. Thousand Oaks, Calif.: Sage, 2007.

This comprehensive state-of-the-art scholarly resource on mentoring theory, research, and practice is packed with research findings. I have included it under this section of considering context because of its treatment of mentoring context and connection. Chapters Eight to Thirteen discuss gender and mentoring, the impact of race, informal and formal mentoring, peer mentoring, and e-mentoring.

Keeping the Millennials, by J. G. Sujansky and J. Ferri-Reed. San Francisco: Jossey-Bass, 2009.

Managing and maximizing the talent in today's workforce is no easy job. Sujansky and Ferri-Reed help us understand this soon-to-be-largest segment in our workforce. Millennials, they say, seek spontaneous feedback in real time, want to know what they are doing right and be able to improve and correct in the here and now, and want to be fully engaged in a meaningful way. Mentoring and coaching top their list of the support they need.

You Just Don't Understand: Women and Men in Conversation, by D. Tannen. New York: Ballantine Books, 1990.

Men and women may share a language, but how they use it and what it means reflects different approaches to relationships. Men typically anchor their identity in effective problem solving and action; women tend more toward a focus on the quality of relationships. Understanding and using gender differences respectfully promotes effective communication, indispensable for mentoring. Tannen's descriptions of gender-specific behaviors and language and the ways in which communication between men and women gets blocked offer helpful insights for mentoring.

The Predictable Phases of Mentoring

How Learning Works: Seven Research-Based Principles for Smart Teaching, by S. A. Ambrose and others. San Francisco: Jossey-Bass, 2010.

Although set in the context of teaching, the seven principles laid out in this book apply to mentoring: (1) students' prior knowledge can help or hinder learning; (2) how students organize knowledge influences how they learn and apply what they know; (3) students' motivation determines, directs, and sustains what they do to learn; (4) to develop mastery, students must acquire component skills, practice integrating them, and know when to apply what they have learned; (5) goal-directed practice coupled with targeted feedback enhances the quality of students' learning; (6) students' current level of development interacts with the social, emotional, and intellectual climate of the course to have an impact on their learning; and (7) to become self-directed learners, students must learn to monitor and adjust their approaches to learning.

Managers as Mentors: Building Partnerships for Learning, by C. R. Bell. San Francisco: Berrett-Koehler, 2002.

Written for managers who have assumed responsibility for mentoring employees, this book is full of techniques, strategies, and steps for building the careers of direct reports and making the role of mentor both comfortable and possible. Grounded in a partnership philosophy, the book helps in understanding power-free facilitation of learning, consultation, and connected mentoring. It examines personal strengths as a mentor, how to give advice and feedback, and the importance of deep listening.

Blended Coaching: Skills and Strategies to Support Principal Development, by G. Bloom, C. Castagna, E. Moir, and B. Warren. Thousand Oaks, Calif.: Corwin Press, 2005.

Bloom and his colleagues developed blended coaching to support the professional development of principals. The book demonstrates how effective coaches move between facilitative and instructional depending on where the learner (in their case, a principal) is at a given time. Designed for a school environment, it has applicability to mentoring as well, especially the reflective prompts and insightful exercises.

Transitions: Making Sense of Life's Changes (rev. 25th anniversary ed.), by W. Bridges. Cambridge, Mass.: Da Capo Press, 2004.

This classic book offers many insights into the transition process and concrete strategies and processes for making successful transitions. Mentors can use this book's learnings to guide mentees through the process of recognizing the new beginnings, making sense out of them, and learning from them.

Promoting Journal Writing in Adult Education, ed. L. M. English and M. A. Gillen. New Directions in Adult and Continuing Education, no. 90. San Francisco: Jossey-Bass, 2001.

Mentors who develop proficiency in journaling are more likely to engage in reflective mentoring practice and enhance their development as mentors. The authors identify the features of journal writing, its benefits and use, and how it can be best applied to facilitate adult learning.

The Business Coaching Toolkit: Top Ten Strategies for Solving the Toughest Dilemmas Facing Organizations, by S. G. Fairley and B. Zipp. Hoboken, N.J.: Wiley, 2008.

The tools presented in this easy-to-read book make a good companion to *The Mentor's Guide*. The chapter on SMART goals will be especially useful during the negotiating phase of the relationship. The authors make the business case for better goal setting, delve into SMART goals, offer a SMART goals worksheet, and suggest ten top ways to use SMART goal setting.

Masterful Coaching, Third Edition, by R. Hargrove. San Francisco: Jossey-Bass, 2008.

If you are looking for a step-by-step tactical resource packed with resources you can use tomorrow in conversations with your mentee, this is it. The guidance Hargrove provides is as masterful as the title of the book suggests. "From Defensiveness to Learning" and "Create and Extraordinary Coaching Relationship" are particularly useful chapters.

Mentoring: The Tao of Giving and Receiving Wisdom, by C. A. Huang and J. Lynch. New York: HarperCollins, 1995.

Maintaining trust, compassion, and connection is foundational to an effective mentoring relationship. An underlying theme of this book is the centeredness that results when both partners have clarity of intent and like-mindedness of purpose. Centeredness is used to frame the mentor's roles and to suggest ways to provide meaningful communication and connection between the partners.

Mentoring at Work: Developmental Relationships in Organizational Life, by K. E. Kram. Glenview, Ill.: Scott, Foresman, 1988.

This classic book provides a realistic view of the mentoring process based on years of research in corporate settings. The book focuses on the role of workplace mentoring relationships in promoting personal development during early, middle, and later career stages. It examines the potential benefits and limitations and illustrates various forms of development relationships through case studies and analysis.

Facilitative Coaching: A Toolkit for Expanding Your Repertoire and Achieving Lasting Results, by D. Schwarz and A. Davidson. San Francisco: Jossey-Bass/Pfeiffer, 2009.

Here's another toolkit with exercises you can use to support, challenge and empower your mentee to create and own their vision. It delivers just what it says: "a toolkit and instructions for expanding and building your repertoire." Although the audience is coaches, many of the exercises are perfect for mentors. You will have fun with this one.

Mentoring Teachers Toward Excellence: Supporting and Developing Highly Qualified Teachers, eds. J. H. Shulman and M. Sato. San Francisco: Jossey-Bass, 2006.

The thirteen case studies in this book are of special interest to those who mentor teachers and staff development specialists. The case studies showcase the dynamics and development of the mentoring relationship in educational settings and touch on such important topics as maintaining boundaries, conflict, difficult conversations, and strategies for mentee support.

Creating a Mentoring Culture: The Organization's Guide, by L. J. Zachary. San Francisco: Jossey-Bass, 2005.

In this book, I provide a comprehensive guide for thinking about mentoring from a broad and deep strategic perspective and to enable organizations to create a culture in which mentoring is a well-honed and practiced competency.

The Mentee's Guide: Making Mentoring Work for You, by L. J. Zachary. San Francisco: Jossey-Bass, 2009.

This book gives mentees guidance in what to expect in a mentoring relationship, how to make the most of their relationship, and how to ask for what they need. It includes stories with over thirty mentors and mentees and digs into the day-to-day realities of a mentoring relationship, with all its exhilarations and frustrations.

NOTES

Preface to the Second Edition

1. Daloz (1999).

2. Daloz (1999); Mezirow, Taylor, and Associates (2009); Caffarella (2002).

3. Merriam, Caffarella, and Baumgartner (2007).

4. Merriam et al. (2007, p. 97).

5. Brookfield (1986).

Chapter 1

1. Parks Daloz (2000, p. 81).

2. Knowles (1980).

3. Merriam, Caffarella, and Baumgartner (2007); Wolf (2005).

4. A number of models, theories, and definitions of emotional intelligence exist today. The concept originated with Salovey and Mayer (1990), and Daniel Goleman (1995) popularized it.

5. Palmer (1998, p. 29).

6. Knowles (1975), building on the work of Tough (1968) and Houle (1972).

7. What are its goals (Brookfield, 1993, 1995; Mezirow, 1995; Collins, 1996)? Is it a process (Brookfield, 1984; Spear, 1988; Garrison, 1997; Grow, 1994)? What are the attributes of a self-directed learner (Owen, 2002; Guglielmino, 1997; Tennant and Pogson, 1995; Poulton, Derrick, and Carr, 2005)?

8. Lowry (1989).

9. Mezirow and Associates (1990).

10. This model, also called conscious competence ladder and four stages of learning, has been attributed to many authors (most notably Donald

Kirkpatrick) and appears under various names (conscious competence ladder, levels of competency, four stages of learning).

11. According to Brookfield (1986, p. 64), "One important element in facilitating adult learning is helping learners become aware of their own idiosyncratic learning styles."

12. Perry (1970).

13. Corey (1980).

14. Berends (1990, p. 8).

15. Huang and Lynch (1995, p. 57).

16. Bateson (1989, p. 34).

17. Bateson (1989, p. 78).

18. Lindeman (1989); Merriam (2008).

19. Knowles (1980).

20. Brookfield (1986, p. 63).

Part One

1. Hargrove (2008, p. 116).

2. "More than ever before, the field of mentoring now recognizes the critical nature of context and the role contexts plays" in shaping the relationship. "Context involves not only the system within which mentoring relationships are embedded but also the structure and medium by which mentoring relationships are enacted within and outside organizations" (Ragins and Kram, 2007, p. 675).

3. Daloz (1999).

4. Mezirow and Associates (2000, p. 3).

5. "The importance of context is not just that it is interactive with one's learning. There are structural dimensions to our social context, often unseen and unacknowledged, that subtly affects learning" (Merriam, Caffarella, and Baumgartner, 2007, p. 430).

6. Fairley and Zipp (2008).

7. Johnson, Rose, and Schlosser (2010, p. 64).

8. Merriam, Caffarella, and Baumgartner (2007, p. 428).

9. For a more in-depth treatment of context and its relationship to learning, see Merriam, Caffarella, and Baumgartner (2007).

10. Nye (2011, p. 11).

Chapter 2

1. American Society for Training and Development Member Mailbag (1999).

2. Mezirow (1978).

3. The book *Kiss, Bow and Shake Hands* (Morrison, Conaway, and Borden, 1994) describes the customs, business practices, cognitive styles, protocols, greetings, and behaviors for sixty countries and is an excellent reference for those who are engaged in cross-cultural mentoring. *The Essential Guide to Training Global Audiences* (McClay and Irwin, 2008) offers tips on program design in thirty-two different areas or countries of the world. Many of these tips apply to mentoring relationships as well as programs.

4. G. Sandvik, personal communication, 1998.

5. M. Oyler, personal communication, Nov. 1999.

6. The names and inclusive dates of these generations tend to vary a bit in the popular literature.

7. Erickson (2009).

8. Hewlett, Sherbin, and Sumberg (2009).

9. Erickson (2009, p. 88).

10. Erickson (2009, p. 76).

11. Egeler (2003).

12. Sujansky and Ferri-Reed (2009, p. 183).

13. Erickson (2009); Egeler (2003).

14. Roland-Martin (1985); Parks Daloz (forthcoming).

15. Babcock and Laschever (2007, p. 39).

16. Hansman (2002, p. 45).

17. Hofstede (2001).

18. Ensher and Murphy (2005, p. 58).

19. Blake Beard (2009, p. 15).

20. Daloz (1999, p. 242).

Chapter 3

1. Huang and Lynch (1995, p. 5).

2. Ball and Gotsill (2011); Creps (2008).

3. J. Kraft, personal communication, Jan. 2011.

4. McClay and Irwin (2008).

5. Palloff and Pratt (2007).

6. Palloff and Pratt (2007, p. 230).

7. Progoff (1975); Quinn (1996).

Chapter 4

1. Light (2010).

2. Whyte, (2004, p. 20); Wells (1997).

3. Brookfield (1995).

4. Brookfield (1995, p. 2).

5. Mezirow, Taylor, and Associates (2009).

6. Bardwick (1998, p. 10).

Chapter 5

1. Knowles (1975).

2. Galbraith (1991).

3. Knowles (1980).

4. Heath and Heath (2010, p. 20).

5. Apgar (2008).

6. Smith (1995).

7. Covey and McChesney (2004).

8. Lencioni (1998, p. 51).

9. Owen (1992).

10. Apgar (2008).

Chapter 6

1. Daloz (1999); Taylor (1998).

2. Hunter and Larson (1996, p. 120).

3. Daloz (1999).

4. Wells (1997).

5. Daloz (1999).

6. Brookfield (1986).

7. Parks Daloz (2000, p. 128).

8. Zander and Zander (2000).

9. Barnett, O'Mahony, and Matthews (2004) comment that when all three are combined, we maximize our reflective powers.

10. Rose (1992).

11. Bell (1996).

12. Loder (1989).

Chapter 7

1. Fairley and Zipp (2008, p. 78).

2. Daloz (1999, p. 212).

3. Schön (1983).

4. Chandler, Eby, and McManus, *Wall Street Journal*, June 12, 2010.

5. Eby (2007, p. 325).

6. Brookfield (1995).

Chapter 8

1. Murray (2001).

2. Deal and Key (1998, p. 5). For more on celebration, see Kouzes and Posner (2007).

3. Deal and Key (1998, p. 207).

4. Gibran (1964, p. 19).

REFERENCES

Allen, T. D., and Eby, L. T. (eds.). *The Blackwell Handbook of Mentoring: A Multiple Perspectives Approach.* London: Blackwell, 2010.

Ambrose, S. A., and others. *How Learning Works: Seven Research-Based Principles for Smart Teaching.* San Francisco: Jossey-Bass, 2010.

American Society for Training and Development Member Mailbag. *The Successful Global Trainer.* Alexandria, Va.: American Society for Training and Development, Aug. 1999.

Apgar, D. *Relevance: Hitting Your Goals by Knowing What Matters.* San Francisco: Jossey-Bass, 2008.

Babcock, L., and Laschever, S. *Women Don't Ask: The High Cost of Avoiding Negotiation and Positive Strategies for Change.* New York: Bantam Dell, 2007.

Ball, K., and Gotsill, G. *Surviving the Baby Boomer Exodus: Capturing Knowledge for Gen X and Y Employees.* Boston: Cengage, 2011.

Bardwick, J. "Changing Culture." *Executive Excellence,* Aug. 1998, p. 10.

Barnett, B. G., O'Mahony, G. R., and Matthews, R. J. *Reflective Practice: The Cornerstone for School Improvement.* Moorabbin, Australia: Hawker Brownlow Education, 2004.

Bateson, M. C. *Composing a Life.* New York: Atlantic Monthly Press, 1989.

Belenky, M., Clinchy, B., Goldberger, N., and Tarule, J. *Women's Ways of Knowing: The Development of Self, Voice, and Mind.* New York: Basic Books, 1986.

Bell, C. R. *Managers as Mentors: Building Partnerships for Learning.* San Francisco: Berrett-Koehler, 2002.

Berends, P. B. *Coming to Life: Traveling the Spiritual Path in Everyday Life.* San Francisco: HarperSanFrancisco, 1990.

Blake Beard, S. "Mentoring as a Bridge to Understanding Cultural Differences." *Adult Learning,* 2009, *20* (1–2), 14–18.

Bloom, G., Castagna, C., Moir, E., and Warren, B. *Blended Coaching: Skills and Strategies to Support Principal Development.* Thousand Oaks, Calif.: Corwin Press, 2005.

Bridges, W. *Transitions: Making Sense of Life's Changes.* Reading, Mass.: Addison-Wesley, 2004.

Brookfield, S. D. "Self-Directed Learning: A Critical Paradigm." *Adult Education Quarterly*, 1984, 35(2), 59–71.

Brookfield, S. D. *Understanding and Facilitating Adult Learning: A Comprehensive Analysis of Principles and Effective Practices.* San Francisco: Jossey-Bass, 1986.

Brookfield, S. D. "Self-Directed Learning, Political Clarity and the Critical Practice of Adult Education." *Adult Education Quarterly*, 1993, 43, 227–242.

Brookfield, S. D. *Becoming a Critically Reflective Teacher.* San Francisco: Jossey-Bass, 1995.

Caffarella, R. S. *Planning Programs for Adult Learners: A Practical Guide for Educators, Trainers, and Staff Developers.* (2nd ed.) San Francisco: Jossey-Bass, 2002.

Cervero, R. M., Wilson, A. L., and Associates. *Planning Responsibly for Adult Education: A Guide to Negotiating Power and Interests.* San Francisco: Jossey-Bass, 1994.

Chandler, D. E., Eby, L., and McManus, S. E. "When Mentoring Goes Bad." *Wall Street Journal*, June 12, 2010.

Collins, M. "On Contemporary Practice and Research: Self-Directed Learning to Critical Theory." In R. Edwards, A. Hanson, and P. Reaggatt (eds.), *Boundaries of Adult Learning: Adult Learners, Education and Training.* New York: Routledge, 1996.

Conceição, S.C.O. (ed.). *Teaching Strategies in the Online Environment.* New Directions for Adult and Continuing Education, no. 113. San Francisco: Jossey-Bass, 2007.

Corey, E. R. "Case Method Teaching." Harvard Business School Case Study 9–581–058. Boston: Harvard Business School, 1980.

Covey, S., and McChesney, C. *The Four Disciplines of Execution: The Secret to Getting Things Done, on Time, with Excellence.* New York: Franklin Covey Company, 2004. CD-ROM.

Creps, E. *Reverse Mentoring: How Young Leaders Can Transform the Church and Why We Should Let Them.* San Francisco: Jossey-Bass, 2008.

Daloz, L. *Mentor: Guiding the Journey of Adult Learners.* San Francisco: Jossey-Bass, 1999.

Deal, T. E., and Key, M. K. *Corporate Celebration: Play, Purpose and Profit at Work.* San Francisco: Berrett-Koehler, 1998.

Eby, L. T. "Understanding Relational Problems in Mentoring: A Review and Proposed Investment Model. In B. R. Ragins and K. E. Kram (eds.), *The Handbook of Mentoring at Work: Theory, Research and Practice.* Thousand Oaks, Calif.: Sage, 2007.

Egeler, D. *Mentoring Millennials: Shaping the Next Generation.* Colorado Springs: NavPress, 2003.

English, L. M., and Gillen, M. A. (eds.). *Promoting Journal Writing in Adult Education.* New Directions in Adult and Continuing Education, no. 90. San Francisco: Jossey-Bass, 2001.

Ensher, E., and Murphy, S. *Power Mentoring: How Successful Mentors and Protégés Get the Most Out of Their Relationships.* San Francisco: Jossey-Bass, 2005.

Erickson, T. *What's Next Gen X? Keeping Up, Moving Ahead and Getting the Career You Want.* Boston: Harvard Business School Press, 2009.

Evans, N. J., and others. *Student Development in College: Theory, Research and Practice.* (2nd ed.) San Francisco: Jossey-Bass, 2010.

Fairley, S. G., and Zipp, B. *The Business Coaching Toolkit: Top Ten Strategies for Solving the Toughest Dilemmas Facing Organizations.* Hoboken, NJ: Wiley, 2008.

Galbraith, M. W. *Facilitating Adult Learning: A Transactional Process.* Malabar, Fla.: Krieger, 1991.

Garrison, D. R. "Self-Directed Learning: Toward a Comprehensive Model." *Adult Education Quarterly,* 1997, *48*(1), 18–33.

Gibran, K. *The Prophet.* New York: Knopf, 1964.

Ginsberg, M. B., and Wlodkowski, R. J. *Diversity and Motivation: Culturally Responsive Teaching in College.* (2nd ed.) San Francisco: Jossey-Bass, 2009.

Goleman, D. *Emotional Intelligence: Why It Can Matter More Than IQ.* New York: Bantam, 1995.

Goleman, D. *Emotional Intelligence: Why It Can Matter More Than IQ.* (10th anniversary ed.) New York: Bantam, 2006.

Goleman, D., Boyatzis, R. E., and McKee, A. *Primal Leadership: Realizing the Power of Emotional Intelligence.* Boston: Harvard Business School Press, 2002.

Grow, G. "In Defense of the Stage Self-Directed Learning Model." *Adult Education Quarterly,* 1994, *44*(2), 109–114.

Guglielmino, L. M. "Contributions of the Self-Directed Learning Readiness Scale (SDLRS) and the Learning Preference Assessment (LPA) to the Definition and Measurement of Self-Direction in Learning." Paper presented at the First World Conference on Self-Directed Learning, Montreal, Canada, 1997.

Hansman, C. A. (ed.). *Perspectives on Mentoring: Trends and Issues.* Columbus, Ohio: ERIC Clearinghouse on Adult, Career, and Vocational Education, 2002.

Hargrove, R. *Masterful Coaching.* (3rd ed.) San Francisco: Jossey-Bass, 2008.

Heath, C., and Heath, D. *Switch: How to Change Things When Change Is Hard.* New York: Broadway Books, 2010.

Hewlett, S. A., Sherbin, L., and Sumberg, K. "How the Gen Y and Boomers Will Reshape Your Agenda." *Harvard Business Review,* July-Aug. 2009, *87*(7–8), 71–75.

Hofstede, G. *Culture's Consequences: Comparing Values, Behaviors, Institutions, and Organizations Across Nations.* (2nd ed.) Thousand Oaks, Calif.: Sage, 2001.

Houle, C. O. *The Design of Education.* San Francisco: Jossey-Bass, 1972.

Huang, C. A., and Lynch, J. *Mentoring: The Tao of Giving and Receiving Wisdom.* San Francisco: HarperCollins, 1995.

Hunter, B., and Larson, H. *In the Company of Friends: Celebrating Women's Enduring Relationships.* Sisters, Ore.: Multnomah Books, 1996.

Johnson, W. B., Rose, G., and Schlosser, L. Z. "Student-Faculty Mentoring: Theoretical Approaches and Methodological Issues." In T. D. Allen and L. T. Eby (eds.), *The Blackwell Handbook of Mentoring: A Multiple Perspectives Approach.* London: Blackwell, 2010.

Justice, I. *EPowerment: Achieving Empowerment in the E World.* Bloomington, Ind.: iUniverse, 2010.

Knowles, M. S. *Self-Directed Learning: A Guide for Learners and Teachers.* Chicago: Follett, 1975.

Knowles, M. S. *The Modern Practice of Adult Education: From Pedagogy to Andragogy.* River Grove, Ill.: Follett, 1980.

Kouzes, J. M., and Posner, B. Z. *The Leadership Challenge.* (4th ed.) San Francisco: Jossey-Bass, 2007.

Kram, K. E. *Mentoring at Work: Developmental Relationships in Organizational Life.* Glenview, Ill.: Scott, Foresman, 1988.

Lehman, R. M., and Conceição, S.C.O. *Creating a Sense of Presence in Online Teaching: How to "Be There" for Distance Learners.* San Francisco: Jossey-Bass, 2010.

Lencioni, P. *The Five Temptations of a CEO: A Leadership Fable.* San Francisco: Jossey-Bass, 1998.

Light, J. "Bosses Overestimate Their Managing Skills." *Wall Street Journal,* Nov. 1, 2010. http://online.wsj.com/article/SB1000142405274870381760457558476412 8883620.html.

Lindeman, E. C. *The Meaning of Adult Education.* Norman: University of Oklahoma, 1989.

Loder, J. E. *The Transforming Moment*. (2nd ed.) Colorado Springs, Colo.: Helmers & Howard, 1989.

Lowry, C. M. *Supporting and Facilitating Self-Directed Learning*. Columbus, Ohio: ERIC Clearinghouse on Adult, Career, and Vocational Education, 1989. http://www.ntlf.com/html/lib/bib/89dig.htm.

Lund, C. L., and Colin, S.A.J. II (eds.). *White Privilege and Racism: Perceptions and Actions*. New Directions for Adult and Continuing Education, no. 125. San Francisco: Jossey-Bass, 2010.

McClay, R., and Irwin, L. *The Essential Guide to Training Global Audiences*. San Francisco: Jossey-Bass/Pfeiffer, 2008.

Merriam, S. (ed.). *Third Update on Adult Learning Theory*. New Directions for Adult and Continuing Education, no. 11. San Francisco: Jossey-Bass, 2008.

Merriam, S. B. "How Adult Life Transitions Foster Learning and Development." In A. Wolf (ed.), *Adulthood: New Terrain*. New Directions in Adult and Continuing Education, no. 108. San Francisco: Jossey-Bass, 2005.

Merriam, S. B., Caffarella, R. S., and Baumgartner, L. M. *Learning in Adulthood: A Comprehensive Guide*. (3rd ed.) San Francisco: Jossey-Bass, 2007.

Mezirow, J. "Perspective Transformation." *Adult Education*, 1978, *28*, 100–110.

Mezirow, J. "Transformation Theory of Adult Learning." In M. R. Welton (ed.), *In Defense of the Lifeworld*. New York: State University of New York Press, 1995.

Mezirow, J., and Associates. *Fostering Critical Reflection in Adulthood: A Guide to Transformative and Emancipatory Learning*. San Francisco: Jossey-Bass, 1990.

Mezirow, J., and Associates. *Learning as Transformation: Critical Perspectives on a Theory in Progress*. San Francisco: Jossey-Bass, 2000.

Mezirow, J., Taylor, E. W., and Associates. *Transformative Learning in Practice: Insights from Community, Workplace, and Higher Education*. San Francisco: Jossey-Bass, 2009.

Morrison, T., Conaway, W. A., and Borden, G. A. *Kiss, Bow or Shake Hands*. Holbrook, Mass.: Bob Adams, 1994.

Murray, M. *Beyond the Myths and Magic of Mentoring: How to Facilitate an Effective Mentoring Program*. (New and rev. ed.) San Francisco: Jossey-Bass, 2001.

Nye, J. S., Jr. "Contextual Intelligence: It's Crucial for Effective Leadership." *Leadership Excellence*, Jan. 2011, p. 11.

Owen, H. *Open Space Technology: A User's Guide*. Potomac, Md.: Abbott Publishing, 1992.

Owen, T. R. *Self-Directed Learning in Adulthood: A Literature Review*. Columbus, Ohio: ERIC Clearinghouse of Adult, Career, and Vocational Education, 2002. (ED 441 000)

Palloff, R. M., and Pratt, K. *Building Online Learning Communities.* (2nd ed.) San Francisco: Jossey-Bass, 2007.

Palmer, P. J. *The Courage to Teach: Exploring the Inner Landscape of a Teacher's Life.* San Francisco: Jossey-Bass, 1998.

Parks Daloz, L. A. "Mentoring Men for Wisdom: Transforming the Pillars of Manhood." In E. Tisdell and A. L. Swartz (eds.), *Wisdom and Adult Education.* New Directions in Adult and Continuing Education. San Francisco: Jossey-Bass, forthcoming.

Parks Daloz, S. *Big Questions, Worthy Dreams: Mentoring Young Adults in Their Search for Meaning, Purpose, and Faith.* San Francisco: Jossey-Bass, 2000.

Perry, W. G. *Forms of Ethical and Intellectual Development in the College Years: A Scheme.* New York: Holt, 1970.

Poulton, M., Derrick, M. G., and Carr, P. B. "The Relationship Between Resourcefulness and Persistence in Adult Autonomous Learning." *Adult Education Quarterly*, 2005, *55*(2), 116–128.

Progoff, I. *At a Journal Workshop.* New York: Dialogue House, 1975.

Quinn, R. E. *Deep Change: Discovering the Leader Within.* San Francisco: Jossey-Bass, 1996.

Ragins, B. R., and Kram, K. E. (eds.). *The Handbook of Mentoring at Work: Theory, Research and Practice.* Thousand Oaks, Calif.: Sage, 2007.

Roland-Martin, J. *Reclaiming a Conversation: The Ideal of the Educated Woman.* New Haven, Conn.: Yale University Press, 1985.

Rose, A. "Framing Our Experience: Research Notes on Reflective Practice." *Adult Learning*, 1992, *3*(4), 5.

Salovey, P., and Mayer, J. D. "Emotional Intelligence." *Imagination, Cognition, and Personality*, 1990, *9*(3), 185–211.

Schön, D. *The Reflective Practitioner.* New York: Basic Books, 1983.

Schwarz, D., and Davidson, A. *Facilitative Coaching: A Toolkit for Expanding Your Repertoire and Achieving Lasting Results.* San Francisco: Jossey-Bass/Pfeiffer, 2009.

Segal, J. *The Language of Emotional Intelligence.* New York: McGraw-Hill, 2008.

Shulman, J. H., and Sato, M. (eds.). *Mentoring Teachers Toward Excellence: Supporting and Developing Highly Qualified Teachers.* San Francisco: Jossey-Bass, 2006.

Smith, H. W. *The Ten Natural Laws of Successful Time and Life Management: Proven Strategies for Increased Productivity and Inner Peace.* New York: Warner Books, 1995.

Spear, G. E. "Beyond the Organizing Circumstance: A Search for Methodology for the Study of Self-Directed Learning." In H. B. Long and others (eds.),

Self-Directed Learning: Application and Theory. Athens: Department of Adult Education, University of Georgia, 1988.

Sujansky, J. G., and Ferri-Reed, J. *Keeping the Millennials.* San Francisco: Jossey-Bass, 2009.

Tannen, D. *You Just Don't Understand: Women and Men in Conversation.* New York: Ballantine Books, 1990.

Taylor, E. W. *The Theory and Practice of Transformative Learning: A Critical Review.* Columbus Ohio: Center on Education and Training for Employment. (ED 423422), 1998.

Tennant, M., and Pogson, P. *Learning and Change in the Adult Years: A Developmental Perspective.* San Francisco: Jossey-Bass, 1995.

Tough, A. M. *Why Adults Learn.* Toronto: Ontario Institute for Studies in Education, 1968.

Wells, S. "Building Trust." *Executive Excellence,* Sept. 1997, p. 11.

Whyte, D. "Five Conversations on the Frontiers of Leadership." *Leader to Leader,* 2004, *33,* 20–24.

Wolf, A. (ed.). *Adulthood: New Terrain.* New Directions in Adult and Continuing Education, no. 108. San Francisco: Jossey-Bass, 2005.

Zachary, L. (ed.). "Examining and Expanding Mentoring Practice." *Adult Learning,* 2009, *20*(1–2), 5–9.

Zachary, L. J. *Creating a Mentoring Culture: The Organization's Guide.* San Francisco: Jossey-Bass, 2005.

Zachary, L. J., with Fischler, L. A. *The Mentee's Guide: Making Mentoring Work for You.* San Francisco: Jossey-Bass, 2009.

Zander, B., and Zander, R. S. *The Art of Possibility: Transforming Professional and Personal Life.* New York: Penguin Books, 2000.

INDEX